Canada: The State of the Federation 1993

Edited by
Ronald L. Watts and
Douglas M. Brown

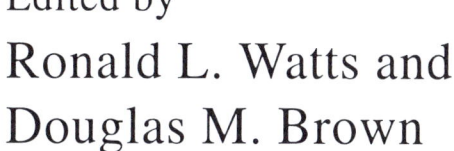

Institute of
Intergovernmental
Relations

Institut des
relations
intergouvernementales

Canadian Cataloguing in Publication Data

The National Library of Canada has catalogued this publication as follows:

Main entry under title:

Canada, the state of the federation

1985-

Annual.

ISSN 0827-0708

ISBN 0-88911-565-6 (1993)

1. Federal-provincial relations - Canada - Periodicals.* 2. Federal government - Canada - Periodicals. I. Queen's University (Kingston, Ont.). Institute of Intergovernmental Relations.

JL27.F42   321.02'3'0971   C86-030713-1

The Institute of Intergovernmental Relations

The Institute is the only organization in Canada whose mandate is solely to promote research and communication on the challenges facing the federal system.

Current research interests include fiscal federalism, constitutional reform, the reform of federal political institutions and the machinery of federal-provincial relations, Canadian federalism and the global economy, and comparative federalism.

The Institute pursues these objectives through research conducted by its own staff and other scholars through its publication program, seminars and conferences.

The Institute links academics and practitioners of federalism in federal and provincial governments and the private sector.

L'Institut des relations intergouvernementales

L'Institut est le seul organisme canadien à se consacrer exclusivement à la recherche et aux échanges sur les questions du fédéralisme.

Les priorités de recherche de l'Institut portent présentement sur le fédéralisme fiscal, la réforme constitutionnelle, la modification éventuelle des institutions politiques fédérales, les nouveaux mécanismes de relations fédérales-provinciales, le fédéralisme canadien au regard de l'économie mondiale et le fédéralisme comparatif.

L'Institut réalise ses objectifs par le biais de recherches effectuées par son personnel et par des universitaires de l'Université Queen's et d'ailleurs, de même que par des conférences et des colloques.

L'Institut sert de lien entre les universitaires, les fonctionnaires fédéraux et provinciaux et le secteur privé.

© Copyright 1993

CONTENTS

v		*Preface*
vii		*Dedication*
ix		*Contributors*

I Introduction

3   1. Overview
      Ronald L. Watts

II Constitutional Debate and the Referendum

19   2. The People and the Charlottetown Accord
      Richard Johnston, André Blais, Elisabeth Gidengil and *Neil Nevitte*

45   3. When More Is Too Much:
      Quebec and the Charlottetown Accord
      Gérard Boismenu

61   4. Let There Be Light
      J. Peter Meekison

87   5. Tensions in the Canadian Constitutional Process:
      Elite Negotiations, Referendums and
      Interest Group Consultations, 1980-1992
      Michael B. Stein

117 6. An Experiment in Intrastate Federalism:
      The Cabinet Committee on Canadian Unity
      Herman Bakvis and *Roselle Hryciuk*

III Immediate Issues

153   7. Aboriginal Policy and Politics:
The Charlottetown Accord and Beyond
J. Anthony Long and *Katherine Beaty Chiste*

175   8. Current Issues in Federal-Provincial
Fiscal Relations
Paul A.R. Hobson

193   9. The NAFTA, the Side-Deals, and Canadian Federalism:
Constitutional Reform by Other Means?
Ian Robinson

IV Chronology

231   10. Chronology of Events 1992-93
Anne Poels

PREFACE

This is the eighth volume in the annual series of the Institute of Intergovernmental Relations entitled *Canada: The State of the Federation* appearing early each autumn. The previous number reviewed the "Canada round" and concluded with an analysis of the Charlottetown Accord. This volume starts with a chapter examining the referendum campaign itself followed by four chapters looking retrospectively at the issues and processes involved in the effort at constitutional renewal and prospectively at the implications of the outcome for the constitutional evolution of Canadian federalism. These are followed by three chapters addressing major issues which currently confront the operation of Canadian federalism: aboriginal policy and politics, the revision of federal-provincial fiscal arrangements, and the impact of the proposed North American Free Trade Agreement. As in previous volumes, the final chapter consists of a chronology listing the most significant developments in intergovernmental arrangements over the year 1 July 1992 to 30 June 1993.

The editors wish to express their gratitude for the cooperation and promptness of all the authors in this volume in meeting our deadlines and in complying quickly to the revisions suggested by our independent peer reviewers. We also thank the referees for responding so rapidly to our requests. We are indebted to the following people who read one or more of the contributions and provided comments to the authors: Kathy Brock, Donna Dasko, Paul Chartland, Roger Gibbins, Janet Hiebert, Guy Laforest, John Meisel, David Milne, Patrick Monahan, Kenneth Norrie, Evelyn Peters, Alasdair Roberts, Gordon Robertson, Daniel Soberman, Katherine Swinton, Hugh Thorburn, and Robert Young.

The preparation of this volume has been the result of an excellent team effort at the Institute. We would like to thank Valerie Jarus for text preparation and formatting, Daniel Bonin for preparing the "sommaires," Marilyn Banting for proofreading and Patti Candido and Mary Kennedy for their assistance.

Ronald L. Watts
Douglas M. Brown
September 1993

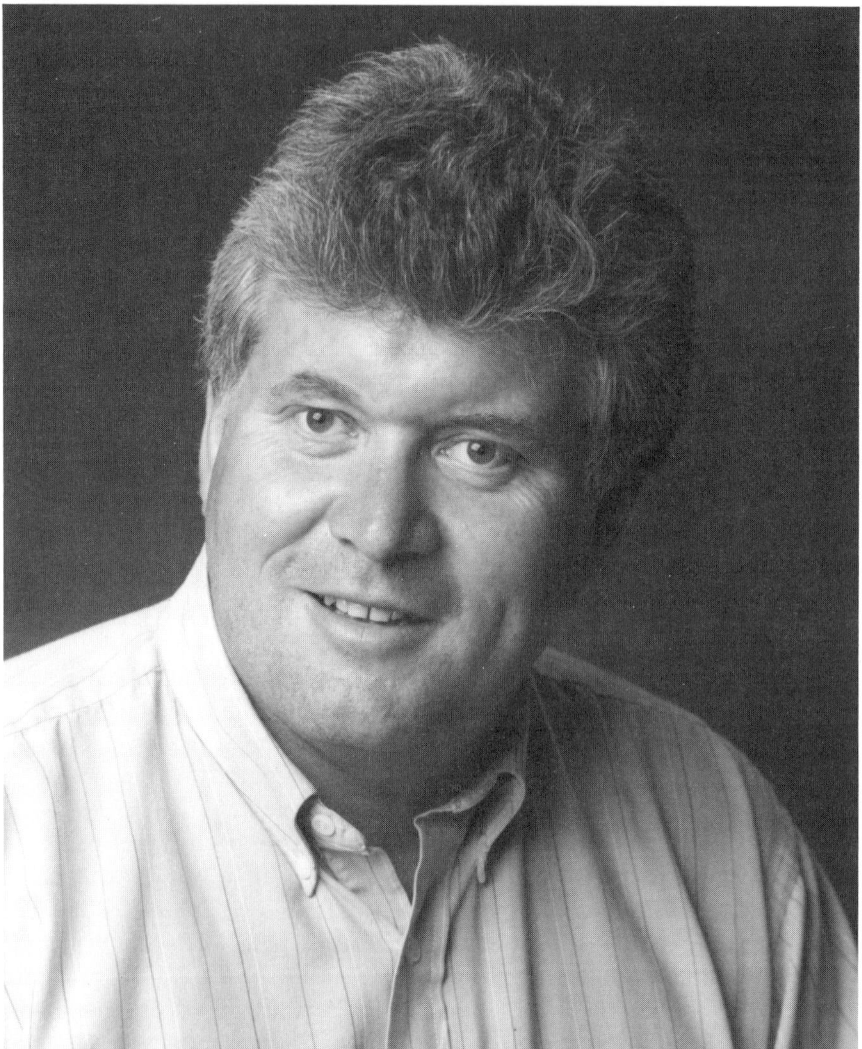

DOUGLAS D. PURVIS (1947-1993)

Douglas Purvis, Head of the Department of Economics and Director of the John Deutsch Institute for the Study of Economic Policy at Queen's University and a member of the Advisory Council of the Institute of Intergovernmental Relations died on 11 January 1993. Doug took a very active interest in the work of the Institute of Intergovernmental Relations, giving us wise advice and collaborating in the organization of colloquia and conferences.

The Institute and I personally have lost a close and dear friend and we dedicate this volume to him.

Ronald L. Watts
Director
Institute of Intergovernmental Relations
Queen's University

CONTRIBUTORS

Herman Bakvis is Professor of Political Science and Public Administration at Dalhousie University.

André Blais is Professeur titulaire, Département de science politique, Université de Montréal.

Gérard Boismenu is Professeur agrégé, and a member of the Groupe de recherche et d'étude sur les transformations sociales et économiques, Département de science politique, Université de Montréal.

Douglas M. Brown is Executive Director, Institute of Intergovernmental Relations, Queen's University.

Katherine Beaty Chiste is Research Associate, Faculty of Management, University of Lethbridge.

Elisabeth Gidengil is Assistant Professor, Department of Political Science, McGill University.

Paul A.R. Hobson is Associate Professor, Department of Economics, Acadia University.

Roselle Hryciuk recently received her MA degree in Political Science from Dalhousie University and for the year 1993-94 is working in the House of Commons, Ottawa, as a Parliamentary Intern.

Richard Johnston is Professor, Department of Political Science, University of British Columbia.

J. Anthony Long is Professor, Department of Political Science, University of Lethbridge.

J. Peter Meekison is Professor of Political Science, University of Alberta.

Neil Nevitte is Professor of Political Science, University of Calgary.

Anne Poels is Librarian, Institute of Intergovernmental Relations, Queen's University.

Ian Robinson is a Post-Doctoral Fellow at the Institute of Labor and Industrial Relations, University of Michigan and the Department of Political Science at Northwestern University.

Michael B. Stein is Professor, Department of Political Science, McMaster University.

Ronald L. Watts was Director of the Institute of Intergovernmental Relations until September 1993 and is Professor, Department of Political Studies, Queen's University.

I

Introduction

1

Overview

Ronald L. Watts

On trouvera difficilement fait plus marquant que le rejet, par les Canadiens, de l'Accord de Charlottetown, lors du référendum du 26 octobre 1992; il allait donc de soi que cet événement se retrouve au coeur de l'édition 1993 de Canada: The State of the Federation. *La plupart des articles du présent ouvrage offrent une perspective à la fois rétrospective et prospective. Le volume comprend d'abord une analyse spécifique de la campagne référendaire; sont ensuite passées en revue les stratégies «alternatives» appelant tantôt à une révision constitutionnelle tous azimuts, tantôt à une solution adaptative et par étapes de la problématique canadienne, c.-à-d. hors des sentiers battus constitutionnels; on s'interroge également sur le rôle et l'utilité des négociations au sommet et de la participation du public au processus constitutionnel; enfin, des collaborateurs examinent trois questions qui seront au tout premier plan du débat politique au cours des deux prochaines années, soit, en l'occurrence, le dossier autochtone, la révision des accords fiscaux fédéraux-provinciaux, ainsi que les répercussions prévisibles de l'Accord de libre-échange nord-américain.*

Canadiens et Québécois auront, dans un même élan, signifié leur rejet de l'Accord de Charlottetown et partant, ils auront exprimé une commune lassitude à l'égard du dossier constitutionnel; si, depuis l'échec référendaire, un calme apparent semble régner sur ce dernier front, il faut s'attendre en revanche, après les élections fédérales du 25 octobre 1993 et celles prévues au Québec d'ici la fin de 1994, que la «question du Québec» détermine à nouveau l'ordre du jour de la politique canadienne et, par conséquent, l'avenir même de la fédération.

INTRODUCTION

The most significant event since the publication a year ago of the previous volume in this annual series was the referendum on the Charlottetown Accord and the rejection of those proposals by a majority of the Canadian people. The previous volume which was sent to press in September 1992 surveyed and analyzed the preceding two years of consultation and negotiations. Those two years had involved concerned Canadians in unprecedented exercises in public participation. The resulting Charlottetown Accord represented the best efforts of their elected leaders to reach a consensus on fundamental reform of Canada's constitutional framework. A theme that ran through the essays in that volume was the profound ambivalence of Canadians about their constitutional future as they approached the referendum, despite the firm consensus of their political leaders.

In the event, on 26 October 1992 Canadians rejected the package of constitutional proposals carefully negotiated and agreed upon by their leaders. Nationally, the "No" vote came to 54 percent. Six of the ten provinces, including Quebec, and one of the two territories, Yukon, voted "No." Three of the Atlantic provinces — Newfoundland, New Brunswick and Prince Edward Island — voted a substantial "Yes," while Ontario voted "Yes" by a very narrow margin. Since most of the items in the Charlottetown agreement required the assent of the legislatures in at least seven provinces representing 50 percent of the population, and a few of the elements needed ratification by every province, it was clear that the agreement had been rejected decisively.

The rejection in October 1992 of the effort to obtain popular support for the Charlottetown Accord marks another critical turning point in the evolution of the Canadian Federation. The public weariness with constitutional issues and the relatively tranquil constitutional scene in the year that has followed has suggested to many politicians and political commentators that for some time constitutional issues will be set aside and that the current constitutional arrangements will be able to continue with only incremental adjustments. Certainly, the aftermath of the demise of the Charlottetown agreement has contrasted with the increased French-English polarization over the status of Quebec, with the heightened aboriginal demands, and accelerating challenge in western Canada to the dominance of central Canada that followed the failure in June 1990 of the effort to ratify the Meech Lake Accord. Nevertheless, underlying the apparent tranquility following the referendum there remains unresolved the fundamental problems and issues that gave rise in Canada to the mega-constitutional politics during the past 25 years and the efforts to reach some resolution that would ward off a potential deeper crisis.

During the coming year two defining political events will again raise these issues and shape the further evolution of the Canadian Federation. The first of these is the federal general election scheduled for 25 October 1993, exactly one year after the referendum. That election will determine whether a weakening in the ability of national political parties to aggregate and integrate regional interests will lead to a consequent reduction in the capacity of the federal government to provide leadership in uniting the country.

The second defining political event will be the Quebec general election which must be held before the end of 1994. Given the Parti Québécois advocacy of sovereignty for Quebec, the stark choice between membership in an unrevised federal structure on the one hand and sovereignty as advocated by the Parti Québécois on the other, will inevitably be an issue in that election.

In view of the significance of the rejection in the referendum of the Charlottetown agreement, it will come as no surprise that that event dominates the contributions to this year's volume. Most of the contributions are both retrospective and prospective in their outlook. They include an analysis of the referendum campaign itself, consideration of alternative strategies of comprehensive constitutional revision and of incremental non-constitutional adaptation, the value of elite accommodation and public participation and the lessons to be learnt in this respect from the Canada round, and analyses of issues that will be in the forefront during the next year or two, particularly aboriginal policy and politics, the revision of federal-provincial fiscal arrangements, and the impact of the North American Free Trade Agreement. The chronology of significant events from July 1992 to June 1993 included in this volume, following practice in previous editions, outlines the ongoing developments in intergovernmental relations during that year.

THE REFERENDUM

After a year and a half of the most intensive, extensive, exhaustive and exhausting round of public consultations and intergovernmental negotiations on the constitution that has occurred in any country during this century, the Charlottetown agreement of August 1992 appeared to indicate that the country's leadership had squared the constitutional circle — to have obtained the agreement of the federal government, all ten provincial governments, the two territorial governments and the leaders of the four major aboriginal groups on a Consensus Report sufficiently inclusive to accommodate all conceivable forms of constitutional disaffection. At the moment the Accord was struck the prospects, according to initial opinion surveys, looked good.

During the course of the campaign for popular endorsement things came unglued, however. In the hurly-burly of the referendum debate the larger vision embodied in the Charlottetown Consensus Report were lost in the media and partisan preoccupations with specific provisions and with concerns about the extent to which each particular group had or had not achieved all its own specific aims. The result was an ensuing preoccupation with assessing losses under the agreement: Canadians seemed to become involved in a competition to see which province, region or group could lay claim to being the biggest losers as a result of the Charlottetown agreement. In the end, the political leaders found that in trying to accommodate every group they had drafted a document that because it required so many compromises made more enemies than friends.

Despite the apparent Canada-wide referendum consensus for rejecting the Charlottetown agreement, the contradictory motivations of different groups for voting "No" in the referendum illustrated vividly the continued contradiction of views held by different groups within Canada. The majority in Quebec, including many Quebec federalists who would prefer not to separate from Canada, voted "No" because the Charlottetown agreement did not give Quebec enough control over its own affairs; many in the rest-of-Canada and particularly in the west voted "No" because in their view it involved too much in the way of special arrangements for Quebec. Many Aboriginal People voted "No" or abstained because the agreement did not go far enough in recognizing their claims; many non-Aboriginal People voted "No" because they felt that the recognition in the agreement of an inherent aboriginal right to self-government was too sweeping and would be too costly. Many Canadians voted "No" from fear that the particular rights of a specific group were not adequately reinforced; others voted "No" because they were opposed to the emphasis upon the rights of specific groups. Efforts to reduce disaffection in one region or for one group seemed only to increase disaffection elsewhere. Thus, in the crucible of the referendum the will of the electorate to accept the concessions and compromises necessary to resolve Canada's structural problems in a united way seemed to leak away.

During the referendum campaign the National Election Study Research Group of political scientists conducted a day-by-day tracking of public opinion and an analysis of the positions of different groups upon the issues involved. The chapter in this volume by Richard Johnston, André Blais, Elisabeth Gidengil and Neil Nevitte is a distillation of that study. They present evidence on shifting support during the campaign and on support for the various elements in the Charlottetown agreement both in Quebec and in the rest-of-Canada. Outside Quebec, the prospects for a "Yes" vote were strong at first with over 60 percent in favour. Subsequently, there was a particularly dramatic collapse of the "Yes" support immediately after Pierre Trudeau's "Maison Egg Roll" speech on 1 October. Later in the campaign, public realization of the weakness of support for a "Yes" vote both in Quebec and elsewhere, as revealed by polls, appears to have contributed further to the decline of the "Yes" share outside Quebec. Public opinion of Brian Mulroney and of other leaders would appear to have been a factor in the negative result, but the outcome was not based solely on a desire to punish political leaders. The "Yes" vote came disproportionately from better-off and better-informed voters, not so much because they liked the content of the Accord as because they were prepared to override their doubts in the interests of avoiding Quebec's separation. On the other hand, within Quebec, the balance of opinion right from the beginning leaned towards a "No" vote, although initially there were some signs of a possible advance towards a "Yes" vote. The possibility of such an advance seems to have been arrested, however, by the leaked Tremblay-Wilhelmy telephone conversation which appeared to confirm that Premier Bourassa had failed to bargain hard enough. In the end the narrow "Yes" majority among non-sovereignists within Quebec was insufficient to offset the virtually total rejection of the Accord by the substantial number of sovereignists.

In this chapter, the authors also consider the question of whether voters can make meaningful and interpretive choices on a document as formidably complex as the Charlottetown Accord. There is extensive evidence of the conservatism of voters in constitutional referendums in most other countries. Furthermore, in the case of the Charlottetown agreement, the failure during the preceding intergovernmental negotiations to decide at the outset whether the Accord would be put to a Canada-wide referendum and the consequent failure to design a document that would be "user-friendly" to the voter led to the production of an agreement that was complex and difficult to understand. This contributed to the reluctance of voters to approve it.

THE IMPLICATIONS OF THE REFERENDUM RESULT

Given that the Charlottetown agreement was the product of such an extensive process of prior constitutional discussion, and that in the subsequent intergovernmental negotiations the great variety of views were reconciled only with extreme difficulty, one implication of the referendum result is that the prospects now for producing another comprehensive proposal for constitutional reform that would obtain public support in the near future, however desirable, are virtually nil. In spite of the earlier widespread public demand for an extensive constitutional reform not only in Quebec but also as reported by the Spicer Citizen's Forum on Canada's Future elsewhere in the country, the referendum result points to just how difficult it is to get agreement within the diverse Canadian society on comprehensive constitutional change. Ironically, even the Reform Party, whose very label was intended to express a desire for fundamental change, advocated a "No" vote during the referendum on the grounds that a moratorium on constitutional deliberations was desirable. What the referendum seems to indicate is the paradox that the Canadian electorate wants transformation but without change! Indeed, the *Economist* of 31 October 1992 described the negative referendum result scathingly as "horrendously Canadian: a populist revolt in favour of the status quo."

Two chapters, those by Gérard Boismenu and Peter Meekison examine the implications for the future of the apparent impossibility of getting Canadians to agree on comprehensive constitutional change.

Gérard Boismenu reviews the process of the Canada round and the compromises embodied in the Charlottetown agreement from a Quebec perspective, showing how the result was a proposal that was inadequate and unattractive to

Quebec. Although for many Quebecers sovereignty may be regarded as no more than a default option, he suggests that the blockage of constitutional reform and the inability to change the status quo could in the end, following the federal and Quebec elections of 1993 and 1994, lead to a "big bang" in the form of pressure within Quebec for a dynamic new alternative.

Peter Meekison, on the other hand, suggests that much might be achieved by abandoning efforts at comprehensive constitutional change in favour of incremental constitutional adaptation. The past 25 years of mega-constitutional politics have demonstrated how difficult it is to achieve comprehensive constitutional reform. Nevertheless, the failure of the referendum has not removed the forces underlying the demand for constitutional reform. The author draws particular attention to the continuing salience of Quebec's concerns, western grievances, and aboriginal self-government. The principal theme of his chapter is that formal constitutional amendment is not the only means by which change can be achieved. There are alternatives available to Canadians and their governments for dealing with their constitutional concerns. Among these are changing conventions, enacting statutes and the greater use of reference cases. Furthermore, he suggests that there is a far greater possibility of rediscovering our traditional means of conflict resolution through relying upon intergovernmental negotiation and agreement. Indeed, if governments were so inclined, a number of the provisions contained in the Charlottetown Accord could be put into effect by such means without the need for formal constitutional amendment.

Both Boismenu and Meekison agree that the relatively tranquil immediate aftermath of the referendum may be only temporary, masking the approach of what is likely to be a particularly difficult period ahead. With no realistic prospect of comprehensive constitutional reform as a way of tackling our unresolved problems, the alternatives seem to be either an explosion of new pressures in Quebec, suggested as a possibility by Gérard Boismenu, or reliance upon incremental non-constitutional political processes and policy adjustments to address our problems, as suggested by Peter Meekison. Experience in other federations indicates that comprehensive constitutional change is much more difficult than incremental change. For example, Switzerland which has separate procedures for partial revision and total revision of the constitution has managed the former over 90 times since 1848 but of four attempts at total revision, including the protracted effort from 1965 to the early 1980s, it has succeeded only once in achieving a total revision, that more than a century ago in 1874. The Australian movement for comprehensive constitutional revision in the period 1975-88 also came in the end to naught. On the other hand, the Canadian federal system in its first 115 years of history, during which it lacked an agreed formal amendment process, proved remarkably flexible in adjusting pragmatically and incrementally to changing circumstances and conditions. This suggests that an incremental approach to constitutional change should be the preferred strategy. Considerable progress could be made by means of ordinary legislative and administrative action and by intergovernmental agreements on rebalancing the roles and fiscal relationships of the federal and provincial governments, on the development of aboriginal self-government, on improving the economic and social union and on electoral and procedural reforms relating to that body. It has been only during the past two and a half decades that constitutional reform and mega-constitutional politics have become such an obsession for Canadians. Perhaps the 1992 referendum has inoculated Canadians from the disease of wanting to solve all structural and policy problems by re-writing the constitution.

But an important question, however, will be whether sufficient progress can be achieved and quickly enough by such incremental methods. There are, of course, limitations to this approach. The first is whether enough can be achieved and sufficiently quickly in this incremental mode to meet the concerns that gave rise during the past two decades to the intense focus upon constitutional change. The second is that this approach cannot provide the *symbolic* significance and the assurance of constitutional safeguards that formal constitutional amendments would. Nevertheless, given the growing realization of the almost certain immobility in any effort to resolve Canada's structural problems through constitutional amendment, the pragmatic incremental approach may now be the only practicable route left. Indeed, agreement may be easier to achieve through such an approach when the higher stake deliberations of mega-constitutional politics are avoided. Both Boismenu and Meekison warn us, however, that if reliance on such an approach becomes simply an excuse for inaction it is likely to be fatal.

THE ROLE OF ELITE ACCOMMODATION

A major issue in the consideration of future processes for constitutional change or adaptation concerns the appropriate role of the public and of elites in such processes. The 1990-92 Canada round process attempted to establish a blend of extensive prior public input followed by elite intergovernmental negotiation and finally public endorsement by referendum. This represented a conscious effort to avoid the accusations of lack of prior public discussion that were directed at the politicians who produced the Meech Lake Accord. Indeed, during the 1990-92 process there was extensive public consultation and involvement. Furthermore, those participating in the process observed at first hand the constraints that the intergovernmental elites thought they had to work within in order to achieve an agreement that would take account of the great variety of views and positions that had been expressed by the Canadian public prior to the intergovernmental negotiations. Yet, in spite of this, during the referendum campaign the media and public critics attacked the Charlottetown agreement as simply the product of politicians.

This raises two questions. First does the failure of the most recent attempt at constitutional reform represent the end of the tradition of elite accommodation as a means to reconciling differences within Canada? Second, if so, is there any viable alternative process for constitutional change? The alternatives are not clear. Some have advocated a constituent assembly process but that requires prior agreement on the composition of the assembly, the method of selecting delegates and their mandate, all issues on which there is no easy consensus. Furthermore, a study of constituent assemblies and conventions elsewhere undertaken for the Institute of Intergovernmental Relations by Patrick Fafard and Darrel Reid in 1991 suggested that such processes have rarely been successful except in post-revolutionary situations where the establishment of a new political structure is unavoidable.[1]

If the alternatives are not promising what then are the prospects for elite accommodation in contributing to the resolution of constitutional issues? The chapters by Michael Stein and by Herman Bakvis and Roselle Hryciuk analyze the role of political elites in the recent constitutional review process and possible lessons that might be drawn from this experience.

Michael Stein notes that the failure of both the Meech Lake and Charlottetown accords has led many political observers to believe that executive federalism has lost its value as an effective structure for conducting constitutional negotiations in Canada. He takes issue with this new conventional wisdom. He advances an alternative view that executive and summit federalism are a natural organic development of Canadian parliamentary federalism and therefore that when the constitutional issues reemerge, as they are certain to do after the next federal and Quebec elections, executive federalism and elite negotiations will be both necessary and desirable for successful constitutional reform. Such processes allow for creative compromise and mutual accommodation resulting in "win-win" outcomes. An important lesson from recent experience, however, relates to the need to combine somehow these elite structures and processes with mechanisms for popular consultation including referendums and for wider interest group involvement in order to achieve long-term success and legitimacy. Such a blending is difficult to achieve because of the inherent tensions and contradictions between the "non-zero-sum" or compromising logic of elite negotiations and the "win-lose" or maximizing logic of referendums and interest group representations. These tensions are reinforced by recent changes in political culture affecting parties, interest groups and new social movements. Nonetheless, in Stein's view elite negotiation and significant public input are not inherently irreconcilable and he suggests a number of tension-managing devices to facilitate their combination.

Herman Bakvis and Roselle Hryciuk focus specifically upon the role of the Cabinet Committee on Canadian Unity and Constitutional Negotiations chaired by Joe Clark in shaping the federal proposals of September 1991. Those proposals following subsequent modifications made by the joint parliamentary committee and then the intergovernmental negotiations, ultimately became the Charlottetown Accord. The Cabinet committee's role as a federal institution attempting to reconcile regional interests and the impact on its deliberations of bureaucratic influences is examined in considerable depth by the authors on the basis of interviews with a range of officials who participated in the process. They also examine this process in the context of the extensive Canadian literature on intrastate federalism.

IMMEDIATE ISSUES

Whatever the degree to which constitutional issues in general reemerge following the forthcoming federal and Quebec elections, three issues will demand immediate attention. All three will have a pervasive impact upon the evolving character of Canadian federalism in that they involve very broad reaching consequences for the continuing nature of intergovernmental relationships within Canada.

The first of these related to aboriginal policy and politics, a subject considered in the chapter by Anthony Long and Katherine Beatty Chiste. During 1992 the aboriginal public policy agenda was dominated by the negotiations leading to the Charlottetown Accord. But while the leadership of all the national aboriginal organizations supported the Accord's aboriginal provisions, a substantial segment of the grass-roots Indian community did not. The defeat of the Accord in the October referendum had the effect of reconfirming the current ambiguous status of the Aboriginal Peoples within Canada, although the substantive provisions of the Accord will undoubtedly leave their mark on future aboriginal demands and future governmental responses. Pressure for nonconstitutional policy initiatives — such as land claims and community-based self-government — can be expected to accelerate. Without an overarching framework such as the Charlottetown Accord, however, the diverse aboriginal community within Canada is likely to drift further apart. Varying aspirations, cultures and resources are likely to lead different aboriginal communities along different paths. The one potentially harmonizing force is the Royal Commission on Aboriginal Peoples (1991-95) with its broad mandate, and the spotlight within the aboriginal policymaking arena over the next year or two will undoubtedly be focused on the Royal Commission and its deliberations. At the same time there will be a need to sort out the appropriate roles and relationships between the federal and provincial governments in this policy area.

The second immediate issue relates to the forthcoming major review of federal-provincial fiscal arrangements scheduled for completion by April 1994. Paul Hobson considers how the federal government's preoccupation with deficit reduction has compromised the functioning of the transfer system. He notes particularly the undermining of the important redistributive function of the federal government to the detriment of both fiscal equity and economic efficiency within the federation. He points to areas that require particular attention and suggests that there appears to be some scope for developing a greater degree of interprovincial revenue sharing. The chapter is valuable in laying out the issues that will be involved in the forthcoming review of fiscal arrangements and in drawing attention to important recent literature on the subject.

The third immediate issue is the impact of the North American Free Trade Agreement (NAFTA) upon the operation of Canadian federalism. Ian Robinson identifies the principal areas in which the NAFTA would impinge on provincial jurisdiction, and the means available to the federal government to enforce these incursions, relating these changes to those found in the Canada-U.S. Free Trade Agreement (FTA) and in the Tokyo and Uruguay rounds of the GATT. He examines how these agreements will increase market constraints on provincial policy initiative and efficacy. He argues that the implementation of the Canada-U.S. FTA marks the beginning of a new era of Canadian federalism, one that the NAFTA and the Dunkel Draft of the Uruguay GATT will substantially extend and entrench. He suggests that these agreements will usher in a new form of "subordinate" federalism that can be distinguished from the "social" federalism of the postwar era in two ways: first by the changes to the economic and social role of Canadian governments that these agreements seek to enforce, and second by the dramatic shift in the *de defacto* distribution of powers implied by the federal government's claim to possess the necessary powers to enforce these agreements.

THE FUTURE PROSPECTS

Although the possibility of achieving comprehensive constitutional reform in the near future would now appear unrealistic, as many of the contributing authors have noted that the crucial structural problems facing the Canadian federation still remain before us. The issues of Quebec's place within the federation, of aboriginal self-government, of the political framework for economic development and the reduction of disparities, of more representative and responsive federal institutions, and of articulating uniting values are still there. Experience in federations elsewhere that have disintegrated indicates that the repeated refusal to resolve basic problems may accentuate internal grievances and frustrations cumulatively to the point where eventually disintegration may become unavoidable. The referendum result, therefore, has not put these issues behind us.

Furthermore, because of the contradictory positions of the different groups that supported a "No" vote in the referendum, the political leaders have been given no clear guidance on the direction required for a resolution that would obtain the support of most Canadians. The conflicting and contradictory positions of the various "No" advocates — the Quebec sovereignists represented by the Parti Québécois and Bloc Québécois, the Reform Party, the Trudeauites, and the National Action Committee on the Status of Women — give no coherent alternative path for the future.

Does this indicate a gloomy prospect for Canada's future? The *Economist* suggested that to Canada the referendum result may mea: no consensus, no end to uncertainty, and even possible eventual fragmentation.

Optimists, on the other hand, have expressed the hope that after a few years of concentrating attention instead upon the economic issues that we have been neglecting and of allowing our existing political institutions another chance to work, Canadians will somehow decide to resolve their differences and stay together. Certainly after their recent experience few politicians will want in the near future to touch constitutional issues only to be kicked in the teeth for trying to meet the conflicting demands of citizens. Canadians may remain deeply divided over their sense of identity but in all of Canada, including Quebec, the referendum has left them united in their constitutional fatigue. In this respect an encouraging result of the referendum is the way in which the situation contrasts with that following the demise of the Meech Lake Accord. Because of the breadth of the rejection of the Charlottetown agreement across Canada it has not been followed by the same heightened polarization of views that followed the failure in 1990 to ratify the Meech Lake Accord. At least for the time being the heat has been taken out of the issue. When one compares this to the situation in 1990 this has been a not inconsiderable achievement for which those involved in the constitutional negotiations can take some credit since the process they followed contributed to this result.

But while apparently normal politics may continue for a short period, the fundamental issues remain unresolved and two watershed elections that must be held within the next year or so are likely to bring constitutional issues back sooner than many expect or wish. The first is the federal election scheduled for 25 October 1993. If that election were to produce a majority government with an overarching support from all the major regions, the prospects for resolving interregional issues might be much improved. On the other hand, if in that election the electorate were to turn its back on the mainline parties and produce, as many are forecasting, a fragmented Parliament with primarily regional parties such as the Bloc Québécois and the Reform Party playing a crucial role in the dynamics of Parliament, then the prospects for continued federal cohesion would indeed be seriously diminished. An examination of the disintegration of federations elsewhere reminds us that a tell-tale sign of imminent dissolution has been the demise of national parties and the rise of predominantly regional political parties operating within their federal institutions. Such situations have generally led to the failure to moderate regional cleavages and to a cumulative regional political polarization and often to eventual fragmentation.

The second critical election will be that due in Quebec before the end of 1994. Jacques Parizeau, the leader of the sovereignist Parti Québécois, sees the vote as a green light for sovereignty and that the Quebec election will be fought on that issue. While post-referendum opinion surveys indicate that declared separatists still make up only about one-third of the Quebec population, those same surveys indicate that a substantial number of those who still call themselves federalist would support continued federalism only if Quebec were to get more powers than Charlottetown offered. With little prospect of agreement from the rest-of-Canada on such additional powers before the next Quebec election, the Quebec electorate is likely to be faced then simply with the stark choice between the status quo and sovereignty. In the past, Quebecers focused on relatively soft options: a revised decentralized federal system advocated by Robert Bourassa's Liberal Party and sovereignty with a close economic association with Canada as advocated by Jacques Parizeau's Parti Québécois. Now with the referendum closing the door on any realistic possibility of a revised federalism and with the lack of sympathy in the rest-of-Canada for sovereignty-association as an alternative, Quebecers will probably have to make the more dramatic choice between the Canadian federation as it is and unmoderated sovereignty.

Despite Premier Bourassa's declaration on referendum night that he would continue "to build Quebec within Canada" and his clearly federalist stance on several occasions since, the Quebec Liberal Party has been left as a result of the referendum with little in the way of attractive alternatives in the form of "renewed federalism" to counter the proposals of the sovereignists. Another complication is the question of who will provide the federalist leadership within the Quebec Liberal Party following Premier Bourassa's retirement and what position the Quebec Liberal Party under new leadership takes in the forthcoming Quebec election. At the same time it is worth taking note of Stephane Dion's recent suggestion that, faced in the next provincial election or in the referendum following a Parti Québécois victory with the hard choice between the current federal structure unchanged and complete sovereignty, a majority of Quebecers may prove reluctant to vote for complete sovereignty when the full implications of its consequences are clear.[2]

As we are already seeing in the autumn of 1993 with the commencement of the federal general election and with the announcement of Premier Bourassa's retirement, the coming 12 months will be a period when there are likely to be major developments in the further evolution of Canadian federalism.

NOTES

1. Patrick Fafard and Darrel Reid, *Constituent Assemblies: A Comparative Survey*, Research Paper 30 (Kingston: Institute of Intergovernmental Relations, Queen's University, 1991).
2. Stephane Dion, "The Quebec Challenge to Canadian Unity," *P.S.: Political Science and Politics*, xxvi, 12 (March 1993): 42-43.

II

Constitutional Debate and the Referendum

2

The People and the Charlottetown Accord

*Richard Johnston, André Blais,
Elisabeth Gidengil and Neil Nevitte*

Ce chapitre analyse le déroulement de la campagne référendaire ainsi que le soutien accordé au Québec et dans le reste du Canada envers plusieurs éléments de l'Accord de Charlottetown. Le brusque effondrement des appuis en faveur de l'entente, immédiatement après le discours de Pierre Trudeau à la Maison du Egg Roll, se sera avéré l'un des faits les plus spectaculaires de cette campagne. Cette chute du OUI signifiait qu'une majorité de Canadiens s'opposaient à l'Accord de Charlottetown au niveau de ses grands principes. Plus tard, au cours de la campagne, les sondages révèlent toutefois que l'option du OUI aurait pu réaliser une certaine remontée dans l'opinion publique. Le jugement porté à l'endroit de Brian Mulroney et des autres chefs politiques influença, à coup sûr, le vote des Canadiens; toutefois, il serait exagéré d'y voir purement l'expression d'une sanction appliquée par une population envers ses leaders. Si les partisans du OUI comptèrent parmi les citoyens les mieux renseignés sur la question constitutionnelle, en revanche cette avalanche d'information n'aura pas permis que le contenu de l'Accord soit mieux compris ou accepté de la part des électeurs canadiens. Au Québec, le résultat du vote ne réserva aucune surprise : ainsi, on ne pouvait s'attendre des souverainistes qu'ils approuvent l'entente; de fait, en raison de leur importance numérique, ils parvinrent à contrebalancer la faible majorité d'appuis obtenus par le OUI dans cette province auprès des non-souverainistes.

To whom was the 1992 constitutional referendum result a "No" and for what reasons? Was the "No" inevitable, or could the result have been a "Yes"? Popular commentary on and elite reaction to the result treated it as resounding and remarkably uniform. In fact, the contest was close nationwide and the "Yes" won in four provinces, including Ontario. On the meaning of the result we have a surplus of interpretations: a repudiation of Quebec; a repudiation of all group recognitions; a judgement on Brian Mulroney; a judgement on the whole political class, unelected as well as elected; and a cry of anguish by victims of recession. The result could have been any and all of these and each proposition merits serious consideration.

The referendum raises a more general question about the very possibility of direct democracy. An abiding theme in the empirical study of politics is whether "public opinion" as such even exists, whether voters can make meaningful and interpretable choices on anything, much less on a document as formidably complex as the Charlottetown Accord.[1] There is, moreover, the question of whether voters can act as citizens, whether they can transcend self- or group-interest and prejudice and reason broadly about the consequences of their actions. An intermediate question in this realm asks what shortcuts busy voters can employ to deal with the costliness of information. Can these shortcuts distort the process?

THE COURSE OF THE VOTE

The place to begin is with the path of vote intentions. Daily trackings for Quebec and the rest-of-Canada appear in Figure 2.1.[2] The daily reading in the figure is

Figure 2.1: The "Yes" Share by Day

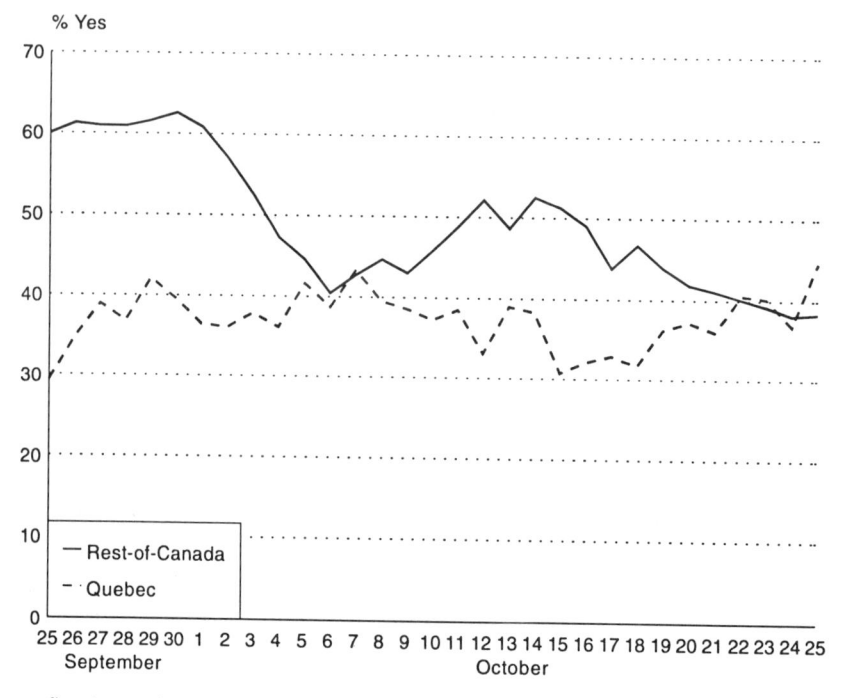

five-day moving average

the five-day moving average "Yes" share, centred on the indicated day.[3] The story differs sharply between the two electorates.

Right from the start, Quebec leaned to the "No." Nothing in the campaign seemed to have an interpretable effect and no trend manifested itself. There is a hint of an uptick after the leaders' debate (12 October). If there was a surge it was reversed in a few days, perhaps as a result of the last Wilhelmy transcripts episode (16 October). The last week did seem to bring a recovery: by voting day, the "Yes" share seems to have been about ten points higher than it was a week before. The surge, if indeed it was a surge, did not suffice. One cannot escape the impression that in Quebec the official campaign was over before it began.[4]

Outside Quebec, prospects for the "Yes" seemed bright at first: a "Yes:No" ratio of about 60:40. But the "Yes" lead outside Quebec collapsed over the first weekend in October, a total drop of 20 points, such that the "Yes" share outside Quebec bottomed out at 40 percent. According to Figure 2.1, the drop was accomplished in five days, from the 1st to the 6th. This understates the speed of the drop: the most obvious reading when the data are not averaged over five days is that the drop was *overnight*, between 3 and 4 October![5]

Then the share for "Yes" began a recovery. According to the moving-average tracking in Figure 2.1, the "Yes" began a surge on the 10th, reached a 50 percent share on the 12th, and began to fall back on the 15th or 16th. Tracking without smoothing suggests a shift to 50 percent "Yes" between the 11th and 12th, a plateauing on the 13th, a move up to 61 percent on the 14th, and then subsidence over the next three days. All of the recovery was erased, in any case. The shifts in question were of too great a magnitude and duration to be just sampling error.[6]

Table 2.1 indicates that the critical regions were Ontario and the Prairie provinces; the Atlantic provinces always stayed on side and British Columbia never came on side. The table gives weekly readings, in deference to the fact that the number of daily completions in each region was very small. In the opening phase, Ontario and the Prairie provinces looked rather like the Atlantic provinces. Once the first October weekend passed, Ontario and the Prairies looked more like British Columbia. The setback for the "Yes" was visible — at least temporarily — everywhere. But it mattered only in Ontario and the Prairie provinces. In British Columbia the province was already in the "No" camp. In the Atlantic provinces, the drop was comparable in absolute size to that elsewhere, but the starting point was just too high to produce a net reversal of direction. Also visible everywhere was the recovery in the second last week. The gain was greatest in Ontario and the Atlantic provinces. The Atlantic region, indeed, ended the campaign virtually where it began. On referendum day, 45 percent voted "Yes" in the country as a whole. In Quebec, the "Yes" stood at

Table 2.1: The "Yes" Share Outside Quebec, by Region

Week	B.C.	Prairies	Ontario	Atlantic
24-27 Sept.	41 (26)	60 (34)	62 (37)	59* (62)
28 Sept. – 4 Oct.	44 (55)	59 (105)	63 (88)	
5–11 Oct.	31 (45)	41 (82)	44 (126)	48 (37)
12–18 Oct.	40 (49)	49 (83)	51 (111)	63 (47)
19–25 Oct.	39 (47)	32 (98)	38 (146)	61 (60)

Number of observations in parentheses

*This number covers the entire period 24 Sept. - 4 Oct.

42 percent. In the Atlantic provinces, the "Yes" held its 60:40 margin; in the west, the margin was 40:60; and in Ontario the outcome was essentially 50:50.[7]

The following basic patterns beg explanation:

- The most important dynamic feature was the early October collapse of the "Yes." What propped the "Yes" up early on? What accounted for its ultimate weakness? Why was the drop so abrupt?
- In the end, support for the Accord outside Quebec followed an east-west gradient. What accounts for this?

THE CHARLOTTETOWN ACCORD AS A BARGAIN

Figure 2.2 helps account for the final result, by suggesting that, piece by piece, the Accord was politically weak. The figure gives support and opposition to four key elements in the document, separately for Quebec and the rest-of-Canada. The percentage disagreeing with a proposal is cast as a negative value; support and "don't know" are cast as positives. On the Senate, preference for the status quo and for abolition are both deemed to be positions in opposition to the proposals in the Accord. First consider the pattern outside Quebec:

- The one element with one-sided support was the recognition of an aboriginal right to self-government.

Figure 2.2: Support for Elements in Accord

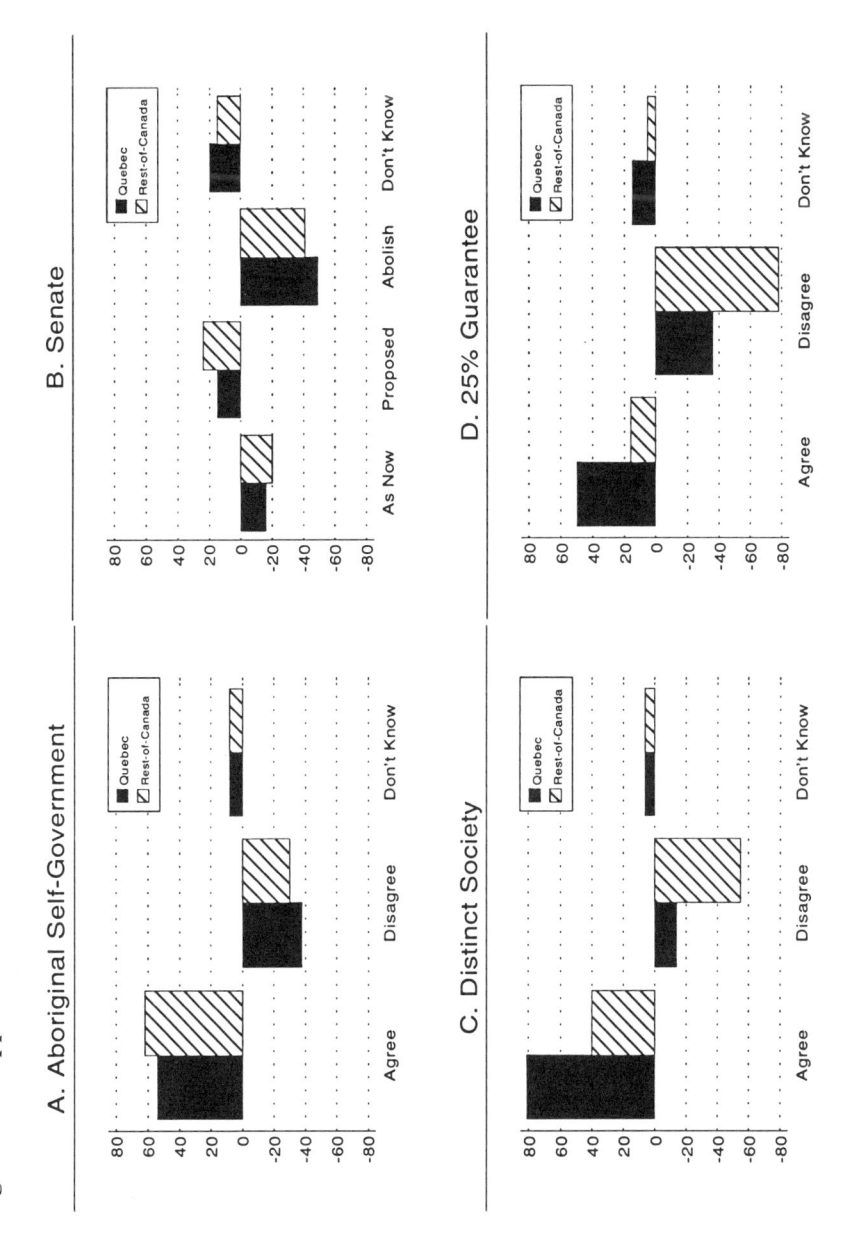

- Senate reform, allegedly the key element for westerners, received only tepid support. The Senate as proposed in the Accord received hardly any more support than the existing body. The plurality preference was for outright abolition of the chamber.
- On recognizing Quebec as a distinct society, opinion was modestly opposed, a 55:40 balance.
- The margin in opposition to the 25 percent guarantee (of seats in the House of Commons) was a stunning 78:16.

Now compare the rest-of-Canada with Quebec:

- On two elements, aboriginal self-government and the Senate, Quebec and the rest-of-Canada were hardly distinguishable. Quebecers were a little less supportive than non-Quebecers of self-government but still supported the proposal. Quebecers were more inclined towards outright abolition of the Senate, less supportive of either the status quo or the new proposals, and slightly more undecided overall. But as in the rest-of-Canada, the clear plurality was for abolition.
- On the other two elements — the ones designed for Quebec — the polarization was striking: a Quebec/non-Quebec gap of roughly 40 points. In each case, the balance of opinion was clearly negative in the rest-of-Canada and clearly positive in Quebec. The principal difference between the distinct society and the 25 percent guarantee proposals was in the overall balance: in both Quebec and the rest-of-Canada, the distinct society distribution was some 25-30 points closer to the approval end of the spectrum. Quebec was consensual around the distinct society clause while the rest-of-Canada was divided. On the 25 percent guarantee the rest-of-Canada was consensual in opposition while Quebec was divided.

On these questions, the various regions of Canada outside Quebec were *not* strikingly at odds with each other. Figure 2.3 gives a simplified picture of opinion on each element by region. Here the regional mean for each element appears, where approval was coded as 1, disapproval as −1, and "don't know" as 0;[8] for an element on which opinion was mostly approving, the mean rating is above zero, and so on. Figure 2.3 confirms that the only element on which opinion was mostly positive everywhere was aboriginal self-government. Even in the western provinces supporters outnumbered opponents. In those same provinces, the opposite was true for the proposal aimed at redressing their alleged representational deficit, the Senate. To be sure, support for the new body was highest — or opposition lowest — in the smaller regions, but not even there did it win many voters over. On the two Quebec-related matters, an east-west gradient was certainly visible. But for neither element was any non-Quebec

The People and the Charlottetown Accord 25

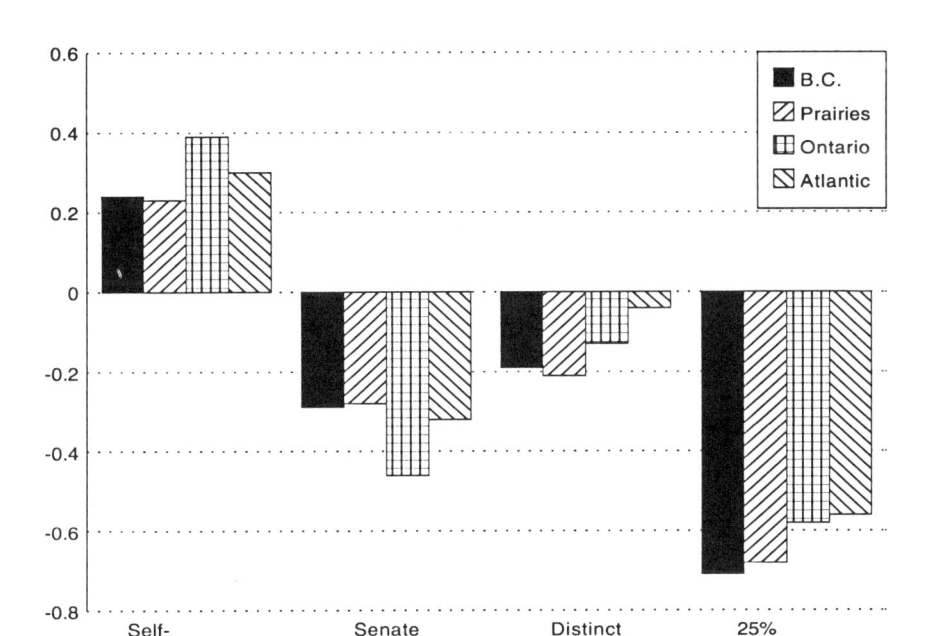

Figure 2.3: Support for Elements by Region

region polarized against any other: all regions opposed both elements; in each region, the balance was much more negative on the 25 percent guarantee than on the distinct society clause.

At first glance, this is not a promising pattern. Only one key element — aboriginal self-government — was supported in both Quebec and the rest-of-Canada. Another element — the new Senate — was opposed both inside and outside Quebec, even in the places for which it was thought to be a concession. Most ominously, on the heart of the package — the two Quebec elements — the country was deeply split. And on one of them, the 25 percent guarantee, there was no hint of a serious division within Canada outside Quebec.

But building coalitions of minorities is what much of politics is about. The critical thing is *asymmetry between support and opposition*: what you support you support intensely and what you oppose you oppose only weakly. The bargain succeeds because it is preferable, for each actor, to have an outcome in which there is no movement at all from the status quo. At a minimum, then, a majority must like at least one element in the package. Different parts of the majority may want different things but, given asymmetry of support and opposition, that should not matter; one thing is enough.

By this standard, the Charlottetown Accord seems to have succeeded. In Quebec, majorities supported three of the four key elements. Outside Quebec, fewer than one respondent in five supported nothing (or opposed everything) in the deal. About one in three supported only one element and a slightly smaller number supported two. Now, if a deal is constructed properly, it should not matter that non-Quebec respondents support only one element, as long as a majority does support at least one.

The trouble is that that one element, as should be clear from Figures 2.2 and 2.3, was usually aboriginal self-government. The proportions supporting other elements were tiny, even for the one thing contrived for a white, anglophone clientele: Senate reform. Aboriginal self-government had to carry a heavy coalition-building burden. But this brings us to a general point.

For a document conceived so clearly and self-consciously as a bargain, the Charlottetown Accord was most peculiar. Typically, elements in a bargain appeal to the self-defined interests of pivotal actors, actors whose withdrawal from the coalition would doom it. It is odd, then, that the most widely supported element was a concession to one of the smallest groups. In sheer numbers, withdrawal of aboriginal voters would be of virtually no electoral significance. Aboriginal Peoples might have practical *non*-electoral clout, by threatening to take us back to the tense summer of 1990. This probably weighed on many non-aboriginal voters, but the implicit threat was also double-edged; resort to unconventional politics could easily undermine support for aboriginal claims. For most voters in 1992, support for aboriginal self-government must have been disinterested, a recognition of a powerful moral claim. Whatever its exact basis, it was support for a *concession* to somebody else. But the same was true outside Quebec for the Accord's Quebec elements: a respondent outside that province who supported, say, the 25 percent guarantee was unlikely to be making a positive statement of approval; more likely, the respondent was saying that he or she can live with it as part of a package or for the sake of constitutional peace.[9]

The one major element in the Accord designed to satisfy the non-aboriginal non-francophone part of the electorate failed to do its job. The meagre support for the proposed Senate admits two readings. One possibility is that the new institution was seen as too much of a derogation from the "Triple-E" ideal, so weak a reed that outright abolition would be better. If a satisfactory question about a "real" Triple-E could be formulated it might win greater support, most importantly, majority support in small provinces. The alternative reading says that Senate proposals — all of them, aside from abolition — rested on a profound elite misapprehension. On this alternative view, the only real thoughts Canadians have about the Senate are about the existing institution and these thoughts are overwhelmingly negative. Polls about the Senate were driven by the elite's definition of the Senate reform agenda, typically, and so offered respondents only something called "Senate reform" as a means of expressing their disdain for the existing institution. Naturally, respondents rose to the bait, but then found their expressions presented in elite discourse (and here, even Preston Manning engages in such discourse) as overwhelming popular support for new Senate arrangements. Instead, for most Canadians the best new Senate is none at all. Our sense is that the second reading is closer to the truth. Just as the 25 percent guarantee was something Quebecers hesitated to accept and never really asked for, so Senate reform was not something really on the minds of Canadians elsewhere, not even in the west.

The discussion so far has made no mention of *shifts* in opinion on key elements. The omission was deliberate: there were no such shifts. The patterns in Figures 2.2 and 2.3 persisted over the entire official campaign.

THE PARTS AND THE WHOLE: OUTSIDE QUEBEC

Yet *something* propped the non-Quebec "Yes" share up in the early going. Opposition to the distinct society clause or to the 25 percent seat guarantee did not kill the overall deal at the start and support for aboriginal self-government did not save it at the end. If the campaign was *not* an exercise in persuasion about elements in the Accord, only the following possibilities remain:

- Considerations telling against the "Yes," for example the 25 percent guarantee, might have become more important.
- Considerations that sustained the "Yes" in the early going might have become less important; for example, opinion on aboriginal self-government might have been important at first but irrelevant later.
- The general burden of proof may have shifted and the Accord may have lost the benefit of the doubt.
- Combinations of the above could have occurred, inasmuch as no one pattern excludes all of the others.

As it happens, all these things did occur. Figure 2.2 showed that the factors with the greatest potential for damage were the Quebec-related ones and both factors became more important. Before 5 October, among voters who opposed one of the two Quebec elements, two in three nonetheless intended to vote "Yes." Even among opponents of both key concessions the "Yes" share was close to 50 percent. After 5 October, these numbers plummeted: among voters opposed to one but only one concession the share dropped below 50 percent; among voters opposed to both Quebec elements the share was only 25 percent. In other words, a respondent who opposed both Quebec elements was only half as likely after 5 October as before to vote "Yes."

At the same time, the factor with the greatest positive potential, aboriginal self-government, got decoupled from the vote, at least in the vital middle of the campaign. Voters did not become less supportive of the principle of aboriginal self-government; but they became less likely to act on the basis of that support.

Support, such as it was, for the new Senate helped brake the decline of the "Yes." At the end, a voter who opposed both Quebec concessions but who approved the new Senate had a roughly 50:50 chance of voting "Yes." But the new Senate just did not enjoy as wide support as did aboriginal self-government.

These shifts admit another, complementary interpretation: that some force stripped away the general arguments in support of the Charlottetown Accord. In a sense, it is no surprise that someone who opposed both the distinct society clause and the 25 percent guarantee was, in the end, very likely to vote "No." What is more surprising is that such a voter had a 50:50 chance of voting "Yes" early on and that even among voters who opposed all four things, about 40 percent intended to vote yes. Before the first weekend in October, then, many voters were prepared to give the Accord the benefit of the doubt. What general arguments were marshalled to bring voters onside and how did they fare?

First, the process that delivered the Charlottetown Accord encouraged voters to ask as a generalization *how well their province did out of the deal*. The negotiations concluded in Charlottetown were much like a first ministers' conference; this naturally directed attention to how one's own premier performed. The near consensus of the federal parties deprived voters of an overarching nationwide division. The contrast with the 1988 debate over the Canada-U.S. Free Trade Agreement is instructive: there the parties divided sharply and these divisions were reflected in sharp contrasts between party groups and weak contrasts between regions and language groups in the electorate at large. The partisan exceptions in 1992, the Bloc Québécois and Reform, were small parties with sectionally concentrated appeals. In the absence of a major-party fault line that transcended provincial boundaries, then, voters may have been encouraged to see cleavages between provinces.[10] Moreover, in a low-information world a general judgement on how one's province did was an obvious conduit for opinion on the Accord's individual elements; one could see it as a running total. But it ought also to have been a cause as much as a consequence of judgements on individual elements: for example, voters might have been more likely to endorse the distinct society clause had they believed their own province to be a winner. As it happens, voters everywhere tended to see their own province as a loser and this perception hurt the chances of the Accord. But, as with support for individual elements, this perception did not move; it was as negative at the beginning as at the end.

Second, proponents felt impelled to move beyond the arguments about the contents of the Accord. What might move someone who liked nothing of substance in the Accord to consider voting for it anyway?

- Most central was the argument that, for all its flaws, the Charlottetown Accord was *the best compromise possible* under the circumstances. Almost by definition an "Accord" is a compromise. To evaluate the compromise is to make the most general possible judgement on the Accord. For many voters, this would be not so much a matter of embracing the logic of a logroll, which includes something for oneself, as accepting the necessity for an accommodation among strategically placed or morally advantaged others. We have already articulated a transcendental logic such as this in relation to certain elements in the package. Now the logic is extended to the package as such: even if you cannot bring yourself to support *any* element in particular, are you prepared to live with the whole package, for the sake of compromise? The general necessity of compromise was an argument repeated *ad nauseam* by proponents. For the most part, it did not work: at no point did a majority accept the argument and, most critically, the proportion accepting it plummetted over the first weekend in October.

- Second was an argument from consequences: even a voter who can imagine a better compromise might still accept that this particular compromise, though suboptimal, would nonetheless allow us to shift the agenda, *to move on to other questions*, while rejection of the Accord would allow the current crisis to continue, with possibly dire implications for the economy. Of all arguments, this one performed best among voters: early on, the balance of agreement/disagreement was close to 60:30; after the first weekend in October, however, the balance was about 50:40.

- Lurking behind the whole process was another argument from consequences, fear of *separation by Quebec* if the Accord went down. Clearly, this fear was not widely shared in the electorate. In the early going, about one voter in three, by a generous estimate, exhibited such fear; at the end, the proportion was under one in four.

Although only one of the three general arguments received majority endorsement by itself and that majority shrank, at every point in the campaign a one-sided majority of voters accepted at least one argument. Over most of the campaign each additional argument accepted added about ten points to a voter's likelihood of saying "Yes." Voters were not, thus, utterly oblivious to general claims about the wisdom and necessity of the Accord, notwithstanding its flaws. But the average number of arguments accepted dropped and did so most dramatically over the critical first weekend in October. This brings us to dynamics.

THE SOURCES OF DYNAMICS

Outside Quebec, three turning points presented themselves for explanation. Most important was the "Yes" collapse in the first weekend of October. It brought the largest shift in vote intention; it increased the relevance of what were all along the most potentially damaging elements in the Accord; and it undermined some of the supporting arguments for the "Yes." The other two points were the "Yes"'s apparent recovery over Thanskgiving weekend and its final collapse, which began the following weekend, around 17 October.

What accounted for the early-October collapse of the "Yes" and of at least two of its key supporting arguments? All indications point to Pierre Trudeau's speech at the Maison du Egg Roll on the night of 1 October. The speech was given in the late evening, Montreal time, and so for most voters it could not have been a news story until the next day, the 2nd, at the earliest. The collapse occurred on the day after that, the 3rd. Awareness of Trudeau's intervention surged just in advance of the collapse of the "Yes." Figure 2.4 links the two by taking the daily percentage aware of Trudeau's opposition, turning the percentage upside down, and superimposing it on the daily "Yes" share. Before the Egg Roll speech around 50 percent of the sample attributed an opposition stance to Trudeau. This seems reasonable in light of the prominence given his mid-September essay in *Maclean's*. The latter was not in fact directly on the Accord, but was initially reported as such and was couched in terms that made inference of opposition perfectly reasonable. In any case, the Egg Roll speech dispelled all doubts. Virtually overnight, awareness of his opposition grew 20 points. No other intervenor was as widely visible to our respondents and for no other was there a surge as dramatic as this. Equally to the point, the gain in his visibility took place in lockstep with the decline of the "No" and led that decline by one day.

Figure 2.5 helps bring out why Pierre Trudeau remains such a pivotal figure. In the figure, our respondents are divided into three groups: those who liked Trudeau very much; those who held him in middling regard; and those who disliked him.[11] At the outset, the more a voter liked Pierre Trudeau, the more likely he or she was to vote "Yes"! We take this to indicate that English Canadians who like Trudeau tend to take the French Canadian project seriously and wish to accommodate it. Although the definition of the project implicit in the Charlottetown Accord was not Trudeau's own, voters may be forgiven if, in the early, low-information context, they were a bit hazy on this. It seems perfectly consistent for someone who likes Pierre Trudeau to give a proposed

The People and the Charlottetown Accord 31

Figure 2.4: Unawareness of Trudeau's Opposition and Support for the Accord

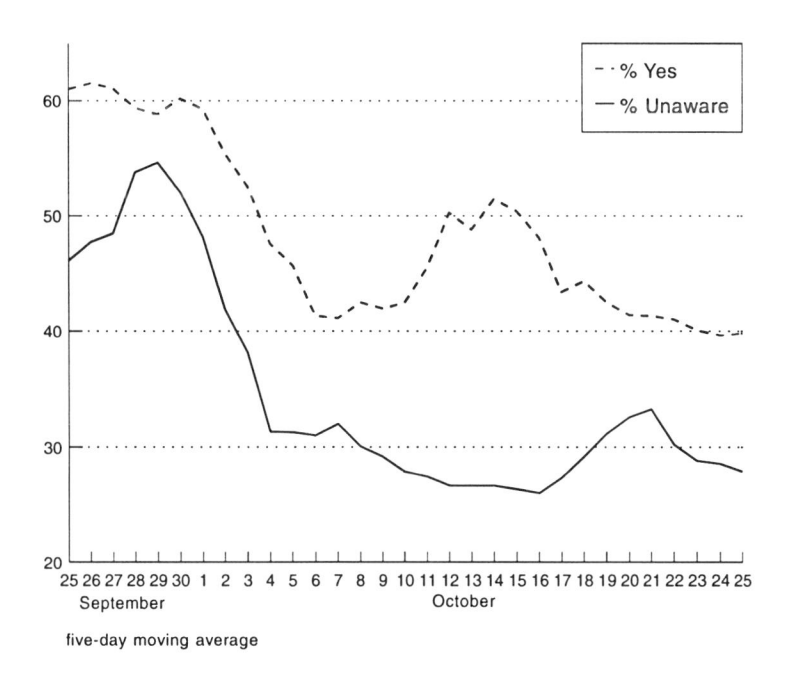

five-day moving average

Figure 2.5: "Yes" Share by Trudeau Ratings

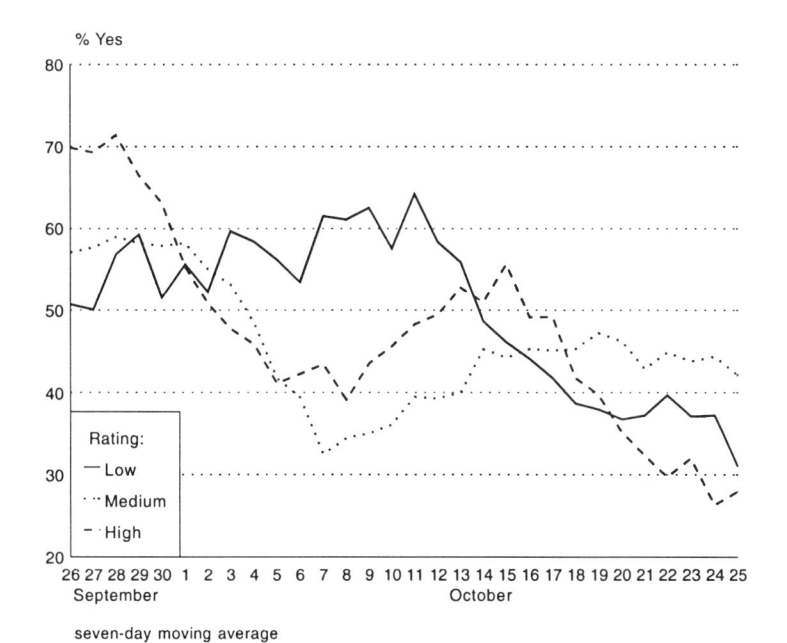

seven-day moving average

accommodation with Quebec the benefit of the doubt. At least it would seem so until Trudeau himself says otherwise.

Once he did say otherwise, the relative positions of the groups shifted dramatically:

- Respondents who disliked Trudeau were not persuaded by the Egg Roll speech. If anything, the "Yes" gained ground in this group right after the speech. But the middle and high Trudeau groups turned against the Accord.
- Among both neutral and pro-Trudeau respondents the "Yes" recovered ground, such that by 15-17 October pro-Trudeau respondents were once again most likely and anti-Trudeau respondents least likely to vote "Yes"; now, though, the "Yes" share in each group had dropped about 15 points.
- At the end, a new configuration emerged, one reminiscent of the coalition against the Meech Lake Accord. Where both neutral and pro-Trudeau respondents shared in the mid-October recovery, only among neutrals was the recovery sustained. Among pro-Trudeau respondents the "Yes" slide resumed. Trudeau fanciers, who started the campaign most likely to vote "Yes," ended up least likely to do so. Closest to them at the end were the group that sustained the "Yes" in mid-campaign: voters who disliked Trudeau. The Charlottetown Accord, like the Meech lake Accord, may have been brought down by a coalition of opposites.

The recovery over the Thanksgiving weekend finds no immediately obvious source in the campaign narrative and may only have been an inevitable, and essentially autonomous, decay of the impulse generated the week before.[12]

The most plausible source for the final collapse of the "Yes" was the barrage of poll information on the 16th and 17th of October: a *Globe and Mail* poll on the 16th and Reid-Southam and Environics-CTV polls on the 17th. This was the first clear indication that the "Yes" would lose. Earlier polls had only hinted at trouble, if they did even that. Before 26 September, polls suggested that the "Yes" would win by a wide margin in the country as a whole, if not in every province. On 26 September an Angus Reid poll gave the first real indication of serious trouble: it placed the all-Canada "Yes" share among decided respondents at 51 percent and polls over the next three weeks confirmed roughly this picture. If on 26 September it became clear that the "Yes" forces faced a real fight, on 16-17 October, it suddenly appeared as if they would lose. We asked respondents their expectations for the result in their province, in Quebec, and in Canada as a whole. For the province and the country as a whole, these expectations plummetted right after 17 October. In turn, the drop in expectations induced a further drop in the "Yes" share.[13]

OTHER FEATURES OF THE VOTE OUTSIDE QUEBEC

Pierre Trudeau was not the only key player. Feelings about Brian Mulroney were also caught up in the vote: the more a voter liked him the more likely he or she was to vote "Yes." Few voters liked him: our respondents typically rated him far below the Accord's other proponents and far below Trudeau. But it would be premature to say that the "No" victory was just a repudiation of Brian Mulroney. First of all, feelings about other key players in the Accord coalition — notably Jean Chrétien, Audrey McLaughlin, and the premier of the voter's province — were even more important than attitudes to Brian Mulroney. Does this just mean that the repudiation was more broad-gauged, that it extended to the whole political class? The problem with this argument is that other leaders, typically, were held in considerably higher regard than Brian Mulroney. Other leaders tended get middling ratings: slightly more voters disliked them than liked them, but the proportion who gave positive ratings was never trivial. And, roughly speaking, the further east one went (outside Quebec) the more highly rated the key politicians (Brian Mulroney aside) tended to be. Attitudes to the political class were clearly important, then, but their importance was not unequivocally negative for the prospects of the Accord.

There remains, moreover, the question of what the very connection between vote on the Accord and attitudes to the political class means. It is too simple to say that the Accord was only a conduit for punishing politicians, a lightning rod whose content was largely irrelevant. Although the Accord must have been such a conduit for some voters, our sense is that most voters truly did grapple with the content of the Accord. Recall from above that clear majorities always accepted at least one general argument for saying "Yes," right down to the campaign's end. And here is where the other meaning of the leader rating-vote relationship lies: busy voters, facing costly information and uncertainty, commonly look to intervenors for guidance. A useful intervenor need not necessarily hold the voter's own interests to heart. For many voters, then, liking or disliking of politicians is a guide to accepting or rejecting their judgement. Rejecting their judgement may have the effect of punishing politicians, but only incidentally.[14]

In addition, judgements on the Accord's public supporters were affected by voters' party commitments, if they had any. Party identification sorted voters in two ways. First, identification with *any* of the three parties in the Accord coalition increased a voter's likelihood of saying "Yes," as compared to identification with Reform or with no party at all. Second, Conservative identifiers were the most likely of all to vote "Yes." Although New Democrats were slower than the Liberals to come around, by referendum day these two party groups were indistinguishable, half-way between non-partisans and Conservatives. And whenever party identification was added to a vote estimation, the predictive power of leader ratings was cut. Neither the vote on the Accord nor the processing of judgements about politicians and their stances were completely detached from the ongoing party struggle in the background.

All other intervenors paled by comparison with members of the Accord coalition and with Pierre Trudeau. Some, such as the women's movement and the business community, had a modest impact in the first few weeks. Curiously, awareness of opposition by the women's movement had a greater effect for men than for women; the impact was *not* a backlash. And women were not summarily more likely to vote "No" than men. The union movement had a modest effect towards the campaign's end, in the sense that awareness of union leaders' support for the Accord modestly increased the chances of a "Yes" vote, other things being equal. But union leaders were bucking their own rank and file: union families were less likely than non-union ones to vote "Yes." Preston Manning had a discernible effect, but not the one he intended: other things equal, awareness of his opposition boosted the "Yes" vote!

Liking Quebec helped a voter mightily in getting to a "Yes" vote and did so in various ways. Party commitments reflected, and may have helped produce, differentials in sentiment about Quebec. Party and group sentiment, in turn, reflected degrees of economic comfort and educational attainment: higher-income voters tended to like Quebec more than lower-income voters did; similarly, the higher the education, the more sympathetic to Quebec one tended to be; unemployment had the opposite effect.

But economic marginality and distress were important in their own right, not just as they affected sympathy for Quebec. In general, the less advantaged one was, the less likely was a "Yes" vote. This suggests that the trough of recession is a bad time to bring forward a major constitutional proposal which is not itself directly about economic recovery. But the pattern is probably not peculiar to economic bad times, not just an indicator of short-term distress. The economic and social differential in response to the Charlottetown Accord corresponded to differences remarked in Maastricht voting in the European community: the socially most marginal voters are least likely to be persuaded by elite consensus on what the country needs. This could indicate one or both of two processes: lower status voters may be less exposed to the arguments originating in the elite; alternatively, they may identify less with the elite and so might reject the elite's arguments, when they do get exposed to them.

And feelings about Quebec were not just ways of articulating degrees of economic comfort or optimism. When voters struggle to compose a response to a complex policy question they listen for clues. One important source of clues is how the question plays into the contours of the polity's group life. In Canada, the most sharply etched discontinuity pits French against English, Quebec against the rest.[15] It should come as no surprise, then, that feelings towards Quebec affected evaluation of the Accord and the chances of a "Yes." As a rule, the less equipped one was to gather substantive information, the more one went straight from simple feelings about Quebec to the vote.[16] And the less one knew, the less one liked Quebec. Again, though, the story is not one of simple rejection. Most Canadians outside Quebec gave that province positive ratings, markedly more positive ones than they were prepared to give to virtually any politician. Only among the least informed were negative ratings as common as positive ones. So feelings about Quebec were clearly implicated in the vote and were most implicated among voters for whom the feelings were most likely to be negative. But the story is not one of a simple backlash.

Each side in the debate believed that getting voters to know more about the Accord worked to their advantage. Each side was right, up to a point. The more a voter knew the more willing he or she was to accept the new Senate or the recognition of Quebec as a distinct society.[17] On the other hand, knowing more about the Accord produced scepticism about its supporting rhetoric: well-informed voters were disproportionately likely to disdain the compromise, dismiss the claim that the Accord would allow us to move on, and reject the possibility of Quebec's separation. But the more one knew about the Charlottetown Accord the more likely one was to vote "Yes." Differences by information level were never large but widened at the end.[18]

QUEBEC

Right from the start, the Quebec electorate must be divided in three: non-francophones, francophone sovereignists, and francophone non-sovereignists. The first group was solidly for the "Yes" and the second solidly for the "No." The relative sizes of these two groups tilted the field of play but the third group decided the outcome. The "Yes" was not helped by the relatively small size of its captive group: although non-francophones represent 18 percent of the total Quebec population, their share of the electorate is closer to 15 percent. Sovereignists constitute a larger share but how much larger is a matter of debate. Here the issue is what a self-described sovereignist means by the term. It seems fairly clear that some Quebecers are confused about what sovereignty entails,[19] but how would respondents who think of themselves as sovereignist react if it were pointed out that a sovereign Quebec would no longer be part of Canada? The sovereignist hard core ought to consist of those who still call themselves sovereignist when confronted with the hard truth. By our estimation these constitute 39 percent of the total electorate (44 percent of francophones).[20] Another 8 percent might be called diffident sovereignists; for this group, it is an empirical question of which is more important: the diffidence or the reflexive self-definition as sovereignist. This leaves 38 percent of the electorate as clearly on the battle ground, francophone non-sovereignists. They may or may not be supplemented by diffident sovereignists.

In our sample, 80 percent of non-francophones voted "Yes." If anything this underestimated the "Yes" share; we suspect that the real share was closer to 85 percent.[21] On the other, sovereignist side, 89 percent voted "No." Although there was subtle variation on this side, more striking was the unanimity: intensity of support for sovereignty amongst self-described sovereignists made only a modest difference; the experimental manipulation mentioned above made no difference; and even ambivalence or indifference on the question mattered little, as 78 percent of those with no opinion on the sovereignty question voted "No."

Given the overwhelming "No" among self-described sovereignists as well as among voters unsure on the question and given the small size of the non-francophone bloc, the "Yes" side needed to win over 70 percent of francophone non-sovereignists to win overall. Instead, the share was 56 percent. By one standard, this was an impressive showing for the "Yes," matched by few electorates in the rest-of-Canada. Perhaps, given the threshold, the task was just impossible. Still, we can ask what kept it so low and the following considerations seem pertinent:

- Just as feelings of attachment to Canada and Quebec are strong predictors of attitudes to Quebec sovereignty, so among non-sovereignists were they factors in the vote. In our sample, 39 percent were more attached to Quebec than to Canada, 14 percent were more attached to Canada than to Quebec, and 48 percent were equally attached to both.[22] Some non-sovereignists clearly viewed support for the Accord as an expression of patriotism: 70 percent of francophone non-sovereignists more or equally attached to Canada voted "Yes," compared to 37 percent of those more attached to Quebec. But the size of the latter group hurt the prospects for the "Yes."

- The great majority of francophone non-sovereignists who turned out in the 1989 provincial election voted Liberal. But 12 percent voted for the Parti Québécois, and this group looked at the agreement with a critical eye: 84 percent voted "No."

- A majority of francophone non-sovereignists saw Quebec as a loser in the Charlottetown Accord. A majority also rejected the claim that the compromise was the best possible, and these positions were closely linked to the vote. Also linked to the vote was perception of the stakes: was a "No" to the Accord a "Yes" to sovereignty? The campaign neutralized this link.

- Among specific proposals, the pattern roughly complemented the one outside Quebec: voters worried more about concessions to other groups than they approved concessions their own representatives had secured. Although a strong majority approved the distinct society clause, few non-sovereignists thought the clause went far enough. At the same time, the Senate proposals were closely linked to the sense of Quebec as a loser, even as Quebecers did not see them as much of a gain for the west. The 25 percent guarantee more than offset losses induced by the Senate proposal, however. Quebecers did not see Aboriginal Peoples' gains as Quebec's losses but neither did their general approval of aboriginal self-government help the "Yes."

- Among non-sovereignists there is little evidence that disappointment with the meagre transfer of power to the province made much difference to the vote.

- In contrast to the rest-of-Canada, the party battle was absolutely central to the Quebec vote, even among non-sovereignists. Feelings about Jacques Parizeau and (especially) Robert Bourassa were crucial to the vote, even controlling other factors (including the 1989 vote). Federal actors were of little to no significance. The only other individual or group to matter was the business community: feelings about the community affected the vote and the community was generally warmly regarded.

- To Robert Bourassa's credibility, two events were potentially critical: Jean Allaire's signing on with the "No" camp; and the Wilhelmy affair(s). We lean to an emphasis on Allaire, as the largest drop in "Yes" support came *before* the Wilhelmy affair and around the time that the "No" team was consolidated. Allaire's presence on the "No" side may have reassured voters that the integrity of the federation was *not* at stake and reminded them that Robert Bourassa had been, to say the least, inconsistent. If the Wilhelmy affair was important, it was so because it strengthened doubts already in place about Bourassa's credibility.

CONCLUSIONS

Did Canadians outside Quebec indeed say "No" to Quebec? to Brian Mulroney? to the political class in general? Some of these questions must be answered in the affirmative. But staking such claims is more complex than it seems at first. And in all discussions, it should be kept in mind that about 45 percent of the non-Quebec electorate said "Yes" to the Charlottetown Accord, notwithstanding the depth of voters' reservations about the document.

There seems to be no escaping the conclusion that the "No" was a rejection of Quebec's demands, at least packaged as they were in 1992, even if Quebec voters also rejected the same Accord. To begin with, neither key Quebec-related element earned majority support outside that province. By itself, this comes as no surprise, and early in the campaign the rejection of these elements did not block majority support for the package of which they were part. But when the

"Yes" collapse began, the most divisive issues were the 25-percent seat guarantee and the distinct society clause. It is also material that, from the beginning (long before reassuring noises came out of Quebec proper), few respondents bought the argument that rejecting the Accord would encourage Quebec's separation from Canada.

Does an emphasis on rejection of the Quebec-specific content in the Accord make the result any less of a rejection of Brian Mulroney? No, but to a great extent only because rejecting Mulroney was so easy at the end. Opinion on the prime minister was a factor all along, to be sure. But early on, his role was partly, perhaps mainly, as a cue-giver about substance. It was the Charlottetown Accord's misfortune that it was tied so closely to Mulroney's reputation, despite his own deep reservations about the settlement. Even so, as long as some combination of general arguments overrode objections to substance, Mulroney's unpopularity was not fatal. It is tempting to speculate that once it was clear that the Accord was going down, voters were free to indulge themselves, as it were, in Mulroney bashing. It is not clear that they would have felt so free had the battle been — or been made by published polls to seem — more closely joined.

Were voters also bashing the rest of the country's political leadership? There is no question that opinion on that leadership mattered; indeed it mattered more than opinion on Brian Mulroney. As with Mulroney some of this impact looks like punishment rather than cue-taking. But the account cannot stop there. An awkward fact is that other leaders were not as uniformly reviled as Brian Mulroney. Most were not as popular as Pierre Trudeau, but most got middling grades and opinion was fairly divided. For political figures about which opinion is divided, the language of punishment is just not appropriate. Voters who intensely disliked the leaders may well have been sending a punitive message. But many voters disliked the leaders only mildly and a large minority gave them a positive rating. In places where politicians continue to be held in relatively high esteem, most notably the Atlantic provinces, the near consensus in the political class helped the Accord.

Did Quebec voters say "No" to Canada? Some did, more or less: sovereignists could hardly be expected to say "Yes" to an Accord designed to negate their very objective. It was only partial mitigation, if any, that for some sovereignists the objective itself was obscure. But as many Quebecers said "Yes" as did voters outside the province and the "Yes" had a powerful patriotic motivation. The non-sovereignists who did say no, themselves a clear minority, did so in part out of reassurance that the stakes were low.

Did voters, in Quebec as well as in the rest-of-Canada, say "No" to all forms of group recognition? Since the referendum, the question has come up in relation to official language communities in New Brunswick, and the claim was made, notably by Deborah Coyne, that such recognition was incompatible with the spirit of the 26 October vote. Some voters, outside Quebec mainly, probably did mean something like this by their vote. For instance, voters who rejected aboriginal self-government also tended to reject the two Quebec items and it is easy to imagine them saying "No" to all such entrenchments. In this sense, the self-government proposals were a litmus test. But by this test, a strong majority could *not* be said to reject group recognition as a matter of principle: majorities everywhere said "Yes" to aboriginal self-government. What else they might say "Yes" to is a matter for conjecture, but the bald claim that "No" meant no recognition of groups simply cannot stand.

Did Canadians fail the test set by their leaders and thus vindicate opponents of direct democracy, either in general or in its specific 1992 manifestation? It *is* true, on the one hand, that the less a voter knew, the less likely he or she was to vote as the political class wished. This pattern surfaces in many ways: differences by education and by measures of respondents' actual knowledge. It is reinforced by information-level contrasts in the importance of "tribal" sentiment; simple feeling towards Quebec was important generally and especially important in low-information groups, as a proxy for substance. All this said, knowledge did not make a voter happier with the Charlottetown Accord. Voters at *all* information levels became *less* persuaded as the campaign advanced of general arguments for the document, and at each stage of the campaign, more informed voters were less willing to accept a general argument for the deal. Strikingly, even though well-informed voters were generally more favourably disposed to Quebec, they were the least persuaded that that province's separation was a serious threat. And the one intervenor who appealed, even if covertly, to tribal sentiment, Preston Manning, was the one opponent who actually helped the "Yes." The data pattern forces us to conclude that many who voted "Yes" did so despite deep reservations. Certainly it does seem true that characteristics associated with entertaining doubts also conduced in the end to giving the Accord the benefit of those same doubts. On one hand, then, we should not delude ourselves about direct democracy: faced with a complex task, many voters will resort to cues and devices that do not pass muster in polite company. On the other hand, many voters struggle mightily with the demands of the choice and many were even prepared to override their doubts and go along with the country's political leadership.

Was the defeat inevitable? It is true that most of the world's ballot measures fail, and it seems reasonable to ask why the Charlottetown Accord should be exempted from this rule. The rule may be misleading, however: most ballot measures are private initiatives placed on US state ballots. Voters naturally distrust such initiatives and the measure commonly stimulates sharp opposition. Conversely, where the political elite forms a consensus on a measure, at least in U.S. states, the measure usually passes.[23] The 1992 Canadian referendum may be a standing refutation of this generalization, if we accept that the

Canadian elite was largely united on the Charlottetown Accord.[24] Then again, it may signal that the 1990s have so discredited political elites that consensus among them is no longer persuasive, indeed may even cause voters to smell a rat. Another possibility is that we have defined the elite too narrowly: given where he sits ideologically, Pierre Trudeau may represent a large body of elite, as well as mass, opinion. But there is another reading of the event worth considering. Canadians did not like much of the Charlottetown Accord's content. And it is not clear that they should have, when one considers where most voters sit, namely, *not* at the bargaining table. Yet almost half the electorate said "Yes," in spite of themselves and even after polls had indicated that the cause was hopeless.

NOTES

Data reported in this paper are drawn from the referendum waves of the 1992-93 Canadian Elections Study, for which the authors are among the co-investigators. Support for the study came from the Social Sciences and Humanities Research Council of Canada, under grants 411-92-0019 and 421-92-0026, the US National Science Foundation, our respective universities, and Queen's University, where the first-named author was a Skelton-Clark Fellow during the referendum and during the writing of this chapter. Fieldwork was conducted by the Institute of Social Research, York University, under the direction of David Northrup and Rick Myles. Special thanks are due to Henry Brady, Joe Fletcher, Ron Watts, Doug Brown, and the anonymous referees. All of the foregoing are absolved from the errors that remain.

1. Key contributions to this debate are: Philip E. Converse, "The Nature of Belief Systems in Mass Publics," in David Apter (ed.), *Ideology and Discontent* (New York: Free Press, 1964); Paul M. Sniderman, Richard Brody, and Philip Tetlock, *Reasoning and Choice* (Cambridge: Cambridge University Press, 1991); and John R. Zaller, *The Nature and Origins of Mass Opinion* (Cambridge: Cambridge University Press, 1992).

2. Interviewing for the referendum campaign wave of the 1992-93 Canadian study began on 24 September and continued to 25 October, the eve of the vote. Sample was released daily and clearance of each day's release was carefully controlled, such that the day of interview was effectively a random event. Altogether, 2,533 interviews were completed, an average of 79 per day. Immediately after the vote, a second wave of interviewing began; 2,226 respondents completed the second interview. About 40 percent of the total sample was drawn from Quebec. Outside Quebec, smaller provinces were modestly overrepresented. The questionnaires included items covering a wide range of considerations: specific elements in the Charlottetown Accord; general arguments; heuristics that might help interpret the event; expectations for the outcome; vote intentions and behaviour; awareness of intervenors; attitudes to a range of persons, places, and groups; general values; perceptions of Canadian society; and basic demographic information.

    For more detail on the study and for wording of individual items see Richard Johnston, André Blais, Elisabeth Gidengil, and Neil Nevitte, *Rhetoric and Reality:*

The Referendum on the Charlottetown Accord (Montreal: McGill-Queen's University Press, forthcoming).

3. All figures and tables are based on decided voters or leaners. On the logic and the practice of moving averages with rolling cross section data, see Richard Johnston, André Blais, Henry E. Brady, and Jean Crête, *Letting the People Decide: Dynamics of a Canadian Election* (Montreal: McGill-Queen's University Press, 1992).

4. There was, however, substantial movement in September, before our fieldwork began: published polls indicate that the "Yes" dropped seven points before the campaign's official start. The five polls done in the last week of August indicated that Quebecers were almost evenly divided: the median "Yes" vote among decided respondents was 47 percent. In the first half of September, by which time the exact wording of the question was a matter of record and each side had articulated its basic theme, the median "Yes" share (three polls) dropped to 43 percent. The four polls between 14 September, the date of the Quebec Superior Court injunction on publication of the Wilhelmy transcript, and the beginning of our fieldwork on the 24th gave a median "Yes" vote of 40 percent. This chronology suggests that the impact of the Wilhelmy affair was limited, indeed that the decline in late September merely continued a trend. We return to this below.

5. For a typical non-Quebec daily sample of about 50 observations. The implied daily 95 percent confidence interval is ±14 percentage points, less than the overnight drop.

6. The shifts between the 11th and 12th and between the 13th and 14th were just inside the 95 percent confidence interval, although well over a standard error in size. The difference between the 14th and the preceding and succeeding low points were well over the threshold of conventional statistical significance.

7. In the Atlantic provinces, the "No" won barely in Nova Scotia. In the west, British Columbia gave the "Yes" only 32 percent.

8. On the Senate, preference for either the existing institution or abolition were deemed disapproval of the body proposed in the Accord.

9. There were, of course, other elements in the package, notably clauses on the economic union and a kind of "social charter." Evidence from other polls indicated that most voters supported these but, like the aboriginal self-government proposals, neither the economic-union nor the social-charter proposals moved many votes.

10. The formulation of the argument in these terms is not original to us. To the best of our knowledge, it originates with Alan Cairns, in his oral presentation to the Advisory Board of the Institute of Intergovernmental Relations, Queen's University, 30 November 1992. Of course, some lines of debate and opposition did transcend provinces, for example NAC's intervention attempted to create debate along general ideological lines.

11. Liking of Pierre Trudeau is indicated by ratings on a "feeling thermometer" which runs from 0 to 100 "degrees," where 50° indicates that the respondent neither likes nor dislikes the person in question. The boundaries for Figure 2.5 are 33° and 66°.

12. Tom Flanagan, in remarks to a seminar at the University of Calgary, suggested that recovery may have been helped along by the two-stage release of the Accord's

legal text. Although the official release date was Tuesday, 13 October, the effective release date was the Saturday before, the 10th: the government of Quebec made the legal text available as the Bourassa-Parizeau debate was looming and Parizeau was refusing to debate a non-existent text. Manitoba also released the text. Officials in Ottawa did not resist early release in these provinces. Indeed, early release in just two provinces might have been tactically ideal. No one could say that the text did not exist, that something was being hidden. But actually getting a copy of the text was still next to impossible. This gave the "Yes" forces a long Thanksgiving weekend of favourable publicity.

13. The estimations on which this claim is based are complicated and do not bear explication here. For more detail, see Johnston, Blais, Gidengil and Nevitte, *Rhetoric and Reality*, chaps. 6 and 7. It is worth emphasizing, however, that voters seemed to focus on the national share, not on the Quebec one nor on the share in their home province.

14. The clearest statements of this argument are Arthur Lupia, "Busy Voters, Agenda Control, and the Power of Information." *American Political Science Review* 86 (1992): 390-403; and "Credibility and Responsiveness of Direct Legislation," prepared for the International Symposia on Economic Theory and Econometrics (1992).

15. Although, strictly speaking, language and province do not coincide, they seem readily conflated in voters' minds, notwithstanding a generation of effort to drive a wedge betwen the two.

16. This corresponds to a recurring pattern in public opinion data: the less informed the voter, the greater the reliance on group likes and dislikes to compose a politically consistent response. The canonical source is Sniderman, et al., *Reasoning and Choice*. For an example in a direct vote context, see James H. Kuklinski, Dan Metlay and W.D. Kay, "Citizen Knowledge and Choices on the Complex Issue of Nuclear Energy," *American Journal of Political Science* 26 (1992): 615-42.

17. Knowledge made no difference to the likelihood of accepting or rejecting aboriginal self-government or the 25 percent guarantee. On each of these, apparently, the consensus was too complete for knowledge to matter.

18. A respondent's level of information here means the number of correct mentions about the Accord in response to the following question in the post-referendum wave: "What proposals in the agreement do you remember the media and politicians talking about before the referendum vote?" The same pattern appears when respondents are stratified by formal education. Respondents with post-secondary education gave the "Yes" a small majority.

19. For further discussion, see André Blais, "Les Québecois sont-ils confus?" *La Presse*, 31 March 1992, p. B1; and Maurice Pinard and Richard Hamilton, "Les Québécois votent NON: le sens et la portée du vote," in (ed.) Jean Crête *Comportement électoral au Québec* (Chicoutimi: Gaétan Morin, 1984). As a recent example, a CROP-La Presse survey (*La Presse* 30 March 1992) revealed that 31 percent of Quebecers think that a sovereign Quebec would still be part of Canada.

20. This estimate comes out of a question-wording experiment administered to the Quebec sample. Respondents were asked if they were very favourable, somewhat

favourable, somewhat opposed, or very opposed to Quebec sovereignty. For one random half, the item ended with the mention of "sovereignty." For the other half the item went on to supply a definition: "that is, Quebec is no longer a part of Canada." When posed the simple question about sovereignty, 47 percent of Quebecers (52 percent of francophones) said they were favourable. When the meaning is supplied, the proportion of "don't knows" dropped (15 percent to 6 percent overall, 17 percent to 7 percent among francophones), as did support for sovereignty (to 39 percent overall and to 44 percent among francophones). If the second variant of the question taps genuine support for sovereignty better than other indicators have done, standard surveys in Quebec overestimate support for sovereignty by close to 10 points. Equally importantly, defining sovereignty strengthens opposition to it: overall, opposition grew from 38 percent to 53 percent; among francophones, the gain was from 31 percent to 49 percent and percentage very opposed more than doubled (28 percent as compared with 12 percent).

21. Our survey followed standard practice in initiating contact in French and so may underrepresent those not fluent in the dominant language, who should have been especially likely to vote "Yes." On the other hand, analyses based on constituency data place the share closer to 90 percent, almost certainly an overestimate. See Maurice St-Germain, Gilles Grenier, and Marc Lavoie, "Le référendum décortiqué," *Le Devoir*, 23 February 1993, p. A7, and Pierre Drouilly, "Le référendum du 26 octobre 1992: une analyse des résultats," in Denis Monière (ed.), *L'année politique au Québec 1992* (Montréal: Département de science politique, Université de Montréal, 1993).

22. Attachment is indicated by scores on feeling thermometers.

23. These assertions are based on David B. Magleby, *Direct Legislation: Voting on Ballot Propositions in the United States* (Baltimore, MD: Johns Hopkins University Press, 1984). This also seems to be the lesson of the closest parallel we can find to the Canadian vote, the 1975 British referendum on continued membership in the European Community. David Butler and Uwe Kitzinger, *The 1975 Referendum* (London: Macmillan, 1976), argue that the near cross-party frontbench consensus in the British Parliament was critical to the measure's success.

24. Not in Quebec, of course, for in that province the elite was deeply divided.

3

When More Is Too Much: Quebec and the Charlottetown Accord

Gérard Boismenu

C'est par un «non» retentissant que la classe politique canadienne essuie le refus de la population canadienne à sa proposition constitutionnelle le 26 octobre 1992. À n'en pas douter, il s'agissait d'une révision constitutionnelle majeure (sujets traités et retombées sur le fonctionnement de la fédération).

Dans ce processus qui a mené à cette proposition, l'attitude du Québec apparaît étonnante à plus d'un point de vue. Pour la population et la classe politique du Québec, l'Entente de Charlottetown est nettement décevante. Le gouvernement Bourassa se lance en campagne en soutenant qu'il a été impossible de faire mieux mais que ce n'est qu'un jalon devant mener à de nouveaux gains lors de négociations ultérieures.

Pour le Québec, il fallait plus, mais plus, est-ce trop? L'une des questions fondamentales qui reste posée, c'est dans quelle mesure est-il possible d'introduire la reconnaissance des communautés nationales dans l'ordre constitutionnel canadien? Lorsque l'on examine certaines concessions au sujet de la question autochtone, on peut imaginer qu'il pourrait être possible d'apporter une réponse à la question québécoise.

La situation politique actuelle est paradoxale. On ne voit pas exactement ce qui pourrait permettre la reprise des négociations constitutionnelles, mais on ne voit pas comment on pourrait y échapper. Pour que l'on sorte de l'impasse actuelle, il faudrait peut-être un big bang *politique qui touche à la fois la classe politique et l'opinion publique au Canada. Mais il se peut fort bien que l'on n'en soit pas encore au* big crunch *préparatoire.*

On 26 October 1992, the people of Canada issued a resounding "No" to the constitutional reform package proposed by the country's political elite. For the first time the Canadian public was asked to decide a constitutional matter by referendum.

This political happening may be analyzed in several ways. We will settle with the painting of a scene in which certain elements will stand out in relief. After an impressionist review of the events that have marked the constitutional saga during 1992, we will bring forth and evaluate the main components of the Charlottetown Accord, with Quebec being the observation post.

The unanswered question that remains but which necessarily must be asked, is to what extent the failure of the referendum will end the constitutional debate? Yet again, many facets are pertinent, but it remains that unclear prospects with regard to elections and the public opinion of political parties and representative movements in Quebec and Canada alike constitute a major element in the spectrum of possibilities. One may analyze the uncertainty of the various players and of the evolving conjuncture, but one cannot escape it.

AN IMPRESSIONIST REVIEW

For a government struggling to survive, as was the case with the Conservative government, the constitutional exercise could have proved extremely difficult — and possibly even fatal. At the same time, the referendum allowed the federal government to take the initiative and it could have turned the political situation to its advantage.

In either case, the Mulroney government was in a difficult situation. After the failure of the Meech Lake Accord, which had dominated Canadian political life from 1987 to 1990, governments (federal and provincial) of Canada-outside-Quebec had to propose a solution for change. Doing otherwise would have suggested that they considered the status quo acceptable. Such a position would have provoked public opinion in a Quebec already polarized by the Meech Lake process. Setting forth a new operation appeared to be a political necessity.

Throughout the debate on the Meech Lake Accord, the non-democratic nature of the constitutional reform process was stressed insistently by critics, particularly in Canada-outside-Quebec. Deliberations held more or less in secret — or at very least, not in public — have been a constant trait of Canadian constitutional history. In the wake of the *Charter of Rights and Freedoms* of 1982, however, a series of groups, associations, spokespersons, intellectuals and so forth presented themselves as promoters or defenders of one side or the other: these "Charter patriots" proclaimed that the constitution was not the business of governments alone, but a heritage that belonged to the entire Canadian population. As a result, one should not — or could not legitimately — modify the constitution without the participation and acceptance of the Canadian public.

The government tried to respond to this objection. First, it established in November 1990 the Spicer Commission — also known as the Citizen's Forum on Canada's Future — which was to settle Canadians' qualms about the constitution. Then followed the Beaudoin-Dobbie Committee, which was to gather reactions to the federal constitutional proposals put forward in

September 1991. Its mission of public consultation eventually took the form of public constitutional conferences, all with a thematic orientation, and held at the beginning of 1992 all across Canada.

Coming from another angle, the Government of Quebec affirmed that the Quebec people were the sole masters of Quebec's destiny. At the same time, however, the Liberal government did not wish to opt for a radical alternative. The signals the Bourassa government sent were contradictory.

At first, Robert Bourassa seemingly shared the population's strong resentment towards the ongoing constitutional process: he refused constitutional negotiations involving 11 governments, did not participate in intergovernmental issues unless they concerned Quebec's immediate interests, and he flirted with constitutional alternatives presuming the sovereignty of Quebec.

But these signals were mixed. At the moment of the adoption of the Allaire Report[1] on the constitution — which favoured a confederation rather than a federation — Robert Bourassa insisted at the party's annual meeting that Canada remained the first choice of the Quebec government. In much the same way, he subscribed to the report of the Bélanger-Campeau Commission[2] which fixed a deadline for a Quebec referendum on political sovereignty; almost concurrently, however, he insisted on the government's freedom to interpret the report's proposals as it saw fit.

In retrospect the attitude of the Quebec government was astonishing. It refused to negotiate in a process involving 11 governments and chose instead to wait for "offers" coming from the rest-of-Canada. The Quebec government thought it did not have to lay out specific conditions. What did the Quebec government really want? There was the constitutional position of the Liberal party, but its leader, Robert Bourassa, emphasized that this was not a government document. In any case, the constitutional position of the Liberal party was no reasonable base for a constitutional discussion within the framework of a federation. What is more, upon completion of the Bélanger-Campeau Report, the Quebec government set a deadline, by the adoption of a law that established that a referendum on sovereignty would be held at the latest by 26 October 1992.

Canada could ignore this threat or start a process of discussion that, at the least, would give the impression of trying to respond to the aspirations of the Quebec people. As much as 1991 could be perceived as a year dedicated to consultation, 1992 could equally well be perceived as a year of choosing.

TIME FOR A "CANADA'S ROUND"

It would be tedious to go over the entire process of constitutional negotiations that followed the death of the Meech Lake Accord. Regardless of how much one discusses the Spicer Commission, the Beaudoin-Edwards Committee, the federal constitutional proposals of September 1991, the Beaudoin-Dobbie

Committee and its numerous constitutional conferences, and so forth — one fact remains: the centre of gravity for the negotiations had moved.

In the discussions leading up to the Meech Lake Accord — that is to say, from 1985 to 1987 — it was understood that negotiations involved nothing more than accommodating the "conditions" required for Quebec to subscribe politically to the constitutional reform of 1982. After the Meech Lake failure, the expression "Quebec round" lost all relevance in favour of "Canada round." A much broader set of questions could now be raised as legitimately as the restricted set of questions that constituted the menu of previous negotiations.

Which is simply to say, the Canadian program was clearly immense and encompassed some tremendously diverse subjects: a preamble to the constitution, a social charter, Senate reform, Aboriginal Peoples' claims, and federal authority in matters of economic union, among others.

From the Quebec side, the question of sharing of powers became a central issue. The Quebec government wanted, in 1987, to avoid any debate on that question. It hoped that the introduction of the interpretative principle of "distinct society" could lead to an expansion of Quebec powers.[3] But the constitutional discussions, which finally led to the Meech Lake failure (and those talks that followed), showed clearly that this potential, to the extent that it existed, could be neutralized in the course of new negotiations. The question of division of powers had therefore to be broached directly. In this fashion, the focus for Quebec was slowly turned from the distinct society clause to the question of division of powers.

Indeed, on 13 June 1991, Gil Rémillard, minister responsible for constitutional affairs, declared that the five conditions posed in 1987 were no longer sufficient and that it was now necessary to move towards changes in the power-sharing agreement. Following suit, the Quebec government devoted considerable time to the question of power sharing in commentaries pertaining to the proposals it had raised.

The space occupied by the subject of power sharing at first led participants in the thematic constitutional conferences held by the Beaudoin-Dobbie Committee to flirt with the idea of constitutional asymmetry. This would permit them to satisfy the demands of Quebec without imposing on the other provincial governments any responsibilities that they did not necessarily wish to assume. The federal minister responsible for the file, Joe Clark, himself proclaimed on 18 January 1992 that he was ready to offer special status to Quebec. This idea, however, was eventually overshadowed by the themes of strong central government, of independent government by Aboriginal Peoples, and of a Triple-E Senate.

ARDUOUS AND LABORIOUS NEGOTIATIONS

Following the March 1992 report of the Beaudoin-Dobbie Committee,[4] the provincial governments, the major players in the constitutional revision process with respect to the amending formulas, were called upon to participate in a process of negotiation — in order to define a position that would establish consensus and that could be proposed to the Government of Quebec.

Even if Joe Clark wanted to move quickly, he agreed, following the first federal-provincial meeting on the constitution (12 March 1992), to look again at his schedule. Furthermore, six newcomers obtained places at the table: representatives of the Aboriginal Peoples and of the Territories.

The negotiation followed a circuitous route. There were some obvious points: the native people imposed the notion of an "inherent right of self-government"; Senate reform constituted a major stumbling block; integration of the so-called "substance" of the Meech Lake Accord was finally accepted; there was a blockage on the question on the right of a veto for Quebec; there was division on the idea of a "social charter" written into the constitution; and the objective of "reinforcing" provincial powers was accepted. Results were a long time in coming.

The Bourassa government abstained from formally participating in these negotiations, but it remained active behind the scenes. The refusal to negotiate in a body of 11 — and now one of 17 — participants was formally supported in a show of quasi-unanimity by the Quebec National Assembly on 18 March 1992. Simultaneously, the frequent meetings with the ministers and premiers of the other governments, the telephone conversations, the exchanges of information of all types — these all gave to the presence of Quebec a sense of character that was at the same time real yet invisible. What is more, the "knife-at-the-throat" strategy — the threat of a referendum on sovereignty if there were no interesting offers (a threat that had been officially adopted by the Quebec government) — seemed to be abandoned little by little as the talks advanced, especially as the moment of truth drew near (the pressing date of the referendum).

Various statements by Robert Bourassa suggested a pulling back. While in Europe in February 1992 he declared in Brussels that if the constitutional offers of English-Canada (or of the federal government) were unsatisfactory, he would hold the referendum on the theme of shared sovereignty within an economic union. Little more than a month later on 19 March 1992, all the while acknowledging his dissatisfaction with the recommendations of the Beaudoin-Dobbie Report — particularly on the sharing of jurisdictions — Robert Bourassa employed his inaugural address for the start of the 19 March parliamentary session to profess faith in federalism and to beseech English Canada to come up with acceptable offers. He came full circle some weeks later when, in an interview given to the newspaper *Le Monde,* he declared on 19 April 1992 his intention to hold a referendum on the federal proposals and not on sovereignty — as was stipulated in the law that he had had voted upon by the National Assembly less than a year beforehand.

The final negotiation session of the 16 "other" participants was on 6 and 7 July 1992. Following that meeting, a document outlining a state of agreement was made public. English Canada succeeded in achieving an agreement on a constitutional revision and in making an offer to Quebec.

This agreement was received coldly by many commentators and analysts in Quebec, and even Robert Bourassa expressed reservations about the presence of "substance" in the Meech Lake Accord, about the Senate proposal, and about the sharing of powers.

On 25 July, Bourassa remarked that he was awaiting responses to the uncertainties that he had expressed. When he did not obtain this satisfaction, he agreed to participate in a first ministers' conference some days later. For the first time (4 August and 10 August 1992), it might be said that, officially, discussions concerned only the process of the constitutional negotiation. After these two days, the Quebec government joined formally in the constitutional negotiations with a total of 17 participants. The sessions took place from 18 August to 22 August in Ottawa and, to refine the final text, on 27 and 28 August 1992, in Charlottetown.

For Quebec, this episode gave birth to arduous negotiations. The content of the negotiations, however, was determined by the agreement already reached by the governments of Canada-outside-Quebec and the Aboriginal Peoples. Any reopening of the principles of this agreement was ruled out. The Quebec government appeared condemned to pluck amendments from the margins of a constitutional document of which it had not been the co-author, which it had not negotiated and which had not been made to respond primarily to Quebec's preoccupations. The discussions conducted during the month of August stemmed directly from the agreement of 7 July.

One must remark upon the scope and importance of the constitutional revision that was being proposed — witness the number of subjects being treated and the overall importance of the repercussions for the Canadian federation.

For the entire federation, a "Canada clause" was introduced — this was to serve as a guide in interpreting the constitution — as well as a social and economic charter. With regard to institutions, the Senate was greatly reformed, the Supreme Court was constitutionalized in terms of status, composition, and nomination, and the proportional nature of representation in the House of Commons was assured. The sharing of powers was approached in terms of federal spending power and the assigning of a few specific jurisdictions. For Aboriginal Peoples, the inherent right of self-government was recognized, which would lead to the establishment of a third order of government. Finally, the amending formula would be modified.

It may be useful at this stage to examine more carefully certain points in the final document that led to the referendum question put to the population on 26 October.

THE "HONOURABLE COMPROMISES"

This agreement[5] is striking by virtue of its extensiveness. In its way, it is a reform at least as substantial as that led by the Trudeau government in 1982 with the *Canada Bill*. The document, at least in terms of issues tackled, fittted in with the long-term priorities and aspirations of the federal government in 1968. Specifically, after the establishment of a charter of rights and liberties, it was understood that a second step was necessary: to modernize the federal institutions. The issue of sharing of powers was considered supplementary. Since the summer of 1980 the idea of a preamble, which would provide a general outline of the Canadian reality, had also been advanced by the federal government.

Now, based on the principles that define the reality, the values, and objectives of the federation, we had a "Canada clause" and a "Social and Economic Charter." In the domain of federal institutions, the Senate, the House of Commons, the Supreme Court, and the amending formula became objects for modifications. Furthermore, there was proposed the institution of a third order of government destined for the Aboriginal Peoples. Finally, there was a series of arrangements relating to the sharing of powers. Obviously, every part of the Charlottetown agreement concerned Quebec's institutional interests, but a more limited number related to the province's traditional demands.

A COPIOUS CANADA CLAUSE

Those who were opposed to the Meech Lake Accord in 1990 saw the introduction of the Canada clause in the constitutional framework as an effective means to counter any potential interpretive criterion regarding the distinct society clause. In the Charlottetown agreement, this clause (a. 1)[6] was presented as a long article for the interpretation of the constitution, in its entirety, and of the Charter of Rights, in particular.

Beyond the attachment declared for the parliamentary regime, federalism, and the primacy of law, the clause includes two categories of specifications: those that involve the socio-political composition of the Canadian people, and those that recall the principles of liberty and equality.

The Aboriginals are designated as "Peoples," thus suggesting that there are several groups. From this they can, on one hand, promote their languages, cultures, traditions and, on the other, maintain the integrity of their societies. In this context, notions such as culture, language, and tradition are only elements of a society defined more broadly, a society that appears indefinite, multidimensional, and certainly extensive. Moreover, the concept of a third order of government was articulated in order to make concrete the principle of an inherent right of self-government for Aboriginal Peoples.

For a second time, Quebec was described as a distinct society within Canada, a society that unites the entire population within Québécois territory. This distinct society, which is not defined by its ethnic character, corresponds to a modern national community. Nevertheless it was not designated in terms of a nation or a people. The distinct society was rather reduced to a handful of traits: a majority of French-speaking individuals, a unique culture, and a tradition of civil law. The expression "which includes" preceding these traits identifying the distinct society would not make any difference for judicial interpretation. Whereas the notion of society for the Aboriginal Peoples was an open concept — despite its essentially ethnic character — in the case of Quebec this notion was restrained.

Further on, in paragraph 2 of this clause, the National Assembly and the Government of Quebec were provided a joint role in the preservation and promotion of the distinct society. This role, however, risked conflicting with the principle provided in paragraph 1 (d) which committed Canadians and their governments (federal and provincial) to the vitality and development of official-language minority communities throughout the rest of the country. In other words, for Quebec, the government could indeed promote the concept of a distinct society but in a manner compatible with the rights and liberties of the individual, and with the vitality and development of the anglophone population.

What was stressed, as with other issues, was the importance accorded to individual — and collective — rights and liberties, to the equality of the sexes, and to the equality of the provinces (a. 1(1)f,g,h). This last principle is, let us keep in mind, the antithesis of the notion of special status or constitutional asymmetry. It thus seemed that the idea of an asymmetrical constitution that would permit a possible reconciliation of the traditional claims of the Quebec government and of the position of the other provinces had been definitely rejected.

In sum, we had the recognition of Aboriginal Peoples through a new order of government, a distinct Quebec society defined in a restrictive fashion and in which the juridical and political potential seem completely neutralized — and, finally, by the legal equality of the provinces, the renunciation of any notion of constitutional asymmetry.

AN EQUAL SENATE

The institution that would have undergone the most significant change was, without doubt, the Senate. Its members were to be elected, provincial representation was to be equal, and its role in legislative work would have been considerable and real. Each province would have had the right to representation by six senators (a. 8), to which was added one senator for each Territory. It was anticipated that eventually the question of aboriginal representation in this body would have to be discussed (a. 9).

The place of the Senate in the legislative process would have been quite complex. It would ratify or reject legislative bills according to variable conditions. As well, the Senate could initiate legislative bills so long as they did not relate to budget issues. This body, where Quebecers would occupy only 9.7 percent of seats (as compared to the present 25 percent) would be required to play a singularly important role in the legislative process and in the selection of principal appointments to the major institutions of Canada.

In return, Quebec would have been guaranteed to benefit forever from a representation of 25 percent in the House of Commons. For the time being, this provision would be quite symbolic, because it confirmed the current situation and the situation anticipated for at least the next 30 years. In the long run, however, it constituted a guarantee against minoritization in the main federal legislative body as a result of regional demographic evolutions in Canada.

SHARING OF POWERS:
STARTING POINT OR ULTIMATE CONCESSIONS?

For the Quebec population, this question of powers is the acid test of any constitutional revision. This is not so much because other issues are without import. It is because in the context of negotiations — even those of a give-and-take nature — this seminal matter becomes a platform for establishing that there are sufficient reasons to accept all the other issues in dispute. Moreover, the neutralization of the distinct society clause helped bring this chapter further into the picture.

On the subject of the spending power, the principles in the Meech Lake Accord (a. 25) would have been maintained. That is to say that for a new co-financed program established in an area of exclusive provincial jurisdiction, the provincial government would have had the right to compensation so long as this government set up a program "compatible with national objectives." The Accord called for a framework to guide future federal interventions in areas of exclusive provincial jurisdiction.

On another point, in establishing legislative controls for both provincial and federal governments, intergovernmental agreements would have been protected for a period of five years maximum, but with the possibility of renewal. This mechanism would be evoked in several domains (a. 26).

First, let us consider training and upgrading of the labour force (a. 28). The Accord began by establishing on one side or another exclusive responsibilities: to the federal government — the Unemployment Insurance Commission; to the provincial government — the training of workers. The provinces could limit federal expenditures in this last area by employing intergovernmental agreements. But at the same time this did not signify the abandonment of the sector by the federal government; it was stated that the federal government would have the authority to establish national policy objectives in the area of labour market development. These objectives might become a focus of consultations but, when all is said and done, they would be in force for provincial programs even when agreements on federal limits had been negotiated. In fact, a provincial government that "negotiated agreements to constrain the federal spending power should be obliged to ensure that [its] labour market development programs are compatible with the national policy objectives."

Next, the area of culture requires attention (a. 29). The Accord began by establishing that the provinces would have exclusive jurisdiction on cultural questions relating to their own territory. At the same time, however, the federal government would continue to hold responsibility for matters of Canadian culture. Notably, it maintained full authority for Canadian cultural institutions (such as the National Film Board or the Canada Arts Council), as well as for the grants and contributions that apply to these institutions. In this division between national and provincial cultural matters, the responsibility of provincial governments for cultural matters within the province would be acknowledged within agreements ensuring harmonization with federal responsibilities.

Six legislative areas (forests, mines, tourism, housing, recreation, and municipal and urban affairs), which were already thought to be under provincial jurisdiction according to a current interpretation of the 1867 constitution, were to be now considered areas of exclusive provincial interest (a. 30 to 35). This signified that the provinces would have the power to limit federal expenditures in these matters by virtue of intergovernmental agreements. This arrangement seemed less designed to exclude the federal government than to coordinate its presence with the various provincial governments. In reality, up to the point that the federal government actually negotiates or renegotiates the form that its intervention will take, it would always be a major player in these fields.

Two other domains were designated as having shared jurisdiction: telecommunications (a. 37) and regional development (a. 36). When needed, negotiations between the two orders of government were to give way to intergovernmental accords, protected for five years. In addition, immigration (a. 27), which is already a concurrent jurisdiction, would also give way to federal-provincial agreements.

What is surprising about these constitutional arrangements is that the language used does not correspond to the usual sense extracted from the words. At first, when one designates a domain as exclusively provincial, one might well think that this means the jurisdiction is under the sole control of provincial political institutions. This is just not so. In fact, a concurrent presence of the two orders of government was accepted. What we had, in the end, was a particular form of shared jurisdiction.

Provincial exclusiveness gave the right to provincial governments to enter into negotiations before heading into intergovernmental agreements. These accords, however, would have been by nature administrative, with special power to renegotiate every five years and, in so doing, define the place the federal government would occupy. What is more, the negotiations could always result in a failure to agree: thus the federal government would remain in this sense a major player — indeed, a constancy.

From another side, there would have been a certain federal tutelage exercised in provincial jurisdictions. For example, for labour training and the limitations on the federal spending power, it would have been the federal government that established national norms, and for culture, the large institutions would remain under federal control. Furthermore, for all the jurisdictional sectors labelled exclusive or shared, the federal government would define the conditions under which it would consent to intergovernmental accords. In a sense, then, the federal government was granted a sort of freedom-of-the-city in many provincial jurisdictions.

AN UNATTRACTIVE PROPOSAL

For the population and the political elite of Quebec, the results of the negotiations of July-August 1992 were clearly at a remove from traditional claims; and they were, in any sense, a very long way from the proposals of the governing Liberal party. The Bourassa government threw itself into a referendum campaign with "offers" which, only with difficulty, would extract great concessions. It had, on the other hand, to sustain proposals that had little resonance for the dominant political representation within Quebec, and for the constitutional vision most anchored in the Québécois political arena. What is more, it had to go against the expectations of the Liberal party, which had kept these self-same expectations alive throughout the previous two years.

When the federal Conservatives started their campaign, draped in the flag of an ambitious reform campaign, Quebec governmental forces preached a pell-mell resignation; it was impossible to do better but, given the various elements, it was nothing other than a marker along the way to a possibility of winning through subsequent negotiations. The proposal, it was understood, was not attractive.

What is more, there was the perplexity and the feeling of resistance towards the idea of Senate reform and the creation of a third order of government. Just what was to be gained by reforming this second House of Parliament — one that virtually consecrated a somewhat miniscule minority of Quebecers, and one that in itself refuted the binational character of non-aboriginal Canadians? Could one leave it to various tribunals to define a third order of government, its powers and its territories? These were questions that were left dangling. Could one accept the definition of a distinct society — such as presently defined — in the Accord and its character as purely symbolic? Was Quebec more ahead of the game with the sharing of powers? Would it be better to look at other alternatives rather than confirming the current entanglements based on official support?

The big and difficult question was: Does Quebec win? Even the most favourable responses were nuanced. On the government side there was an inclination to say "this is just a beginning." These proposals were greeted with difficulty.

Throughout the Quebec bureaucracy, there was an assortment of critical — indeed unfavourable — judgements on the continuation of negotiations and on the "gains" that might be had.

The result is all-too-well-known. The agreement was rejected by almost 56 percent of the electorate in Quebec. All four western provinces also rejected the Accord, as did Nova Scotia. And, as for Ontario, it recorded a weak majority. Overall, the Accord was opposed by 54 percent.

IS MORE TOO MUCH?

For Quebec, more was necessary. But more — was it too much? First of all, let us begin to point out that Quebec society was not on a death march; Quebec is neither destined to be part of Canada, nor to be independent. The path it will follow depends on a multitude of factors — among them, the manner in which it faces the constitutional question.

We can say that for many Quebecers sovereignty is no more than a default option. This is the attitude, it seems to me, of about 20 percent that represent the "swing voters" in the current make-up of our two-party system. And these are those who largely hold the key to the future. Globally, there is a widespread but deep attachment for Canada, but a Canada capable of recognizing the socio-political reality of Quebec and of permitting its institutions to assure a cultural flowering — linguistically, but also socio-economically. If Quebec is still a part of Canada it is because a majority believes, even to this day, that this challenge can be met. But it would be presumptuous to take this fact for granted in Canada-outside-Quebec.

If we put the political sovereignty of Quebec in brackets for a moment, can anyone imagine a scenario that would make sense for those wishing to meet this challenge? We could here and now — and henceforth — say that the die is cast and that it remains simply to draw conclusions: submission or secession? Elsewhere, Kenneth McRoberts has concluded in a recent study that Canada-outside-Quebec has hardened its attitude towards Quebec over the last 20 years and that a renewal of federalism that takes into account Quebec's traditional demands is improbable. This hardening may be explained in part by demographic changes and the economic rise of the west, but as McRoberts states "the growth of English Canadian resistance to duality and distinct status was primarily the responsibility of governments, most notably that of Pierre Elliot Trudeau."[7] He succeeded in convincing English Canadians to adopt his vision of the country and the place Quebec should have in it. This clear-minded evaluation leads us directly to an impasse.

But if one does not accept this conclusion, one must still address the fundamental question: to what extent is it possible to introduce a recognition of national communities into the Canadian constitutional order.

A negotiation among three national communities: (English) Canadians, Quebecers, and Aboriginal Peoples could be a path to explore.[8] Such a prospect could be fruitful in the sense that no party would have the pretence of imposing on any other any real expression of nationhood nor their model of identity.[9] A search for perfect symmetry would be illusory.

Discussions on a political pact creating a multinational and polyethnic state that would not clean the table of its present constitution, represents an hypothesis full of risks and ambushes. Such an hypothesis would demand a certain amount of work to dismantle Trudeauist certainties, but is it not also extravagant?

As for the Canada-outside-Quebec proponents, they are juggling here and there with the idea of negotiation among nations.[10] It is true, however, that they represent a minority.

But when one examines carefully the "closedness" of English Canada — which presents itself in the form of Charter patriotism, with uniform citizenship and juridic equality among the provincial governments — that closedness appears, in certain places, nevertheless, capable of making concessions when negotiating the aboriginal question.

For the Aboriginal Peoples, in the Charlottetown Accord concessions were made to recognize one or more ethnic nations, to subordinate the application of the *Charter of Rights and Freedoms* to ancestral law and to the freedoms relating to the utilization or protection of their languages, cultures, or traditions (a. 2), to subordinate eventually their political citizenship to ethnic adherence (electoral body and eligibility) (a. 46), to establish a correspondence between one nation (even ethnically based) and a state level with sovereign powers

(a. 41), to leave — should the case arise — the judiciary to define the jurisdictions of these governments and their territory (a. 41, 42).

To satisfy the claims of Quebec, it seems to me that the concessions required would not be so significant: the nation is more a territorial society than a kinship society; political citizenship has no reserves; for freedoms, it might be supposed that, in one way or another, the question of commercial sign language might be solved; there is already a correspondence (recognized in Meech and Charlottetown) between the provincial government and the Québécois community. It would be necessary to accompany provincial jurisdictions with shared jurisdictions in which the provincial must be preponderant[11] — for example: regional development, social security, labour training, culture and immigration.

One can envision diverse mechanisms. What is important from the start is to establish principles from which one can build constitutional reform. The time for building without vision has lasted long enough. In any case, in these matters, the people speak and make their will clear above and beyond these questions, even if one tries to camouflage them.

WHAT AWAITS US IN THE FUTURE?

If there is a pause at this moment, it will not last long. This is not quite the time for sleepiness. When the status quo guards the gates it becomes a beckoning for future unrest. Let us recall certain facts.

The political parties, federal as well as provincial, have practically nothing to propose to reform Canadian federalism. In a general sense, setting apart the sovereignist movement in Quebec and the Reform party in the west, the political elite was favourable to the Charlottetown agreement; it was disaffected by the result obtained. Even before the referendum result was confirmed, the anticipated defeat said to these people that one should definitely consider posting a moratorium on all constitutional negotiations. The current policy is more of a "wait-and-see" outlook.

How long is one supposed to remain contented with this attitude? Or, how long can such an attitude continue to be accepted? As much rests at stake in this as in the whole current constitutional debate.

On the Quebec side, the Liberal party will be tempted to set aside the whole constitutional question. For the party to settle for the present constitutional debâcle might appear to be political suicide, but without a credible alternative it seems to be the route they are ready to take. However, the die has not been thrown yet. Adding to this uncertainty is the possibility of a change in the leadership of the Liberal party in the coming months — because of the serious health problems of Robert Bourassa. This, of course, would favour internal debates on the question.

According to this scenario, the new Liberal leader could have difficulties in reconciling the gap between inflexible federalists and strong nationalists within the party. The ambiguities of Robert Bourassa permitted him to play both — and if it were possible — several sides of the fence. A new leader could well disappoint a clientele so well versed in this school of politics. This could be one of the factors that leads to the defeat of the present government in the next election — which must be held by the fall of 1994. And, broadly speaking, the electorate's fatigue towards a Liberal government in its second mandate could be another factor leading to a defeat.

As noted above, for now, we have put in brackets the option of the political sovereignty for Quebec. These brackets are clearly artificial. One might estimate that the chances of the Parti Québécois winning the next election are reasonably good. If this is the case, the constitutional question will once again go back to square one. The new government will give the issue high priority in its agenda. Ways of obtaining independence are specified in a recent PQ publication.[12] But one can suppose that a majority vote in favour of sovereignty would be followed by negotiations well before setting in place conditions for sovereignty and common institutions. One cannot exclude negotiations that could touch upon common institutions evoking a confederation. In any case, it is certain that an electoral victory for the Parti Québécois will change the conditions of negotiations and, at the very least, render them inescapable.

Beyond that, for how long can we permit ourselves to be spectators — more or less passive — in the face of the various options and proposals, such as those advanced by the Aboriginal Peoples in order for them to concrete a third level of government despite the Charlottetown impasse. A call for patience will not suffice. Already we have witnessed many zones of tension. The installations of gaming houses on reserves creates a pretext for a new political crisis.

The current political situation is also paradoxical. No one quite sees exactly what it might take to revive the constitutional negotiations. The Charlottetown agreement was insufficient for Quebec and, it seems, for the Aboriginal People; the political elite was disavowed the moment there was a referendum by a majority of Canadians. Given the fact that the referendum route is almost indispensable in terms of major constitutional reform, it is difficult to see who could sway public opinion.

The situation is also paradoxical because no one knows how to stop these new negotiations in the very near future. The aboriginal question is going to raise its head, no doubt. The possible election of the Parti Québécois might also provide a degree of amplification. Besides that, the next federal election may give us a thoroughly uncommon House of Commons, with five political parties represented substantially and a minority government in the lead. In this possibility, one could say that the crisis of legitimacy and representation of the traditional political elite might spill over into a parliamentary crisis.

Do these conditions — partially or totally joined together — announce a horizon that is politically blocked or the opening to a dynamic new alternative? It is impossible to say. For those who would square the current circle, it is perhaps necessary to have the equivalent of what might be called the "Big Bang" that will simultaneously touch public opinion and the political elite. The question is: Are we steeled enough for the preparatory stage of the "Big Crunch"?

NOTES

I am grateful to my colleague Alain Noël for helpful suggestions on a previous draft of this chapter.

1. *Un Québec libre de ses choix,* Rapport du Comité constitutionnel du Parti libéral du Québec, 25e Congrès des membres du Parti libéral du Québec, janvier 1991, 74 p.
2. Commission sur l'avenir politique et constitutionnel du Québec, *L'avenir politique et constitutionnel du Québec,* Rapport remis au Président de l'Assemblée nationale du Québec, mars 1991, 180 p.
3. G. Boismenu, "Through a Glass, Darkly: The Meech Lake Mirage," in A.B. Gollner & D. Salée (eds.), *Canada Under Mulroney. An End-Of-Term Report* (Montreal: Véhicule Press, 1988), pp. 48-64.
4. *Un Canada renouvelé,* Rapport du Comité mixte spécial du Sénat et de la Chambre des Communes, février 1992, 211 p.
5. For this section we refer to the *Consensus Report on the Constitutional Consensus,* Charlottetown, 28 August, of which the definitive text was made public when the referendum campaign had just begun.
6. Editors' note: "a." refers to numbered article in the *Consensus Report*, ibid.
7. K. McRoberts, *English Canada and Quebec: avoiding the issue* (North York: Robarts Centre for Canadian Studies, 1991), p. 14.
8. For a developed discussion see: G. Boismenu, "Is The Reconciliation of Ethnicity, Nationality and Citizenship Possible?" in J. Laponce and J. Meisel (eds.), *Ethnicity and Canadian Constitution,* forthcoming.
9. Greg Marc Nielsen writes: (trans.): "The symbolic representation of each event differs according to whether one belongs to one or the other of the existing political cultures ... The two societies are thus relatively separate. But, at the same time, on the symbolic plan, their statements are profoundly inseparable, given their communal institutional history. How does one explain one without reference to the other?" *Possibles,* 16, 2 (1992): 67-68
10. P. Resnick, *Toward a Canada-Quebec Union* (Montreal: McGill-Queen's University Press, 1991); C. McCall et al. "Three Nations," *Canadian Forum* (March 1992): 4-6.
11. The system proposed by the Task Force on Canadian Unity in 1979.
12. Parti québécois, *Le Québec dans un monde nouveau* (Montreal: VLB Éditeur, 1993).

4

Let There Be Light

J. Peter Meekison

Le 26 octobre 1992, les Canadiens ont rejeté l'entente de Charlottetown, mettant fin ipso facto à un quart de siècle de négociations constitutionnelles. Or, l'échec du référendum sur cet accord ne signifie pas pour autant que toutes les questions discutées en ce domaine, au cours de ces vingt-cinq dernières années, ont été renvoyées du même coup aux calendes grecques. Certes, on note peu d'empressement de part et d'autre à rouvrir le débat constitutionnel; néanmoins, d'autres avenues s'offrent aux Canadiens et à leurs gouvernements pour traiter ce dossier.

Cet article avance pour l'essentiel que la procédure formelle de modification de la constitution ne représente qu'un moyen, parmi d'autres, d'effectuer un changement à ce chapitre. De fait, on pourrait arriver à un résultat similaire en modifiant les usages établis, en promulguant de nouvelles lois et en recourant davantage à la jurisprudence existante. En outre, les ententes et négociations intergouvernementales s'avèrent, et de loin, la meilleure façon de renouer avec la procédure traditionnelle de résolution des conflits.

Au reste, advenant que les gouvernements décident d'agir sur le plan constitutionnel, plusieurs dispositions contenues dans l'entente de Charlottetown pourraient être appliquées sans qu'il soit nécessaire de procéder à une modification formelle de la constitution.

The defeat of the Charlottetown Accord on 26 October 1992 brought a decisive end to a 25-year search for constitutional perfection.

When the vote was over, many Canadians gave a collective sigh of relief, believing that, at last, governments could address more pressing issues like the economy, the deficit, unemployment and the environment. But to others, the constitutional agenda remained unfinished business. During the past quarter century, the route chosen for change has been formal amendment to the *Constitution Act*. This process, however, has recently proven unsuccessful. Now, the question arises, are there ways to make needed changes to our system of government other than by formal amendment to the constitution? The answer is a resounding yes!

The first part of this paper explores some of the methods governments have at their disposal to bring about constitutional revision. These are ordinary legislation, convention and reference to the courts.

If the past quarter century can be characterized as the era of constitutional reform, the period immediately preceding it can be characterized as the era of cooperative federalism. It is my contention that governments can address much of what was found in the Charlottetown Accord through intergovernmental agreements, as was done during the era of cooperative federalism. A number of issues such as interprovincial trade barriers, fiscal federalism and labour market training are strong contenders for such agreements.

The final portion of the chapter is intended to serve as a reminder that the principal reason for the intensive constitutional debate was, and still remains, national unity. Constitutional reform was seen as the means to achieve this goal. Until Quebec indicates in some way its acceptance of the 1982 constitutional amendment which patriated Canada's constitution, the subject of constitutional reform will never completely disappear. A similar argument can be made about Aboriginal Peoples and the constitution. Their quest for aboriginal self-government has been intensified, not diminished, by the defeat of the Charlottetown Accord.

In summary, while some Canadians feel the constitutional debate has ended, others feel that, far from having ended, a constitutional crisis of major proportions looms ahead.

Despite agreement on the need for constitutional reform, many scholars have been critical of the process chosen and pessimistic about the possibility of Canadians reaching agreement on constitutional amendments.

The titles of only a few books written between the demise of the Fulton-Favreau formula and the collapse of Meech Lake illustrate this point. *The Future of Canadian Federalism* (1965); *Confederation at the Crossroads* (1968); *One Country or Two?* (1971); *Canada in Question: Federalism in the Seventies* (1972); *Divided Loyalties* (1975); *Must Canada Fail?* (1977); *Unfulfilled Union* (1982); *And No One Cheered* (1983); *Canada Notwithstanding* (1984); *The Federal Condition in Canada* (1987); and *A Deal Undone* (1990) do not indicate a particularly optimistic view. In fact, collectively they convey a message of despair about our political and constitutional future. All the works cited relate in one way or another to Quebec or to constitutional reform.

Closely related to this pessimism is the theme of Canada in crisis. For more than 25 years Canadians have been told they are in the midst of a crisis. It seems that every time the subject of reform is raised, those examining the question conclude that Canada is undergoing a crisis far worse than any previously encountered.

In their *Preliminary Report,* published in 1965, The Royal Commission on Bilingualism and Biculturalism stated:

> The Commissioners ... fully expected to find themselves confronted by tensions and conflicts. They knew that there have been strains throughout the history of Confederation.... What the Commissioners have discovered little by little, however, is very different: they have been driven to the conclusion that Canada, without being fully conscious of the fact, is passing through the greatest crisis in its history.[1]

In 1972 the Joint Parliamentary Committee on the Constitution, established in 1970 by Prime Minister Trudeau, declared that Canada "is in the midst of the most serious crisis in its history."[2]

The Pepin-Robarts Commission established in 1977 by Prime Minister Trudeau after the Parti Québécois (PQ) electoral victory in 1976, released its report entitled *A Future Together* in January 1979. They, too, emphasized that Canada was in the midst of a crisis. They also issued the warning, "We recognize that even crises can become tedious and difficult to believe in if they go on too long and nothing seems to happen."[3]

In 1991, the Spicer Commission, established by Prime Minister Mulroney after the demise of the Meech Lake constitutional accord, released its report. One observation stands out.

> This part is the commissioners' voice. And we must tell you clearly: Canada is in a crisis. This is a crisis identified and experienced by the people of Canada as immediately as a drought affects a farmer. This is a crisis of identity, a crisis of understanding, a crisis of leadership. We have arrived at this conclusion not because participants used the word crisis — few of them did — but because what they told us adds up, mercilessly, to this conclusion.[4]

The Beaudoin-Dobbie Committee, the Special Joint Committee of the Senate and House of Commons responsible for reviewing *Shaping Canada's Future Together,* stated:

> Canada is at a critical point in its history. Either it continues on the path of unity, a strong nation, confident of its future and of its people, or it engages itself on a drastically new path, one laden with uncertainty and doubt.[5]

So, one can track the theme of constitutional crisis back over the past quarter century. This sense of immediate or imminent disaster, reported by five very diverse groups, all of which crossed Canada holding public hearings, has coloured how Canadians perceive constitutional reform. They simply do not believe the prophets of doom, because all predictions thus far have proven false.

During this so-called crisis period, Canadians have witnessed a number of failures — Quebec's rejection of the Fulton-Favreau amending formula in 1965; Quebec's rejection of the Victoria Charter in 1971; the collapse of constitutional negotiations in 1980 and subsequent unilateral federal action; Quebec's rejection of the agreement on patriation of the constitution reached in 1981; the failure, in 1987, after four years of negotiation to reach agreement on aboriginal self-government; the failure of the Meech Lake Accord in 1990; and the rejection by the electorate of the Charlottetown Accord in 1992. For 25 years we have assumed that Canada is going to disintegrate if agreement is not reached. We have tried mightily to avoid this catastrophe by attempting to reform the constitution. In other words, we have had our fingers in the constitutional dike for almost a generation.

With the defeat of the referendum, we have pulled our fingers out and, amazingly, there are no visible leaks in the dike. What we do not know, however, is what is happening underneath the surface. Has there been significant structural damage which for the time being is invisible and undetected?

The referendum defeat represents a watershed, bringing to a sudden and convincing end the long era of constitutional reform which has monopolized centre stage one way or another since our centennial. It is significant that a generation of Canadians and thousands of new Canadians have witnessed continuous discussions about constitutional reform. To them such debate must appear a normal facet of Canadian political life. It became very clear after the referendum that the public was in no mood to continue this debate. They would rather wait and see what happens next, then deal with the issue. But, they reason, if past experience serves as a guide, nothing catastrophic is likely to happen.

Our search for renewed federalism, reform or accommodation with Quebec — call it what you will — may therefore be at an end or, at the very least, sidetracked for the foreseeable future.

This view is reflected in a statement by Premier Klein of Alberta after meeting with Premier Bourassa. He said:

> Perhaps there should be a reasonable post-mortem of the process — not the package itself, but the process and what went wrong. Perhaps when the time is right ... five, 10, 15 years down the road, put it back on the front burner when the Canadian people are more receptive.[6]

A similar view is reflected in the following exchange between Gil Rémillard, Quebec's minister of intergovernmental affairs, and Premier Rae of Ontario. In response to questions in the National Assembly, Rémillard once again emphasized the importance to Quebec of constitutional reform.[7] To the possibility of reopening constitutional discussions, Premier Rae responded that Mr. Rémillard just "didn't get the message."[8]

While some political leaders are clearly avoiding the issue, others are continuing to remind Canadians that discussions are far from over. Headlines include: "Parizeau maps out route to sovereignty," "PQ predicts independent Quebec by 1995," "Bouchard predicts new union for Quebec and rest of Canada," "Natives look to themselves for new deal: Less talk more action in

1993," "Ground lost since death of accord, Mercredi says."[9] Nor should one ignore the Rt. Hon. Joe Clark's warning:

> Some of the anger [over the referendum] is gone. [But] That phrase "calm before the storm," came up very frequently in a series of meetings I held recently in Quebec. I think it is the case generally.[10]

It is a fact that both the PQ and Bloc Québécois are committed to Quebec independence. Whether or not they will succeed is unknown. One way or another, though, they intend to keep the public's attention focused on the inevitability of Quebec's separation from the rest-of-Canada. Aboriginal Peoples are equally determined to achieve self-government and secure the promises held out to them in the Charlottetown Accord and associated political accords. To emphasize this point, both the Assembly of First Nations and the Inuit Tapirisat of Canada walked out of an intergovernmental conference in Inuvik in July 1993 because they felt the Government of Canada no longer seemed to accept the principle of the Aboriginal Peoples' inherent right of self-government.[11]

The rejection of the Charlottetown Accord also brought an end to efforts to achieve Senate reform. Nevertheless, the subject of Senate reform continues to surface, as it did when Senators decided to increase their expense allowances by $6,000 in the summer of 1993. The prevailing option this time, however, appears to be abolition of the Senate rather than its restructuring.[12] To many westerners, however, abolition of the Senate would end their hopes of having a more equitable voice in national decisionmaking. Debate about the structure and role of the Senate will continue.

What we need to understand is that forces underlying the demand for constitutional reform have not disappeared simply because the Charlottetown Accord was defeated. Quebec's concerns, western grievances and aboriginal self-government still remain as unfinished business. How and when they will be addressed is uncertain but they *will* resurface. In many respects, our current situation is comparable to being in the eye of a hurricane. The last 25 years carried us here. In the next few years, we will once more be in stormy seas. Or will we?

ALTERNATIVES TO THE MEGA-AMENDMENT OR "LET THERE BE LIGHT"

Consider this question. "If formal constitutional reform — the mega-amendment — is *not* attainable, are there other ways to bring about constitutional change?" The answer, as I have said, is yes. If this route is successful, the demand for formal constitutional solutions should fade. Of equal importance, the emotions aroused as we have attempted formal amendments should also fade.

There are four basic ways that constitutional frontiers can be shifted: formal constitutional amendment, convention, statute and judicial interpretation. Let me examine the latter three in greater detail. One cannot predict what changes will be thought necessary or pursued through these processes, so rather than develop a new list of subjects for consideration I have tried to use matters that, in one way or another, have been central to previous constitutional negotiations. Indeed, in my opinion, governments can implement much of what was contained in the Charlottetown Accord without resorting to formal constitutional amendment.

CONVENTION

Much of our constitution consists of convention or usage. These practices have evolved over time and, while not part of the written constitution, are equally important. To a great extent, the functioning of cabinet government is influenced by convention. Other examples include alternating the Governor General and Chief Justice of the Supreme Court of Canada between English- and French-speaking individuals.

When the federal government released its paper on constitutional reform in September 1991, it contained references to parliamentary reform.[13] For whatever reason, there was no apparent interest in pursuing this subject during the multilateral constitutional process and there are no references to it in the Charlottetown Accord. Nevertheless, there continues to be demand from the public for parliamentary reform.

One way to achieve this objective is to modify a number of the conventions by which parliamentary government operates. For example, the public has demanded more free votes and a corresponding reduction in the tight party discipline now present. Any changes here will lead to new understanding of votes of non-confidence. It should be recognized that there is no reason, other than political unwillingness, why coventions governing matters such as votes of confidence, budget secrecy and the functioning of parliamentary committees cannot be changed. Indeed, both the Liberal Party of Canada and Prime Minister Kim Campbell have made a number of proposals in this area.[14]

STATUTE

Statutes also form a major part of our constitutional fabric, for they add substance to the bare bones of the basic document. Examples such as the *Canada Elections Act, Official Languages Act* and the *Supreme Court Act* come readily to mind. Such statutes represent important constitutional building blocks.

Although electoral reform was not central to the recent constitutional discussions, the topic has generated considerable interest. Is our current system fair? Do election results reflect the popular vote? Should there be a separate system of representation for Aboriginal Peoples? Such questions were addressed by the Royal Commission on Electoral Reform and Party Financing (the Lortie Commission) in its report of November 1991. There is nothing in the constitution that limits us to single member districts and a single non-transferable vote. We could, instead, institute a system of proportional representation or an alternative ballot by statute.

It is of interest to note that neither the Lortie nor the Macdonald Royal Commission supported the idea of introducing proportional representation.[15] With either change, the composition of Parliament would be fundamentally altered to make its representation more closely reflect the popular vote, a concern that surfaced after the 1979 and 1980 federal elections. Canada is not alone in questioning its electoral system. Italy is attempting to move away from proportional representation while New Zealand is considering adopting it.[16]

The Charlottetown Accord contained a number of constitutional amendments, the main purpose of which could be accomplished by statute. For example; the *Supreme Court of Canada Act* could be amended to provide for a provincial nominating process and the *Bank of Canada Act* could be amended to have the Governor's appointment ratified by either house. Parliament could pass an act guaranteeing the sanctity of intergovernmental agreements. A statutory framework authorizing governments to conclude agreements harmonizing telecommunications regulations is another possibility. To be sure, statutes would not provide the same degree of protection as a constitutional amendment, but our choices are to jettison an entire idea or achieve our policy objectives another way. At some point, an element of trust and opportunism must be reintroduced into the realm of federal-provincial relations.

JUDICIAL INTERPRETATION

Since Confederation, judicial interpretation has had a profound impact on the division of powers and our constitutional evolution. The courts act as our constitutional referees. Individuals and corporations occasionally challenge the constitutionality of government actions or legislation. Governments also have the ability to refer constitutional questions to the courts for review and determination. The courts have ruled on matters such as communications (radio), aeronautics, anti-inflation, off-shore resource ownership, and export taxes on natural gas and patriation, all through reference cases. What needs to be remembered here is that governments can initiate legal proceedings, the outcome of which will alter our constitutional boundaries. While governments can frame the questions to be answered, they have no control over the outcome.

Since there is an element of risk associated with references, it is likely that this alternative to constitutional reform will be used sparingly.

Just as there are examples of instances where cases have been referred to the courts, there are examples of situations where provinces decided it was not in their interests to take the matter to court. Two non-challenges that come to mind pertain to the *Canada Health Act* of 1984 and the *Canada-United States Free Trade Agreement Implementation Act* of 1988.

Alberta, for example, did not directly challenge the *Canada Health Act* even though the province had traditionally challenged similar exercises of the federal spending power. The Act prohibited practices like extra billing which Alberta then permitted. Despite provincial concern, it was not in the province's interest to go to court. Why? Because it was a lose-lose situation. If the provinces *won* the case they might have succeeded in dismantling the national health care system and ending up by paying 100 percent of the costs. If the provinces *lost* the case — a more likely scenario — the federal spending power would have been clearly established within whatever limits were set by the courts.

Although there were federal-provincial discussions leading up to the Free Trade Agreement between Canada and the United States, the treaty itself was implemented by a federal statute. Speaking to this issue in 1987, the then Attorney General of Ontario, Hon. Ian Scott, said, "In short, whether or not the agreement amounts to a constitutional amendment in any formal sense it represents, in my view, de facto constitutional change — and a constitutional change of very significant magnitude."[17] Despite Ontario's opposition to the Free Trade Agreement, it did not initiate a court challenge. Why? While one cannot overlook the fact that the 1988 federal election was fought over this issue, the most likely reason is that the province would have lost. If so, Parliament's legislative jurisdiction over trade and commerce, particularly international trade, would have increased. This would not have been in Ontario's interest. Political sabre-rattling was as far as Ontario was prepared to go.

A recent case that helped to define federal jurisdiction over the environment is the Oldman Dam decision of 1992.[18] In this case, an interest group took the federal government to court because, in its opinion, the government had not fulfilled its obligations to carry out an environmental impact assessment. The court agreed with the position presented by the Friends of the Oldman River Society. The importance of this case is considerable, particularly in light of the recommendation from the Beaudoin-Dobbie Committee that the environment *not* be added to the list of items to be discussed under the division of powers. They said,

> At the present time, there is no subject heading in the Constitution dealing with this matter [environment]. But, both the federal and provincial governments, under various heads of power, share responsibility for the environment. We agree with

this sharing of responsibility and see no need for constitutional change in this area.[19]

If the parliamentary committee's view prevails in the future, individuals will continue to turn to the courts to adjust constitutional boundaries.

The foregoing discussion outlines some of the alternative processes to formal amendment to the constitution. In each instance, governments have to decide if they want to initiate change. Part of their willingness to do so will depend upon the public's demand for change.

A RETURN TO COOPERATIVE FEDERALISM

In the previous section, several alternative processes to formal amendment were described. Although these approaches will permit the solution of some problems, they may not necessarily be the most effective means of addressing all the difficulties currently confronting our federal system. Other approaches which are best characterized as intergovernmental in nature may sometimes be more suitable. It is my contention that, through intergovernmental negotiation, governments can conclude agreements which are similar in scope to a number of the provisions contained in the Charlottetown Accord.

The genius of post-war Canadian federalism has been the development of a series of federal-provincial agreements covering a wide range of policy fields ranging from health care to social assistance. National policies have emerged — not always harmoniously — but they have been developed. Health care, energy pricing, and fiscal arrangements are good examples. As one observer remarked 30 years ago, "This leads us away from the preoccupation with the lawyers' constitution to some analysis of the politician's or administrator's constitution."[20]

Since the failure of Charlottetown, there are three policy areas that remain issues of major concern for governments. They are interprovincial trade barriers, the federal spending power and labour market development and training.

Dispute in these areas will not disappear just because formal constitutional amendment cannot be reached. Indeed disagreements appear to have intensified since the referendum. Rather than expending our energy searching for constitutional solutions to our problems, we may be more successful in falling back on what has proven successful in the past — intergovernmental negotiation and agreement — cooperative federalism.

A brief history of attempts to resolve disputes in the three policy areas reinforces this point.

INTERPROVINCIAL TRADE BARRIERS

The federal government added the subject of interprovincial trade barriers to the constitutional agenda in 1980. At that time, governments were unable or unwilling to reach agreement.[21] The Macdonald Royal Commission studied the issue and, in 1985, recommended against constitutional solutions. To quote the Commission:

> We have reservations about placing further responsibilities on the courts in an area where complex economic and political trade-offs often seem to be required. Many practices that have attracted attention in relation to the economic union fall into grey areas that even a strengthened section 121 cannot easily reach.[22]

Instead the commissioners recommended a Code of Economic Conduct. A committee of federal-provincial ministers responsible for economic development under the aegis of the first ministers' conference was to be responsible for developing the Code.

During the negotiations leading up to the Charlottetown Accord the federal government pressed very hard for provincial agreement to the proposals contained in its September 1991 position paper. Just as in 1980, most provinces, while accepting the principle of the common market, resisted any constitutional limitations to their legislative authority to protect or preserve particular aspects of their economies. For example, P.E.I. wanted to protect its limits to land ownership, Alberta wanted to protect its natural resources, Saskatchewan wanted to protect its Crown corporations and British Columbia wanted to protect its social assistance programs. The list of exceptions grew to the point that the proposed cure was worse than the problem. In a rather prophetic statement, the Royal Commission predicted this eventuality. They said, "A constitutionalized code formulated today would probably include so many opting-out, *non obstante* and exemption clauses that it would perhaps only legitimize what it was designed to prevent."[23] As the provinces' list of exceptions increased, the federal government's enthusiasm for a constitutional provision decreased. At the meeting in Charlottetown, first ministers deleted the subject from the main agreement and added it to a companion "Political Accord" for further review at a future first ministers' conference.[24]

In the course of the negotiations on interprovincial trade barriers, the idea of devising a dispute resolution mechanism took root. Although most provincial governments were determined not to have the courts review their trade policies, they appeared to be amenable to the creation of some kind of intergovernmental tribunal. The Macdonald Commission used GATT mechanisms as their model, but negotiators of the Charlottetown Accord proposed one patterned after that in the Canada-U.S. Free Trade Agreement. While I see little prospect of governments resurrecting the detailed provisions of the "Political Accord," I do see a much greater prospect for governments agreeing to a code of conduct and a dispute resolution mechanism.

That interprovincial trade barriers remains a contentious issue is reflected in the following statement by Premier McKenna of New Brunswick in late November 1992. He said, "Those provinces that want to put up barriers will have barriers put up against them.... We can't wait to have unanimity from 10 provinces, so let's introduce interprovincial free trade with those who want it."[25] Such language is the basis for both political and legal conflict. Indeed these words were not idle musings. In the spring of 1993 New Brunswick announced its "Quebec Reciprocal Treatment Policy." Speaking in the New Brunswick legislature, the minister of economic development said:

> The following statement is to be included in all applicable tender documents and advertisements of tenders: *Note to Quebec bidders only: Until the preferential restrictions in Quebec currently applying to non-Quebec businesses and labour are repealed, only those having their principal place of business in New Brunswick are allowed to bid unless specifically invited.*[26]

In the spring of 1993, the federal and provincial governments established a schedule to eliminate trade barriers.[27] The actual negotiations began in June 1993 and are scheduled to continue for about a year. New Brunswick's drawing the line in the sand may force all governments to reassess their policies before further retaliatory measures are taken. That such an eventuality might occur is reflected in various news accounts. Ontario is concerned about Quebec's restrictive policies limiting Ontario business and labour opportunities, while New Brunswick is concerned about Ontario's policies with respect to marketing Moosehead beer, despite the fact that an all-province agreement was reached in 1990 on domestic beer sales.[28] Reports from the June conference have not been encouraging. It appears that British Columbia insists on maintaining certain barriers affecting regional development.[29] Although problems continue to exist, my sense is that governments have made the political commitment to solve this problem once and for all. What we are seeing today is the preliminary skirmishing.

THE FEDERAL SPENDING POWER

The issue of the federal spending power was one of the original topics placed on the constitutional agenda in 1968 and it has remained there ever since. It was one of Quebec's five demands listed in 1986. The question is not whether the federal spending power exists — it does — but rather how it can be controlled.

During both the Meech Lake and Charlottetown negotiations, the limits developed (provincial opting-out with federal compensation) were a matter of considerable controversy. Many Canadians felt that if such a clause were included in the constitution, national programs such as health care could be dismantled while others such as day care would never get introduced.

Another reason why this topic was prominent during the Charlottetown negotiations results from the 1990 federal budget. At that time, the federal government unilaterally introduced a ceiling on the Canada Assistance Plan (CAP) for the three wealthiest provinces — Ontario, British Columbia and Alberta. Parliament approved this policy by statute. The provinces had two choices — to accept the decision or to take the federal government to court. The provinces affected did, in fact, take the federal government to court — and lost.[30] It should come as no surprise that throughout the negotiations leading to the Charlottetown Accord the provinces pressed for a provision that would protect intergovernmental agreements from unilateral changes for their duration.

The reason the spending power is so important is that it goes to the heart of our federal system and touches upon most aspects of public policy. That is why, throughout the Charlottetown Accord, one finds reference to the federal spending power, including the following: the limits to new national shared-cost programs,[31] the so-called six policy fields such as forestry[32] and most importantly the agreement to establish "a framework to govern expenditures of money in the provinces of Canada in areas of exclusive provincial jurisdiction."[33]

If people doubt the importance of the spending power and the increasing apprehension of the provinces, they should pay close attention to Premier Rae's remarks when he claimed the federal government owes Ontario $2 billion for welfare payments under CAP.[34] Nor should one ignore Premier Klein's comments about user fees for health care which he made shortly after his successful leadership race.[35] The subject of user fees for health care has also surfaced in both the Conservative leadership race and the 1993 Alberta provincial election.[36] While one can dismiss all such statements as political posturing, they can also be seen as trial balloons sent up to test the political waters. They also serve to underline the rather precarious nature of our social safety net and highlight potential areas of federal-provincial conflict.

Closely-related to the question of the spending power is the burgeoning public debt because it limits the funds available for social programs and leads to intergovernmental dispute. The C. D. Howe Institute has referred to the size of our public debt as a crisis.[37] While some dismissed the C. D. Howe report as alarmist, prudence would suggest that it be given some credence. Here is the reaction of the minister of finance, Don Mazankowski, to the report. According to one newspaper account:

> "Canadians will not tolerate any increase in taxes," said Mazankowski....
>
> But he was "quite intrigued" by the suggestion of some economists in the report that it's time to look seriously at "wholesale" cuts in federal transfers.

> The government has repeatedly cut the growth in those payments used to fund old age security, higher education, and health care.[38]

This comment leads one very quickly into the political minefield known as offloading or, put another way, shifting the burden of expenditure from one level of government to another — usually from the federal to the provincial governments. The various provincial budgets introduced this spring have all contained reference to this problem, some in particularly harsh terms. The federal government is blamed for provincial deficits and, by inference, the need to increase provincial taxes. The B.C. budget refers to "federal offloading"; Saskatchewan talks about "a diminishing federal financial commitment"; New Brunswick mentions the "arbitrary ceiling provision" on equalization payments; and Newfoundland talks about the "unilateral federal EPF restraint measures." To Quebec, "Federal transfers are part of the problem of Quebec's public finances. They should be part of the solution." Alberta said, "Current federal-provincial fiscal arrangements blur responsibilities, fail to give provinces adequate revenue to meet their responsibilities, penalize some provinces in providing national programs, and do not allow provinces sufficient flexibility. All of this leads to waste and duplication."[39]

Offloading involves more than expenditure reductions and intergovernmental transfers. It also raises the question of what should or will be the federal government's continuing role in the policy fields of health, post-secondary education and social assistance. When Parliament approved the *Canada Health Act* of 1984, provinces were instructed to eliminate policies such as extra billing and other user fees or face equivalent reductions in federal transfers. The time may be rapidly approaching when federal cash contributions will be at such a low level that provinces will simply refuse to accept the funding and its conditions and will establish their own programs. Policy control over shared-cost programs by the federal government is ultimately linked to federal expenditures, and a reduction in funding serves only to weaken the control.

The possibility of a major federal-provincial dispute over the financing of our most important shared-cost programs would increase tensions in the federal system and reduce the federal government's ability to influence national standards. Thomas Kierans of the C. D. Howe Institute states, "Fiscal federalism is in danger of disintegrating and time to salvage it is running out."[40]

The constitutional and fiscal agendas are inevitably intertwined, make no mistake about that! If for no other reason than to restore public confidence, a review of the use of the spending power appears timely. A good place to start is with the commitment to establish the framework found in section 37 of the Charlottetown Accord which stated:

> The government of Canada and the governments of the provinces are committed to establishing a framework to govern expenditures of money in the provinces by

the government of Canada in areas of exclusive provincial jurisdiction that would ensure, in particular, that such expenditures

(a) contribute to the pursuit of national objectives;
(b) reduce overlap and duplication
(c) respect and not distort provincial priorities; and
(d) ensure equality of treatment of provinces while recognizing their different needs and circumstances.

While finance ministers are the logical persons to initiate such a study, it should not be conducted as merely another part of the periodic renegotiation of fiscal arrangements. The nature of the framework contemplated in section 37 appears to be a much more fundamental restructuring of the spending power with very real consequences for the functioning of fiscal federalism. In my opinion, the deficit issue has served to highlight the importance and timeliness of such a review.

LABOUR MARKET DEVELOPMENT AND TRAINING

Of all the proposed changes to the division of powers in the Charlottetown Accord, the one to labour market development and training was the most profound. With the failure of the referendum, the federal government very quickly reasserted its authority over this field. The subject was discussed at a January 1993 meeting of ministers responsible for labour market training where ministers stressed the need for cooperative and coordinated action.[41] The first tangible agreement was reached in early August 1993 between the federal and Quebec governments.[42] Under the agreement, the main responsibility for job training would be turned over to the province, a role the province had sought for many years. The agreement parallels the provisions found in the Charlottetown Accord and was achieved through intergovernmental negotiation which does not require legislative approval.

At the same time that there have been pressures to devolve responsibility for labour market development and training to the provinces, groups like the Business Council on National Issues and the Canadian Chamber of Commerce have been arguing for the creation of a federal role or presence in the field of education.[43] In its 1991 publication entitled *Learning Well ... Living Well*, the federal government linked its national unity and prosperity initiatives together. The authors, while fully acknowledging the provinces' exclusive jurisdiction over education, raised the possibility of an expanded federal role "in promoting excellence and supporting provincial efforts to improve the acquisition of knowledge and skills."[44]

One of the last reports published by the now defunct Economic Council of Canada painted a rather dismal portrait of the current state of Canadian education. It notes that, "Canada is the only federal country without a federal ministry of education."[45] There is a growing belief in Canada that federal involvement in setting national standards and coordinating provincial efforts would raise Canada's standard of education. Another straw in the wind was a speech by Conservative leadership candidate, Jim Edwards, now President of the Treasury Board, to the Empire Club calling for a system of national tests.[46]

To this point in our history, education has been seen as an area of exclusive provincial jurisdiction. Any idea of federal involvement was dismissed as totally unrealistic because of the potential for constitutional wrangling. Commenting on Ontario's recently-established Royal Commission on Education, Michael Valpy, a columnist with the *Globe and Mail*, said "the mosquito of the Constitution is interfering with Canadians coming together as a whole people to hold a national inquiry into this subject."[47]

As with everything else today, the assumption that the federal government cannot participate in education needs to be questioned. The demands by business lobby groups and expressions of concern by parents cannot be simply swept aside. The question that needs to be answered is whether or not such concerns and demands are justified and what can be done about them if they are. In looking at the various statements, one finds a demand for national standards and a greater federal role in training. While the federal government has some constitutional responsibilities (undefined) through its responsibility for unemployment insurance, how and where to draw the line between these responsibilities and education has never been clearly spelled out. What is becoming increasingly clear, however, is the need for increased federal-provincial dialogue in this area.

The preceding discussions on interprovincial trade barriers, spending power and labour market training have a common theme: federal-provincial cooperation and negotiation. In one instance — the removal of interprovincial trade barriers — some new form of dispute resolution mechanism (other than the courts) is called for. In labour market training, it appears the first federal-provincial agreement is about to be reached. There is every reason to believe that other instruments of flexibility may emerge. It is not inconceivable that some form of intergovernmental secretariat will be established to act as the coordinating organization reporting to first ministers' conferences. Does this sound far-fetched? Not really. Better structures or institutions than the first ministers' conference do not come readily to mind. To date, such conferences have been the means by which policy differences have been resolved. I would expect that matters like administrative interdelegation, mirror legislation and new areas for intergovernmental agreements including telecommunications, a code of economic conduct and labour market training will be pursued. Indeed, the failure of constitutional reform may force governments to become more pro-active in developing mutually acceptable solutions.

Two precautionary notes should be sounded. First, after the CAP experience, thought will have to be given to a means of protecting intergovernmental agreements. Second, the issue of transparency needs to be addressed. After their experiences with constitutional reform, the public will expect to be kept informed and most likely involved in influencing decisions related to reaching such intergovernmental accords.

THE AMENDING FORMULA: PROSPECTS FOR MORE MODEST USE

Canadians' experience with the amending formula of 1982 is relatively limited. It was first used in 1983 to secure changes to the aboriginal provisions of the 1982 constitutional accord. When applied to mega-amendments such as those proposed in 1987 and 1992, success has eluded us. I do not place the blame on the amending formula but instead on the constant expansion of the constitutional agenda and the apparent imperative to solve all problems at once.

Constitutional queuing, or addressing one issue at a time such as Quebec's concerns, was ruled out when Meech Lake failed. If we want to have reform on the scale previously contemplated, it is difficult to see how one can avoid a mega-amendment along the lines of Charlottetown because there are so many linkages and trade-offs among the competing interests.

We should perhaps accept the fact that amendments that are properly characterized as *major reforms* are unlikely to find favour. Therefore the amending formula should be used for less grand purposes — to solve a very specific problem comparable to the insertion of section 92A that was precipitated as a result of two Supreme Court of Canada decisions on natural resources. An early candidate, in my opinion, is an amendment to protect intergovernmental agreements similar to the one found in the Charlottetown Accord (section 126A).[48]

There is another fact about the amending formula that deserves mention. Parliament alone can amend certain parts of the constitution using its authority under section 44 of the *Constitution Act, 1982*. For example, section 51 of the *Constitution Act, 1867* specifies the composition of the House of Commons. Parliament last amended this section in 1985 and I am confident that few were aware that, as this proposal went through the legislative process, it was in fact a constitutional amendment. I raise this example because the composition of the House of Commons received considerable attention during the referendum debate. In other words, there is nothing to prevent Parliament from examining (and changing) the distribution of seats, gender balance or aboriginal representation if it wishes to do so. Indeed, in 1991 the Lortie Royal Commission recommended an amendment to section 51 concerning aboriginal representation.[49]

A part of the amending formula that needs greater scrutiny is section 43, which applies to amendments affecting some but not all provinces. In 1987 it was used to amend the provisions of Newfoundland's 1949 terms of union with respect to denominational schools. More recently, it has been used at the request of New Brunswick to make that province officially bilingual.[50]

The Charlottetown Accord included a bilateral amendment to section 16 of the *Charter of Rights and Freedoms* as it applied to New Brunswick. The amendment gave equal status to the "English linguistic community and French linguistic community," and affirmed the authority of the legislature to preserve and promote these communities. Immediately after the referendum failed, New Brunswick requested a constitutional amendment under section 43. The federal government obliged in February 1993 and the amendment was proclaimed on 12 March 1993. What should have been a more or less routine matter (New Brunswick voted in favour of the referendum) was challenged in federal court by Deborah Coyne, a fierce opponent of both Meech Lake and Charlottetown. She claimed the Crown did not have the authority to act.[51] Her suit was withdrawn in late June 1993 because it had apparently been filed in the wrong court.

The case would have been interesting because it would have explored the limits of section 43. For example, could this section be used to confer some form of special status on Quebec? While this interpretation is unlikely, it raises some intriguing possibilities. Another potential change that could be introduced under this section is an amendment to the Alberta Act protecting Alberta's Métis Settlements, a provision lost with the defeat of the Charlottetown Accord. In short, one should not discount a more limited use of the amending formula.

ONE NATION — OR TWO?

Before concluding this chapter, I should mention the darker side of the constitutional debate. We can solve our constitutional problems in a variety of ways but even these attempts can be derailed by our lack of unity over basic goals for our country and a lack of charity towards each other's aspirations. Put plainly, Canada could be on the verge of self-destruction. Unfortunately this claim has been made so often that it is now often discounted. My purpose is not to give the claim credence but to explore it and some of its implications.

After the 1992 referendum, *The Economist* made the following observation:

> Journey's end, it seems, is a bog. When 54% of its people and six of its provinces said No on October 26th to the set of constitutional proposals on which they had been asked to vote, Canada reached the end of the road it has been traveling for the past dozen years. The bog in which it now comes to rest is deeper and stickier even than the one from which it started, and it is not clear there is a way out. Canada may well be mired for years.[52]

Although it will take a long time for a detailed and comprehensive analysis of the referendum to emerge, certain public opinions were made fairly clear during the fall of 1992. One is that Quebec got too much in the form of "concessions," the one most frequently mentioned being the guarantee of 25 percent of the seats in the House of Commons. Some critics thought the Canada clause and its distinct society provisions established a hierarchy of rights. Another concern was that too much power, again because of Quebec's demands, had been devolved to the provinces — that Canada was becoming too decentralized and, hence, more ungovernable. In Quebec one heard the opposite argument. Quebecers felt there was insufficient recognition of their historic demands for greater legislative responsibility. Charlottetown was not even close to meeting the proposals of the Quebec Liberal Party's Report (Allaire) of January 1991.

Although the referendum is behind us, one must ask whether or not the two visions of our federal system — centralization or decentralization just mentioned — are reconcilable. If Charlottetown did not strike the appropriate balance with respect to the division of powers, it is difficult to see what alternatives are available. For one thing, the "have not" provinces were most reluctant to see further devolution of federal authority and, in fact, they insisted on guarantees that federal funding would continue if they requested it. The provisions on culture in the Charlottetown Accord clearly highlighted the tensions between these two opposing views. Even Alberta, which to this point has championed province-building, showed no particular desire to pursue the transfer of additional federal powers to the provinces. Quebec was more or less by itself on this agenda item.

Another worrisome trend is the erosion or outright rejection of any special consideration for Quebec. Nobody denies that Quebec is a distinct society. It is — but there is a very obvious reluctance to recognize and protect its distinctiveness in the constitution, and that reluctance is becoming more and more wide-spread. A key reason is that Canada today is fundamentally different from the Canada of its 1967 centennial when recent constitutional discussions began. One need only examine the development of multiculturalism over the past two decades, the shifting patterns of immigration or the louder voice of the Aboriginal Peoples to discern reasons for a growing disenchantment with policies that give protection to Quebec's distinct society. It is interesting that "nearly a third of Canadians reported in the 1991 census that their ethnic background was neither British nor French."[53]

In a perceptive article, journalist Richard Gwyn, suggests that the two-nations idea is passé. He said:

> Canada is understood better as an ethnic, European-style nation in Quebec, and a "rest of Canada" well on the way to becoming a multiethnic world nation....
>
> All that's certain is that Quebec and the rest of Canada now are marching to quite different drummers in quite different directions, which is a real problem.[54]

In his book, *Charter versus Federalism: The Dilemmas of Constitutional Reform,* Alan Cairns reaches a comparable conclusion when he argues that Canada, except Quebec, has embraced the Charter.[55] What appears to be occurring is a gradual drifting apart of Canada's two solitudes. During the 1980 Quebec referendum campaign, there was a tremendous outpouring of affection for Quebec. People genuinely and generously wanted to know what Quebec wanted and were prepared to accommodate those demands. During the 1992 referendum campaign the opposite sentiment surfaced. One would frequently hear, "If they want to go, let them."

An issue over which there has been significant conflict is language policy. In 1988, Quebec's Bill 178, or sign law, had a profound effect on the rest of Canada and can be listed as one the chief reasons for the demise of the Meech Lake Accord. Since the Bill's constitutionality depended on the use of the notwithstanding clause contained in the Charter, it had a five-year time limit. It could be amended or renewed as-is. The Bourassa government introduced legislation in the spring of 1993 amending the legislation and softening the restrictions. Perhaps what is of greater significance is that in 1993 the government did not feel the need to use the notwithstanding clause. The passage of Bill 86 represents a shifting position in Quebec on language policy. Despite efforts by the PQ to arouse public opinion on this issue, the debate was rather low key and the government was able to have the legislation approved without much difficulty.[56]

The language issue is not confined to Quebec. Problems have appeared in Ontario with that province's new bilingual highway signs.[57] There continue to be problems across Canada in minority language education. Francophones on the prairies have turned to the courts to enforce their rights under section 23 of the Charter. This spring the Supreme Court of Canada ordered Manitoba to give francophones control over their schools "without delay."[58] Victor Goldbloom, Commissioner of Official Languages, in his 1992 report, while acknowledging the great progress made by provinces in the area of minority languages, stated:

> A few months ago, all provincial governments were prepared to make a *constitutional* commitment to fostering the vitality and development of official language minority communities. It does not seem unreasonable today to expect them to provide legal underpinning to well-established policies on essential services in the minority language.[59]

This is yet another example of non-constitutional solutions to matters of public policy. Voluntary changes in policy positions have far greater symbolic significance than court-imposed decisions.

What of the future? A number of possibilities come to mind. The most frequently mentioned, particularly by the Parti Québécois (PQ), is that the PQ would be elected in the next Quebec election. Within a year, they would hold a referendum on sovereignty and the referendum would pass. What would happen next? We would negotiate — but what would we talk about? The PQ has always advocated, from Réné Lévesque to Jacques Parizeau, some kind of continuing link with Canada. Whether or not the rest-of-Canada would agree is unknown.

There is no way to predict the public mood if Quebec, through a referendum, decides it wants out of Confederation. While it makes sense to maintain some kind of economic links such as customs, transportation and currency, one cannot assume that a break-up will necessarily be amicable. Nor can one assume that solutions will be based on logic as opposed to emotion. It is reasonable to expect, however, some kind of cooperation. After the initial shock and the ensuing economic uncertainty wear off it should be evident that some kind of association is better than building fences between us. Moreover, each separate polity will need to establish, or reinforce, some form of linkages with the United States. It is unlikely that a completely different relationship would evolve among the three nations.

An alternative would be some form of asymmetrical federalism or special status for Quebec. This concept is not a new one; indeed it has been debated for years. Under it, Quebec would assume responsibility for an unspecified number of subject areas not available to the other provinces. Interestingly enough, this approach found favour last year in the first of the public conferences held to review the federal government's position paper of September 1991.[60] The difficulty with pursuing this course today is reconciling it with the concept of provincial equality which has also taken root. Commenting on *Maclean's* year-end survey, pollster Allan Gregg stated:

> In short, the differences appear irreconcilable. At the very least, we might logically conclude that any new constitutional package that is predicated primarily on a partnership between English and French will be doomed to failure in English Canada. Conversely, a new proposal founded on the principle of equal provincial partnership will surely create fissures and debate in Quebec that are unlikely to produce any kind of consensus in that province.[61]

If this dichotomy remains, I hold out little hope for the alternative of asymmetrical federalism.

Let me return, therefore, to M. Parizeau's scenario. I would argue that, once negotiations conclude between Canada and Quebec, there would need to be yet another referendum to ratify what has been agreed to, just as there was in October 1992. It seems almost inconceivable that the public will agree in advance to whatever the two sides negotiate. Moreover, once these hypothetical negotiations commence, there is no way to predict with any degree of accuracy what will emerge as the final agreement, or if an agreement will be reached at all. Both domestic and international pressures are unknown, as is the identity of the negotiators. While some are forecasting possible outcomes and, in some instances, dictating solutions, most commentary is highly speculative.

A number of scholars are giving serious attention to what was once a taboo subject. Just as there were books on the future of Canadian federalism, a number on Canada without Quebec have been published recently. Included are: *Toward a Canada-Quebec Union* (1991); *Deconfederation, Canada Without Quebec* (1991); *Canada Remapped, How the Partition of Quebec Will Reshape the Nation* (1992) and *Negotiating With a Sovereign Quebec* (1992).[62] While the works offer different perspectives, they do not shrink from confronting the fracturing of the Canadian polity.

Indeed, in *Deconfederation*, Bercuson and Cooper advocate Quebec's separation as being in the best interests of Canada and Quebec. To quote, "Indeed, the departure of Quebec is the necessary condition for serious thinking about Canada's future as a country."[63] So much for 125 years of history! Thinking what was once the unthinkable, is not only occurring with greater frequency, but apparently to some is the preferred or inevitable outcome.

Before concluding, I should make a brief reference to the aboriginal question. There is no doubt that expectations of Aboriginal Peoples are high and solutions will not be readily forthcoming.

The Royal Commission on Aboriginal Peoples was established in 1991. It will not release its report until the spring of 1995. The Commission's mandate is extensive, covering virtually all aspects of the relationship between Aboriginal Peoples and Canadian society. Their mandate is to make recommendations that will lead to reconciliation. To some extent, the Charlottetown negotiations eclipsed the Royal Commission's activities, but now, with the failure of the Charlottetown Accord, there is much greater pressure on the Commission to propose recommendations that will be acceptable to both Aboriginal Peoples and other Canadians.

CONCLUSION

There appears to be little enthusiasm on the part of Canadians and their governments to resume constitutional discussions. Paradoxically, constant reminders of our constitutional disagreements continue to surface. These two realities create a dilemma if solutions are to be found. Prudence suggests that the mega-amendment is not a realistic alternative today. But, the other approaches outlined in this chapter provide a framework by which accommodation can be accomplished if people press for change.

Canadians have spent so much time, energy and emotion on constitutional reform that we have ignored other means of solving our problems. The title of this chapter, "Let there be light," was intended to emphasize this possibility. Although such solutions do not have the permanence of a constitutional amendment, they nevertheless are easier to achieve, can be modified as needed and do not raise needless expectations.

Whether or not there is a willingness on the part of the public to press for the limited agenda I have outlined is another matter. The issues mentioned such as electoral reform and the removal of interprovincial trade barriers are real and require public discussion, parliamentary action and/or intergovernmental agreement. They cannot be ignored or allowed to fester. Indeed, many recent statements by our political leaders suggest that their patience on some of these matters is running out and that for the next few years intergovernmental relations, both federal-provincial and interprovincial, may be marked by conflict as opposed to cooperation. At the same time, fiscal realities may cause governments to put aside their differences and force them, however reluctantly, to work together on common solutions.

There remains one final thought. It was stated at the outset that the pressures that led to our constitutional negotiations have not disappeared. While that is true, my impression is that many of them may have faded in their intensity. If the PQ wins the next provincial election, we will once again be plunged into the depths of constitutional debate. But even here, there are too many unknowns to see into the future. For years now, Canadians have been told the country may break up. If and when they are confronted with the stark reality of Quebec separation, they will then have to be prepared to make the necessary compromises if they wish to remain united. It is difficult to believe Canadians will stand by and watch the disintegration of their country. There is an element of risk associated with the wait and see attitude but, at present, Canadians prefer this position to continued debate on constitutional reform.

The October 1992 referendum brought to an abrupt end the era of constitutional reform. Given the complexity of the federal system and our failure to bring about constitutional reform, the non-constitutional approach appears to provide greater possibility for success in the future.

NOTES

1. Canada, Royal Commission on Bilingualism and Biculturalism, *Preliminary Report* (Ottawa: Queen's Printer, 1965), p. 13.
2. Canada, Special Joint Committee of the Senate and House of Commons on the Constitution of Canada, *Final Report*, 16 March 1972, p. 3.
3. Canada, The Task Force on Canadian Unity, *A Future Together* (Ottawa: Minister of Supply and Services, 1979), p. 11.
4. Canada, Citizens' Forum on Canada's Future, *Report to the People and Government of Canada* (Ottawa: Minister of Supply and Services, 1991), p. 113.
5. Special Joint Committee of the Senate and House of Commons on a Renewed Canada, *Report of the Special Joint Committee on a Renewed Canada*, 28 February 1992 (Ottawa: Minister of Supply and Services, 1992), p. 4.
6. "Set aside Constitution, Klein urges," *The Edmonton Journal,* 3 February 1993, p. A3.

7. Rhéal Séguin, "Quebec seeks new talks on constitutional reform," *The Globe and Mail,* 10 March 1993, p. A4.
8. Richard Mackie, "Rae rejects unity talks based on old demands," *The Globe and Mail,* 11 March 1993, p. A5.
9. *The Globe and Mail,* 22 December 1992, p. A6; *The Globe and Mail,* 25 January 1993, p. A1; *The Globe and Mail,* 11 March 1993, p. A5 ; *The Edmonton Journal,* 2 January 1993, p. A3 and *The Globe and Mail,* 31 March 1993, p. A5.
10. "Prospects for unity uncertain — Clark," *The Edmonton Journal,* 20 February 1993, p. A3.
11. The two organizations issued a press release in Inuvik on 13 July 1993 expressing these concerns after what they deemed to be an unsatisfactory exchange between themselves and the newly-appointed minister of indian affairs, Honourable Pauline Bowes.
12. See an editorial in *The Globe and Mail,* "They have sat too long in that place," 30 June 1993, p. A16 and a Canada-wide mailing from Audrey McLaughlin, leader of the New Democratic Party requesting donations in support of the People's Campaign to Abolish the Senate.
13. Canada, *Shaping Canada's Future Together* (Ottawa: Minister of Supply and Services, 1991).
14. See "Chrétien proposes reforms," *The Globe and Mail,* 20 January 1993, p. A7. See also an editorial in *The Edmonton Journal* criticizing their proposals, "Grits flunk Commons reform," 23 January 1993, p. A14.
15. Royal Commisssion on Electoral Reform and Party Financing, *Reforming Electoral Democracy,* vol. I, (Ottawa: Minister of Supply and Services, 1991), p. 18.
16. "Electoral Reform," *The Economist,* 1 May 1993, pp. 19-21.
17. Hon. Ian Scott, "Notes for Remarks to the Canadian Bar Association," Toronto, 15 December 1987.
18. *Friends of the Oldman River Society v. Canada (Minister of Transport),* [1992] 2 W.W.R. 193 (S.C.C.).
19. *Report of the Special Joint Committee on a Renewed Canada,* Ottawa, 28 February 1992, p. 66.
20. D.V. Smiley, *Conditional Grants and Canadian Federalism; A Study in Constitutional Adaptation* (Toronto: Canadian Tax Foundation, 1963), p. iii.
21. Hon. Jean Chrétien, *Securing the Canadian economic union in the Constitution* (Ottawa: Minister of Supply and Services, 1980).
22. Royal Commission on the Economic Union and Development Prospects for Canada, *Report,* vol. 3 (Ottawa: Minister of Supply and Services, 1985), p. 137.
23. Ibid.
24. *Political Accords: The Multilateral Meetings on the Constitution,* Charlottetown, 28 August 1992, pp. 1-2.
25. "McKenna takes aim at barriers," *The Globe and Mail,* 24 November 1992, p. A3.
26. "Remarks by the Hon. Denis Losier delivered to the Legislative Assembly," 21 April 1993, p. 3.

27. See "Governments agree on comprehensive negotiations to reduce internal trade barriers," *Press Release*, Industry, Science and Technology Canada, Montreal, 18 March 1993.
28. Stephanie Nolen, "Ontario considers retaliating," *The Globe and Mail*, 7 July 1993, p. A3A and "Beer war brewing between provinces," *The Globe and Mail*, 24 July 1993, p. B3.
29. "B.C. opposed to dropping trade barriers," *The Globe and Mail*, 9 June 1993, p. B1.
30. *Reference Re Canada Assistance Plan*, [1991] 6 W.W.R. 1 (S.C.C.).
31. Agreement, section 16 (p. 27). This section incorporates the same provisions as found in Meech Lake.
32. Agreement, section 11 (pp. 17-18) which includes urban and municipal affairs, tourism, recreation, housing, mining and forestry.
33. Agreement, section 37.
34. "How Rae plans to get rid of the Tories in Ottawa," *The Globe and Mail*, 22 January 1993, p. A9.
35. "Medical User Fees Pushed," *Calgary Herald*, 13 January 1993, p. 1.
36. In a speech to the Empire Club of Toronto on 19 May 1993 Jim Edwards touched on this topic by noting that, while he personally did not favour user fees, other leadership candidates had proposed them. (p. 4)
37. "Debt crisis looms, study warns," *The Globe and Mail*, 16 February 1993, p. A1.
38. "Mazankowski hints at transfer cuts as weapon in fight against deficit," *The Edmonton Journal*, 17 February 1993, p. A3.
39. See Alberta, *Budget '93*, 6 May 1993, p. 18; Québec, *1993-1994 Budget*, 20 May 1993, p. 21; Newfoundland, *Budget*, 18 March 1993, p. 5; Saskatchewan, *Budget Address*, 19 March 1993, p. 16; British Columbia, *Budget '93*, 30 March 1993, p. 4; and New Brunswick, *Budget 1993-1994*, 31 March 1993, p. 12.
40. Peter M. Leslie, Kenneth Norrie, Irene Ip, *A Partnership in Trouble; Renegotiating Fiscal Federalism* (Toronto: C.D. Howe Institute, 1993), p. vii.
41. "Ottawa, provinces vow to improve job training," *The Globe and Mail*, 21 January 1993, p. A5.
42. André Picard, "Quebec to run job training," *The Globe and Mail*, 4 August 1993, p. A1.
43. "Business group calls for standard test," *The Globe and Mail*, 24 March 1993, p. A1, and The Canadian Chamber of Commerce, "Policy in Action," 2, 1 (Spring 1993): 4.
44. See Prosperity Secretariat Consultation Paper, *Learning Well ... Living Well* (Ottawa: Minister of Supply and Services, 1991), p. i.
45. Economic Council of Canada, *A Lot to Learn: Education and Training in Canada* (Ottawa: Minister of Supply and Services, 1992), p. 45.
46. Edwards, speech to Empire Club of Toronto, 19 May 1993.
47. "Just what do Canadians want their schools to do?" *The Globe and Mail*, 22 January 1993, p. A2.

48. References are to various sections contained in the *Draft Legal Text* of the Charlottetown Agreement, 9 October 1993, pp. 27-28. Referred to hereafter as Agreement.
49. Royal Commission on Electoral Reform and Party Financing, *Report* vol. I, Recommendation 1.4.14, p. 190.
50. The amendment is found at the very end of the draft legal text, p. 51 and is simply referred to as: "Bilateral amendment — New Brunswick and Canada."
51. "Language-law court challenge launched," *The Edmonton Journal*, 16 February 1993, p. A10. For more information, see University of Ottawa, Canadian Centre for Linguistic Rights, *Bulletin,* vol. 1:1 (April 1993): 7.
52. "Glug glug," *The Economist,* 31 October 1992, p. 18.
53. "Nearly 1 in 3 Canadians neither British nor French," *The Edmonton Journal*, 4 February 1993, p. A3.
54. "Two-nations idea is now out of date," *The Edmonton Journal,* 2 February 1993, p. A3.
55. Alan C. Cairns, *Charter versus Federalism: The Dilemmas of Constitutional Reform* (Montreal: McGill-Queens University Press, 1992).
56. "Quebec government pushes through sign law," *The Globe and Mail,* 18 June 1993, p. A6.
57. "Ontario backlash brews over bilingual signs," *The Edmonton Journal,* 18 February 1993, p. A9.
58. Sean Fine, "Let francophones control schooling, Manitoba ordered," *The Globe and Mail*, 5 March 1993 p. A4.
59. Commissioner of Official Languages, *Annual Report, 1992* (Ottawa: Minister of Supply and Services, 1993), p. 18.
60. Atlantic Provinces Economic Council, *Renewal of Canada: Division of Powers; Conference Report*, Halifax, 22 January 1992, p. 11.
61. Allan R. Gregg "The New Canada," *Maclean's*, 4 January 1993, p. 29.
62. Philip Resnick, *Toward a Canada-Quebec Union* (Montreal and Kingston: McGill-Queen's University Press, 1991); David J. Bercuson and Barry Cooper, *Deconfederation, Canada Without Quebec* (Toronto: Key Porter Books, 1991); Scott Reid, *Canada Remapped, How the Partition of Quebec Will Reshape the Nation* (Vancouver: Pulp Press, 1992) and Daniel Drache and Roberto Heron, eds., *Negotiating With a Sovereign Quebec* (Toronto: James Lorimer, 1992).
63. Bercuson and Cooper, *Deconfederation*, p. 159.

5

Tensions in the Canadian Constitutional Process: Elite Negotiations, Referendums and Interest Group Consultations, 1980-1992

Michael B. Stein

Depuis l'échec des accords du lac Meech et de Charlottetown, plusieurs commentateurs politiques ont soutenu que les négociations au sommet entre acteurs de haut niveau du système fédéral canadien ne constituent plus un moyen très efficace pour la conduite des pourparlers constitutionnels au pays. Ces observateurs sont d'avis qu'en cette ère de souveraineté populaire, les Canadiens n'ont d'autre choix, s'agissant de la réforme de leur constitution, que de s'en remettre exclusivement à des structures de consultation populaire telles que les groupes de travail, les auditions publiques, les assemblées constituantes et les référendums.

L'auteur récuse en partie, quant à lui, cette nouvelle croyance populaire. Il affirme que les négociations au sommet dans le cadre fédéral sont à la fois souhaitables et nécessaires pour mener à bien la réforme constitutionnelle; selon Stein, celles-ci comportent, en soi, une possibilité de compromis entre les acteurs concernés. Auquel cas, on peut qualifier pareil résultat d'éminemment positif. Toutefois, il importe que ce type de négociations aillent de pair avec des mécanismes de consultation populaire, afin de tenir compte du climat politique du moment.

Or, concilier ces deux types de démarche n'est guère chose facile. Il existe des tensions et des contradictions entre, d'une part, la logique fondée sur le compromis qui détermine le processus des négociations constitutionnelles et, d'autre part, la logique tendant à maximiser la fonction référendaire, ainsi que le rôle joué par les groupes de pression. On assiste à un renforcement de ces tensions et contradictions par suite des récents changements survenus sur le plan politique, le tout ayant une incidence sur les partis poltiques, groupes de pression et nouveaux mouvements sociaux. Ces types de conflits sont apparus lors des négociations entourant les accords du lac Meech et de Charlottetown et partant, ont peut-être contribué largement à leur échec. On peut cependant en venir à bout en recourant à divers procédés conçus spécifiquement pour la gestion des tensions.

Since the failure of both the Meech Lake and Charlottetown Accords, many political observers believe that executive federalism has lost its value as an effective structure for conducting constitutional negotiations in Canada. Executive federalism is a term which Donald Smiley first invented and defined as "the relations between elected and appointed officials of the two orders of government in federal-provincial interactions, and the executives of the provinces in interprovincial interactions."[1] In Canadian constitutional negotiations it refers to the numerous meetings, contacts and communications among top federal and provincial officials, ministers and first ministers which have contributed in a central way to the framing of constitutional proposals and the negotiation and implementation of constitutional agreements.

These relations have occurred intermittently over much of this century, and almost continuously in the last 25 years during intensive efforts at comprehensive constitutional renewal. Most such interactions take place in closed meeting-rooms, beyond the reach of the media and the glare of publicity. They are normally unknown to the general public and receive little if any attention within the elected legislatures of the two levels of government. Frequently the agreements produced by these relations are debated in a most cursory fashion by members of the federal Parliament and provincial legislatures, and often are not even ratified by the legislatures. They are, in short, highly elitist structures, whose institution, composition and decisionmaking processes seem to reflect the antithesis of the representative and participatory norms associated with the institutions of liberal democracy in the current age of popular sovereignty.

It is not surprising, therefore, that many Canadians, including both political experts and lay people, believe that it is no longer possible to leave these matters primarily to these political executives. They feel that in this era of popular sovereignty, they cannot allow *their* document, the people's constitution, to be negotiated and fundamentally altered without major input and the ultimate consent of the Canadian population in a referendum. After all, as they see it, the ultimate source of sovereignty and legitimacy in democratic political systems lies with the "ordinary" citizens.

I will discuss the issue as it relates to the Canadian case in six parts: (i) the new mythology of popular sovereignty and consultative processes; (ii) the concomitant critique of executive/summit federalism; (iii) my alternative view: the necessity and desirability of executive/summit federalism in a blended constitutional process of elite negotiations and popular consultations; (iv) the tensions and contradictions between elite negotiations and direct democratic consultations or referendums in constitution-making; (v) the tensions and contradictions between elite negotiations and interest group consultations in constitution-making; and (vi) some possible ways of reconciling these tensions and contradictions.

THE NEW MYTHOLOGY OF POPULAR SOVEREIGNTY

As one of our most acute constitutional commentators, Peter Russell, has pointed out, the perception that popular sovereignty is both desirable and inevitable in the current constitutional climate of Canada is the culmination of Canada's long and somewhat retarded pursuit of decolonization, political maturity, and full democratic development; moreover, it follows a path travelled earlier and often more rapidly in other advanced industrialized countries. The United States was the first modern country to embody the principle of popular sovereignty in its written constitution of 1787, and to attempt to implement it in its institutional practices. This principle was ultimately derived from a Lockean view of political legitimacy based on the notion of popular consent; it may be contrasted with the Burkean concept of "organic constitutionalism" based on an incremental, informal and indirect collective consensus, which shaped the modern British constitution and evolving British institutions.[2]

Since 1787 most countries establishing liberal democratic regimes have embraced the *American* concept of legitimacy and democratic consent. They frequently include in the preamble of their constitution some reference to popular sovereignty, and attempt to incorporate this concept directly into their institutional design and practices. This is the case for democratic regimes of all types: parliamentary-cabinet or presidential-congressional, unitary or federal, or some hybrid of the two. For example Australia, which like Canada adopted a Westminster-style parliamentary-cabinet system and a federal structure when its constitution was first adopted in 1901, also included an explicit reference to popular sovereignty in its constitutional preamble, and adopted an amending formula that provided for ratification by popular referendum.[3] It is widely assumed, therefore, that adoption of a Lockean concept of legitimacy in both regime design and institutional practices is the most normal and sensible constitutional route for new or aspiring democratic countries to follow.

Moreover, there are more practical reasons for assuming that mechanisms of direct democracy and interest group consultation are likely to play a central role in future constitution-making in Canada. As Alan Cairns has pointed out, the Charter of Rights has entrenched a broad range of individual and group rights in our constitution since 1982, and therefore organized groups promoting these rights are likely to demand a greater role in future constitutional discussions.[4] This role may include the direct participation of individual citizens or of interest groups in the constitution-making process at different stages (such as negotiation and ratification), and through a variety of political structures (including legislatures, task forces, courts, constituent assemblies or referendums). It will be very difficult for political leaders to resist such demands.

Finally, some have noted that the very fact that the federal government and several major provinces have already instituted provisions for holding consultative referendums or plebiscites and have applied them at the ratification stage of the Charlottetown Accord has important implications for future constitutional proposals. It suggests that the formal procedure for legislative ratification of constitutional amendment proposals provided in the 1982 Act may now be superceded by a new constitutional convention involving referendums similar to the formal ratification procedure and practice in Australia.[5]

In short, in Canada today, as well as elsewhere (e.g., the European Community), there is widespread acceptance of the ethos of popular sovereignty in constitution-making. Although direct democratic devices such as referendums or plebiscites are the most overt and popular expression of this new ethos, other mechanisms of public consultation involving both organized interest groups and individual citizens have also been widely advocated. These include open and peripatetic legislative and task force hearings at different stages of the constitutional process; different types of constituent assemblies comprised of various combinations of non-partisan groups, experts and "ordinary citizens"; and expanded use of public opinion polling, open-line radio and television programs, and government-subsidized telephone lines soliciting the views of the general public on political issues.

THE CRITIQUE OF EXECUTIVE/SUMMIT FEDERALISM

Simultaneously, there has been strong and widespread criticism recently directed against "closed-door" elite negotiations by politicians or officials in such constitutional matters. These structures are viewed as highly unrepresentative of the mass citizenry or minority groups; insensitive to strong local or regional, racial, ethnic-linguistic, or gender concerns; vulnerable to internal pressure tactics, personality conflicts, or techniques of subterfuge and deception; and ineffective in bargaining and decisionmaking.

A particularly strong target of criticism is the first ministers' conferences in Canada, made up of our federal prime minister, provincial premiers, and the heads of territorial governments, sometimes described collectively as "summit federalism." These conferences are viewed by many as purely public relations gambits by egoistic electorally-oriented politicians who lack the expertise, trust ties, or shared interests necessary for the negotiation of complex and delicate governmental agreements. Because constitutional matters generally involve discussion or bargaining over intangible symbolic goods rather than quantifiable or divisible material objects, the first ministers' conferences are seen as especially unsuitable policymaking structures in this policy sector. They are ill-equipped to achieve the cooperation and mutual understandings that are at the root of the compromises, trade-offs, and linkages essential to successful constitutional negotiations.[6]

Tensions in the Canadian Constitutional Process 91

According to the critics, evidence in support of their contentions about executive/summit federalism in Canadian constitution-making can be found in the entire historical record of constitutional negotiations in Canada. First, there were numerous, although intermittent, failed attempts by our first ministers to negotiate a limited agreement on patriation and an amending formula between 1927 and 1968, at a time when provincial support for constitutional change was generally weak.[7] Second, top officials, ministers and first ministers acting under the aegis of executive or summit federalism were unable to produce an accord over a more comprehensive constitutional renewal package between 1968 and 1980, despite many lengthy efforts by negotiating actors who were strongly committed to constitutional change.[8] In November 1981, a constitutional first ministers' conference (FMC) did manage to produce an accord which provided for patriation, an amending formula, and a Charter of Rights; however, it was a truncated agreement that excluded Quebec, and that was subsequently repudiated by a strong bipartisan majority of the Quebec legislature. Even the Charter contained in the package originally negotiated by the first ministers was initially rejected by important grass-roots interests such as women's and aboriginal groups, because it had unfairly circumscribed rights which they had won at an earlier stage. It required mass mobilization organized by leaders of those groups against some of the recalcitrant premiers to restore the original more comprehensive rights package.[9]

The purest manifestation of summit federalism and its inherent weaknesses in relation to Canadian constitution-making, in the opinion of most critics, occurred during the negotiation of the Meech Lake Accord in 1987. They point out that in the initial bargaining on 30 April, which led to a unanimous agreement, there was little or no consultation between the first ministers and the ministers, officials and experts who accompanied them. The final major compromises, trade-offs, and linkages leading to an agreement were all in fact made by eleven white males behind closed doors, working under intense group pressure.[10] The Accord, as amended at the Langevin Block in June, was subsequently declared to be a "seamless web," susceptible to only cursory scrutiny by the various legislatures involved in the ratification process. Amendments could only be made to the package where "egregious errors" had been discovered. All efforts to subject the Accord to more careful critical examination by organized interest groups and the public-at-large were ultimately rejected by the original signatories on the grounds that any fundamental alteration would unravel the finely-woven and delicately balanced fabric of the Accord.[11] Moreover, a major party to the agreement, the Quebec government, flatly refused to entertain later proposals for modification of the agreement which were designed to address public dissatisfaction towards the Accord; it maintained that it was politically bound to abide by its original five minimum conditions for re-entering the Canadian constitutional family. It is hardly surprising, therefore, according to the critics, that organized interest group opposition directed both to the content and process of Meech Lake constitution-making eventually turned a substantial majority of the Canadian public against the Accord and ultimately managed to defeat it.

Even the highly public and broadly consultative Canada round between 1990 and 1992, culminating in the Charlottetown Accord, has been criticized as a further example of the weaknesses of elite negotiations through executive/summit federalism. The package was negotiated by first ministers in the summer of 1992 only after a lengthy process of public consultations. These included: the hearings of the Citizens' Forum on Canada's Future (chaired by Keith Spicer) in 1990; the hearings of the Special Joint Committee of the Senate and House of Commons on the process for amending the constitution of Canada (co-chaired by Senator Gerald Beaudoin and Tim Edwards, MP) in 1991; the hearings of the Quebec National Assembly Parliamentary Commission on the Constitutional and Political Future (co-chaired by Michel Bélanger and Jean Campeau) in the fall of 1991; the hearings of the Special Joint Committee of the Senate and House of Commons on a Renewed Canada (co-chaired by Senator Claude Castonguay and later Senator Gerald Beaudoin and by MP Dorothy Dobbie), which reviewed the federal government's proposals for reform released in September 1991; and the five Renewal of Canada conferences held in different cities across Canada, in January-February 1992, and composed in part of "ordinary citizens."[12] Yet the agreement ultimately reached in August 1992 by the first ministers was severely criticized for being too comprehensive, insufficiently fleshed out, not available in final legal form until late in the referendum campaign, and containing a number of items that were poorly conceived or unwisely conceded.[13]

One frequently cited example of the latter was B.C. Premier Harcourt's acquiescence in the formula for substantially increased legislative representation for Ontario and Quebec in the House of Commons and the provision for a permanent 25 percent floor for Quebec representation in that body. It was viewed by most British Columbians as operating against the long-run interests and democratic rights of their province, which has the fastest-growing population in Canada. Another was Premier Bourassa's acceptance of the provisions for moderate decentralization in the distribution of powers, which was severely criticized even by his own close advisors, Diane Wilhelmy and Andre Tremblay.

In summary, prevailing opinion in Canada today among many experts and wide segments of the mass public echoes this critique and seems to regard executive/summit federalism as an anachronistic, ineffective, undemocratic and undesirable institution in contemporary constitution-making in Canada. According to this view, the appropriate and desirable structures for framing and ratifying proposals for future constitutional change or renewal must include broad public consultation with organized interest groups, experts and individual citizens through increased use of legislative hearings, public-oriented task forces or commissions, perhaps some type of constituent assembly, and final approval by direct referendum involving the electorate at large. Incorporating them into our constitution-making processes would constitute a giant leap forward in our endless quest for full constitutional maturity and popular sovereignty.[14]

AN ALTERNATIVE VIEW: THE NEED FOR A BLENDED PROCESS

Although the unresolved constitutional issues have been placed on the political backburner since the defeat of the Charlottetown Accord, this situation is only temporary. The issues are very likely to reemerge after the next federal and Quebec elections. At the same time, there will be renewed discussion of the appropriate structures and processes for debating and negotiating them. There is therefore an urgent need to examine critically the prevailing mythology about public participation in constitution-making, and the related critique of executive and summit federalism.

In my view, executive/summit federalism is a natural organic development of Canadian federalism and a valuable structural imperative of contemporary constitution-making in this country. Ronald Watts and Donald Smiley were the first to point out that executive federalism tends to evolve naturally in parliamentary federations as a method of reconciling regional and national interests in intergovernmental policymaking. It serves a functional need by providing an outlet for regional interests in a federation when alternative structures for representing these interests at the national level of government are inadequate.[15] It also reflects the general shift in power from the upper levels of the bureaucracy to elected political executives and their political advisors.

This trend to executive federalism, Ronald Watts notes, is a general phenomenon in all existing parliamentary federations; even countries like Australia, which have elected upper houses reflecting regional interests, have evolved similar structures in recent years.[16] Moreover, the greater concentration of executive power in the hands of governmental leaders and first ministers has produced a more global form of executive federalism, which Stefan Dupre has aptly labelled "summit federalism"; in this structure, intergovernmental consultations and negotiations are conducted largely or exclusively by first ministers.[17] In constitutional matters, probably because the issues involved are viewed as important for all policy sectors and government departments, there is a strong tendency to adopt the more global form of summit federalism for negotiating intergovernmental concerns.[18]

Richard Simeon was among the first to observe that the pattern of elite negotiation or bargaining by first ministers in intergovernmental relations in

Canada closely resembles that of heads of national governments in international relations; he appropriately called this process "federal-provincial diplomacy."[19] In Simeon's view, as in global politics, this form of diplomacy can be especially useful in resolving issues between governments in federal systems when solutions cannot be found by lower level politicians and officials such as ministers or deputy ministers. It also serves as an important legitimizing device.[20]

The structures of executive and summit federalism are also useful in political systems and societies that have consociational or semi-consociational features, as both S.J.R. Noel and Kenneth McRae have noted. Where a democratic society is deeply divided into two or more segments defined by ethnicity, language, religion or class, but there is a strong will at the elite level to maintain its existence as a single nation-state and democratic polity, then there is a natural tendency for such systems to evolve consociational-type arrangements. These include power-sharing and formal coalitions among the different communities, and representation of their leaders on a proportional basis; recognition of collective as well as individual rights and minority as well as majority rights reflecting these segmental differences in the constitution and governing structures of the society; the establishment of strong vertical linkages between political elites and masses in each segment; and regular intersegmental bargaining processes among the elites. In Canada, there are grounds for arguing that the structures of executive and especially summit federalism, along with the federal cabinet itself, have been important in maintaining a semi-consociational arrangement between French and English Canada since at least the late 1960s.[21]

Most of the multilateral negotiations of a non-constitutional nature in executive or summit federal structures in Canada until recently have involved a type of compromise bargaining in which attempts have been made to allocate rewards or outputs on an equitable basis according to some predetermined formula (e.g., in regional equalization or fiscal-sharing arrangements). However, in constitutional bargaining, these rewards or outputs are not readily quantifiable, and this has contributed to much conflict, stalemate and bargaining failure. The general tendency has been for negotiating parties to adopt fixed and rigid bargaining positions, which are incapable of easy resolution. Nevertheless, over the course of the last 25 years of intermittent but comprehensive ongoing constitutional negotiations, there has been a gradual process of "constitutional learning" which involves the incorporation and adaptation of new bargaining strategies and tactics and problem-solving methods developed in other negotiating arenas, such as labour relations or international relations. These techniques and methods have been subsumed by me under the concept of "integrative bargaining."

The concept of "integrative bargaining" was first developed by two labour relations specialists, Walton and McKersie. It was used to refer to the interactive activities surrounding the common objectives of negotiating actors, capable of some integration.[22] The concept was later expanded to encompass problem-solving techniques and mutually beneficial outcomes in bargaining by Pruitt, a social psychologist.[23] In recent years it has been adapted to international negotiations by Oran Young.[24]

As I have explained elsewhere,[25] integrative bargaining involves a process of elite interactions which aim at achieving an "integrative" rather than a purely "distributive" or compromise agreement. The parties to the negotiation are divided by differences that are not so deep as to be fundamentally irrevocable. These differences are therefore susceptible to problem-solving methods and solutions involving mutual accommodation. This type of bargaining tends to produce "win-win" outcomes, in which the overall utilities of the bargaining actors are greater than those achieved by maintaining the status quo. The outcomes are generally obtained by devising creative solutions of mutual benefit embodied in new structures, ideas or institutions. The role of "soft" negotiating parties or "third-party mediators" is often crucial in discovering these solutions.

In distributive bargaining, on the other hand, the parties to the negotiation are generally in fundamental disagreement. The differences between them are "issues" not readily resolvable except by allocating rewards on a quantitative basis. This type of bargaining inherently involves a "fixed" or "zero-sum" exchange, in which there are clear winners and losers. It tends to promote "positional" rather than flexible negotiating styles, and binding arbitration or adjudication by neutral parties that are empowered to resolve the dispute.

I have also argued that "integrative bargaining," as a technique or method used by elites to bring about successful negotiations, is beginning to play a major role in constitution-making in Canada. All of the early efforts at achieving comprehensive constitutional agreement in Canada between 1968 and 1981 reflected "positional" or "non-integrative" patterns of elite bargaining, and they ended in stalemate or breakdown. However, in the first ministers' negotiations of November 1981 a type of integrative bargaining occurred for the first time which helped to break the constitutional logjam and produce the key institutional components of the 1981 accord: a charter of rights modified by a notwithstanding clause or legislative override and a 7/50 amending formula with limited provisions for opting out.[26] However, the integration achieved was only partial, since the accord was unable to win elite or public acceptance in Quebec.

Similarly in the 1987 negotiations leading to the Meech Lake Accord, a process of integrative bargaining occurred at the first ministers' level, culminating in their unanimous agreement. However, because this agreement was principally designed to respond to Quebec's demands, it failed to win wider acceptance among contending elites, organized groups and mass populations of the English-speaking provinces, and therefore was eventually defeated.

The Charlottetown Accord negotiated in the summer of 1992 was probably the most clearcut case of successful integrative bargaining by the political elites in Canada. The package provided mutual benefits for all the major negotiating elites who were party to it, and contained compromise provisions, linkages, and trade-offs acceptable to these leaders and most contending political elites and groups as well. These included novel institutional proposals such as an elected, equal and partially effective Senate for the west, expanded representation in the House of Commons for Ontario and Quebec, a 25 percent floor in representation for Quebec, and aboriginal self-government for Native Peoples. Although it, too, was defeated at the ratification stage in the October referendum, the initial negotiation of the agreement by the political elites of this country was, in my view, a notable achievement in and of itself.

In short, I would argue that in spite of the shortcomings outlined by the critics, all of the elite structures and processes discussed in this section, including executive federalism, summit federalism, federal-provincial diplomacy, intersegmental bargaining by consociational elites, and integrative processes of elite bargaining, have made important and valuable contributions to past efforts at constitution-making in Canada. Moreover, I believe they will continue to help solve our constitutional and national unity conflicts in the future, in conjunction with popular consultative structures. There are several reasons for this. One cannot devise a meaningful constitutional accord in a popular consultative forum such as a task force, legislative hearing, constituent assembly, or referendum, since these types of mass participatory structures are far too unwieldy to produce sophisticated and coherent decisions on issues related to fundamental values and rights, formal institutional mechanisms, or complex technical and legal matters. Moreover, despite their claims to greater democratic legitimacy, such structures are likely to involve disproportionate participation and input by a few well-organized interests at the expense of many others.

It seems clear, then, that elite structures and decisionmaking processes are likely to remain a necessary and central component of constitution-making in Canada in the future. But one lesson, arising from the experiences of both Meech Lake and Charlottetown, must not be forgotten: the elite structures and processes described above are insufficient and incomplete by themselves for constitution-making in today's widely shared culture of popular sovereignty. Elite structures must somehow be combined with mechanisms of popular consultation, including referendums and interest group representations, in order to achieve long-term success and legitimacy.

TENSIONS BETWEEN ELITE NEGOTIATIONS AND DIRECT DEMOCRATIC CONSULTATIONS OR REFERENDUMS

As we have noted above, elite negotiations within executive/summit federal structures encourage constitutional agreements which are overall compromises in a non-zero-sum bargaining context. There is a strong thrust or dynamic towards accommodation and reduction of conflict or competition among the bargaining units. The process of negotiation involves much effort at finding solutions that integrate the interests of bargainers; it is intended to increase overall utilities or satisfaction in comparison to the status quo or some alternative future. During this process, there is an attempt to forge linkages between high and low priority concerns of the different negotiating parties, and to use third-party mediators and problem-solving approaches of various types to find an integrative solution. This solution will not satisfy fully the demands of any single negotiating party, but it will allow all parties to obtain at least part of their demands. In other words, the outcome in elite-type integrative bargaining is viewed as "win-win" rather than as "win-lose"; it is more "satisfying" than "maximizing."[27]

Public consultations involving either direct democratic participation by individual citizens in a referendum or formal representations in hearings by organized interest groups, on the other hand, encourage constitutional interactions in a "zero-sum" bargaining context involving both winners and losers. The dynamic in such processes is towards competition, conflict and maximization of individual or group utilities. The processes of decisionmaking emphasize rational calculations of who are the winners and losers in the accord. There is also a thrust towards assertion of the interests of individuals and popular groups or movements, and maximization of their rights and freedoms against the larger collectivity and its leaders. The principles of equality of the individual citizen and majority rule tend to be asserted against minority ethnic, linguistic or communal group rights. Third-party mediators, closed-door bargaining, and problem-solving communications techniques are regarded with distrust, as instruments used to subordinate individuals and mass-based groups to narrow elite interests. An outcome that falls short of realizing the interests of the individual citizens or popularly-based groups through their negotiating representatives is viewed as a "loss," and therefore requires rejection of the leaders' unsatisfactory accommodations.

There is some support for this argument both in the general theoretical and comparative literature on referendums, and in that dealing with referendums in Canada. For example, Butler and Ranney (1978) noted in the conclusion to their comparative study of referendums that

> Referendums disturb politicians — and us — because they tend to force the decision-makers, the voters, to choose between only two alternatives: they must either approve or reject the measure referred. There is no opportunity for continuing discussion of other alternatives, no way to search for the compromise that will draw the widest acceptance. Referendums by their very nature set up confrontations rather than encourage compromises.[28]

Similarly Hahn and Kamieniecki acknowledge in their study on *Referendum Voting* that "According to opponents of the referendum, too many people with competing interests prevent compromises from being reached on controversial issues. Under present conditions, they contend, the referendum is poorly adapted to achieving compromise on matters of major public concern."[29]

Finally, in the Canadian context, Kathy Brock cites Butler and Ranney in noting that

> While a clear-cut solution to the question posed in a referendum might resolve an impasse, it also precludes a compromise solution characteristic of a bargaining process. Decisions in representative assemblies and first ministers' conferences may be scrutinized, delayed, revised, and negotiated. Thus the final result may reflect a broader selection of public opinion than one arrived at through a referendum procedure. This is important in Canada at a time when public opinion is so divided and citizens are questioning the viability of the political system.[30]

This device of the popular referendum may also be used to illustrate some of the dynamics that operate in such popular consultations, although it also has its own particular and distinctive characteristics. It is an institutional mechanism that involves the entire mass citizenry in political decisionmaking, usually on issues of more fundamental constitutional, moral or broad policy import. The objective in calling a referendum is frequently to try to produce a quick policy decision which also has broad public support. This is achieved by reducing multiple and complex issues to a single basic question that can be answered in simple dichotomous ("yes-no") terms.

According to Gordon Smith, a referendum has four distinctive functional characteristics: first, it tends to force existing parties and groups into two large constituencies or groupings: a "Yes" and a "No" camp. This may reduce the importance of traditional partisan or organized group affiliations in the voters' policy choice. Second, it requires that the decision be made by a stipulated majority of voters. This has the effect of emphasizing the primacy of the majority over the minority; hence majority rights, interests and perceptions tend to be favoured over minority concerns on that policy issue. Third, unlike a plebiscite, which is generally a popular vote on the entire policy record of the government, a referendum, whether binding or consultative, is normally confined to a clearly stipulated and limited policy issue. This may encourage more independence and autonomous voter action than is the case in plebiscites. Fourth, it enables the citizen to have a direct impact on the policy of the government on the issue. Given the direct democratic nature of this policy instrument, it is almost certain to determine the fate of the policy, regardless of its formal status (that is, as mandatory or consultative). The overall effect, then, is to give to the citizen a kind of veto, and therefore a sense of being empowered.[31]

One would expect, then, that in an age in which the ethos of popular sovereignty has become so strong, that the referendum would be perceived as a useful instrument for asserting the power of the individual citizen, mass-based interest groups and new social movements against the political elites. Moreover, studies of advanced industrial democracies in the last two decades point to a general trend towards partisan dealignment and the embracing of new post-materialist values by a growing portion of the citizenry.[32] When these trends are combined with a significant general decline in citizen trust in political elites and leaders,[33] then it is not surprising that *recent* popular referendums in western countries appear to reflect a strong element of mass discontent directed towards the established parties, elite bureaucrats and politicians. I would hypothesize that this phenomenon may have contributed *significantly* to the results in the 1992 referendum in Canada on the Charlottetown Accord.

Unfortunately, there is as yet little available theoretical or empirical literature on referendum participation in Canada that may provide supporting argument or evidence for this hypothesis. Most of the rather skimpy literature on referendums in Canada tends to approach the phenomenon primarily from a historical, legal or institutional perspective.[34] However, Patrick Boyer offers some preliminary observations on the results of the recent October 1992 referendum on the Charlottetown Accord in his comprehensive historical study of referendums in Canada.

In Boyer's view, the referendum proposal was rejected because the Charlottetown package was too comprehensive and too ambitious in its program of constitutional reform. Hence the package on which Canadians were voting contained too many complex and contentious items for voters to handle in a simple "Yes-No" choice. As a result:

> The internal dynamic of the campaign was that the Yes side spoke generally in favour of broad propositions and compromise, whereas those urging a No vote each focussed on one or two specific shortcomings in the accord, and made a strong emotional case on that basis alone. The cumulative effect of many specific and negative attacks, by a variety of groups, on many different points, administered to the accord the death of a thousand small wounds.[35]

Boyer later observes in a similar vein:

> The paradox arose because the package contained so many different elements with dozens of major provisions. At many public meetings during the referendum campaign I was asked by troubled voters why the ballot question could not have broken out (sic) the component parts. A voter might, for instance, have agreed with

aboriginal self-government and disagreed with an elected Senate and distinct society status for Quebec; there was no way a voter could register that opinion. My answer usually was two-fold. First, since parliamentarians would have to make similar "Yea" or "Nay" choice, it was only fitting that individual citizens go through the same choice. Second, the Charlottetown Accord represented a negotiated package; each element in it related to concessions or new rights that had been bargained against other provisions... The fabric of the Charlottetown Accord had been woven together, and the strands could not be pulled apart for balloting purposes without unravelling the whole.[36]

It is interesting to note that Boyer, who is such a staunch promoter of referendums versus what he refers to as "first-minister" federalism and "special interest" groups in constitutional matters, uses the argument of a seamless web to defend the comprehensive referendum device. It is very similar to that used by the negotiators of the Meech Lake Accord to support the process of executive/summit federalism against the advocates of broader interest group or legislative consultation.

In a similar manner, Richard Johnston, a leading author of a forthcoming post-referendum electoral study by a team of Canadian voting behaviour specialists, presented some of their preliminary findings in the March 1993 issue of *Political Science*, a publication of the American Political Science Association. In his concluding reflections, he argues:

> In law, amendments still have to meet a high threshold of provincial agreement. The coalitional net thus still has to be cast widely, more widely, I suspect, than most voters wish. Any package that the electorate might accept seems unlikely to be proposed. Any proposal that makes it through the ministerial processes is likely to fail with the people.[37]

It appears as if he has also detected the same contradictory impulses and tensions facing Canadians in constitution-making as we have noted above. His conclusion in this respect is rather pessimistic; namely, that "formal textual constitutional change [in Canada] is now at an end."[38]

Most other studies that are directly concerned with patterns of referendum voting are foreign and comparative in orientation, such as the studies of the various referendums on joining the European Economic Community in the 1970s. They tend to focus primarily on the relationship between referendum voting and changing party policy positions on the referendum issue.[39] There appears to be no study as yet of voter choice in referenda in a non-partisan context (i.e., one where all the major parties in the polity are united in support of the policy submitted to referendum decision or ratification, as was the case in Canada in 1992). Future studies of the 1992 and 1993 Danish and the 1992 French referendums on the Maastricht Treaty in Europe might prove revealing in this respect.

The general assumption in the comparative literature on referendums is that when they are initiated and organized by the government, they are likely to be successful; in this sense their results are perceived to resemble those of government-sponsored plebiscites. In the matrix of functional variance of referendums developed by Gordon Smith, referendums of this type are categorized as both "controlled" and "hegemonic."[40] The cases of "controlled" and "anti-hegemonic" referendums (e.g., De Gaulle's referendum on regional and municipal reform in France in 1969; the Irish referendum on abolition of the single transferable vote electoral system in 1968) are generally attributed to government miscalculation or mismanagement. There are relatively few cases of "uncontrolled" referendums, "since they provide an ideal vent for the expression of anti-governmental and anti-system feelings."[41] When they are held, it is usually because they are citizen-initiated (e.g., the Swiss referendum on foreign workers in 1970), and they tend to be defeated by an alliance of pro-government or pro-system forces.

The pattern in constitutional referendums in industrialized democracies in recent years, however, appears to be somewhat different. Most of these referendums are government-initiated and organized (that is "controlled"), but the results are either "anti-hegemonic" or narrowly "pro-hegemonic." It appears as if current governments are increasingly being pressured into holding referendums on controversial constitutional proposals. Despite an initial organizational advantage, they frequently lose the referendum contest to the "anti-hegemonic" forces. This appears to have occurred not only in Canada in late 1992 with respect to the Charlottetown Accord, but also in Denmark early in 1992 with respect to the Maastricht Treaty on European monetary union. A similar result was very narrowly avoided in France in late 1992. In Australia, rejection of constitutional proposals introduced by the governing authorities is also a frequent occurrence, particularly in recent years.[42]

THE TENSIONS BETWEEN ELITE NEGOTIATIONS AND INTEREST GROUP CONSULTATIONS

What role have interest groups played in constitutional negotiations and public consultations since 1980? Have they tended to manifest an attitude of "self-interest" utility maximization and a "win-lose" negotiation style on constitutional issues, in contrast to those elite constitutional negotiators involved in genuine integrative bargaining? Put another way, have they been advocates of a broader "public" or a narrower "private" interest?

The most popular and widely-used framework for studying interest group behaviour in general in Canada, that of Paul Pross,[43] does not lend itself readily to a systematic empirical analysis of this question. Pross categorizes interest groups in Canada as falling somewhere on a continuum defined by two opposite polar types "issue-oriented" and "institutionalized" interest groups (or more precisely, they are portrayed as developmentally different types, ranging from "issue-oriented" to "fledgling" to "mature" to "institutionalized" groups). These are differentiated primarily by such factors as organizational features (e.g., financial resources, size of membership), level and target of communication (politicians, officials, advisory boards, task forces/commissions, print/electronic media), and nature of objectives (single, narrowly-defined or multiple and broadly-defined). A major reason for the inapplicability of this framework to the questions addressed in this paper is that it provides little basis for evaluating whether the groups are advancing a "self-oriented" narrow group interest or a broader public or societal interest. In fact, Pross seems to consider all groups, whether essentially "issue-oriented" or "institutionalized," as acting in narrow "self-interest" maximization terms.

Similarly, Alan Cairns' view of interest group behaviour in constitutional matters in Canada also seems inadequate for our purposes. He advances an argument about these groups, presented from an essentially neo-institutional perspective, as part of what Brodie and Nevitte have referred to as his "citizens' constitution theory."[44] In his view, since the adoption of the *Charter of Rights and Freedoms* in 1982, a relatively small number of interest groups whose origin or rationale lies with those explicit equality or collective group rights embodied in the Charter, have generated a demand for broader public participation and consultation in constitutional matters. They have also led the assault on executive federalism and elitist government (the political "insiders") on behalf of the average citizens (the political "outsiders"). And they have successfully defeated their adversaries on two occasions since their emergence as a potent legal and organizational force; first in the struggle against the Meech Lake Accord between 1987 and 1990, and more recently, in the struggle against the Charlottetown Accord in 1992.[45]

The particular "charter-based" interest groups Cairns appears to have in mind are the aboriginal groups (e.g., the Assembly of First Nations) whose rights are protected under section 25 of the Charter, the multicultural groups (e.g., the Ukrainian Association of Canada) whose rights are protected under section 27, gender groups (e.g., the National Action Committee on the Status of Women, or NAC), whose rights are guaranteed under section 28, minority language groups devoted to the preservation or protection of English or French, whose rights are protected under sections 16 to 23, and equality groups (e.g., the disabled, visible minorities), whose rights are protected under section 15.[46]

One obvious difficulty with Cairns' perspective on interest groups in relation to constitution-making is that it is somewhat too narrowly defined; it confines itself almost exclusively to the "charter-based" groups, and leaves no role for other types of groups in the constitution-making process. These would include so-called "public interest" groups (e.g., consumers groups, criminal victims groups) or "special interest" private sector groups (e.g., business interest groups like the Business Council on National Issues, legal, or medical groups).[47] It also discounts the constitutional impact of many groups arising from new social forces or movements in society that are not explicitly protected by the Charter — the so-called new social movements, such as environmental groups or peace groups.[48] This has the effect of eliminating a wide segment of the group universe from performing any leading or causal role in constitutional politics in this country.

A promising alternative framework for analyzing interest groups in terms of their contribution to the public/private interest has recently been developed by Peter Finkle and Kernaghan Webb and their collaborators.[49] They present a more inclusive typology of interest groups intended largely to isolate "objective" criteria on which to base future government funding of such groups. The typology includes three basic group types: public interest groups, charter-recognized groups, and special interest groups.

According to Finkle and Webb, "public interest" groups are defined by seven major distinguishing characteristics: (i) they seek public policies that produce collective benefits, (ii) they pursue what are widely perceived as broad societal interests (i.e., including benefits that are both broad-based in scope, such as the public education of citizens under the age of 19, or narrow in scope, such as assistance to refugees from a given country), (iii) their members or staff have no direct pecuniary interests in the policies that are being pursued, (iv) they have serious difficulties overcoming a "free-rider" problem,[50] and therefore need public funds to be effective, (v) they exist at least as a "fledgling" organization, (vi) no group can claim to have a monopoly in the promotion of the public interest involved, and (vii) their membership is voluntary. Examples of "public interest" groups, according to Finkle and Webb, are the John Howard Society and the Elizabeth Fry Society.

"Charter-recognized" groups are distinguished by four characteristics: (i) they are organized around the pursuit of collective interests recognized in the Charter or in subsequent court decisions, (ii) their main activity is to promote public policies that further their interpretation of collective interests, (iii) no organized group based on these Charter-recognized interests has a monopoly in the promotion of those interests, and (iv) their membership is voluntary. Examples of "Charter-recognized" groups are the Assembly of First Nations and the National Action Committee on the Status of Women.

Finally "special interest" groups are distinguished by the following five characteristics: (i) they mainly seek to advance the pecuniary interests of their members, although there may be positive spillovers or externalities for others in this, (ii) that part of their activity which involves influencing government policy (policy advocacy) may produce collective benefits that are widely distributed, (iii) they often acquire tax-deductible status for expenditures involving the promotion of their group interests, (iv) unlike the two other types of groups, they may acquire a state-granted monopoly over a specific interest domain (e.g., doctors, lawyers), (v) their membership may or may not be voluntary.[51] Examples of "special interest " groups are the Business Council on National Issues and the Canadian Labour Congress.

There are a number of obvious problems with their typology. First, it is not clear how so-called "public interest" groups better represent and advance the "public interest" than a narrower "special" or "private" interest. In a later section, Finkle and Webb attempt to explain this by introducing a concept of "other-regardingness" versus "self-regardingness."[52] However, they also acknowledge that what one individual or segment of the population may consider to be a "public interest" orientation or "other-regarding" attitude, another will view as a "special interest" orientation or "self-regarding" attitude.[53] Susan Phillips et al. suggest a possible way of overcoming this problem by defining "public interest" groups as those "whose members act to influence public policy in order to promote their common interests" *and also* "whose objective is to benefit people beyond their membership."[54] The problem is that "the public interest is a highly evocative term and almost every group tries to argue that their particular demands are in the public interest."[55] Thus, it is not surprising, that there are many competing and rather different definitions of what is meant by the "public interest" in the literature.[56]

Second, apart from the ambiguity in the concept of "public interest," several other terms used by Finkle and Webb, such as "broad societal interest," "collective interest" and "non-pecuniary benefits" are unclear and not readily definable with any degree of precision.

Nevertheless, Finkle and Webb make the valid point that there is some need to use these ambiguous concepts to provide more rational and systematic guidelines for policymakers and analysts dealing with interest groups.

What relevance does their framework have for the problems addressed in this chapter? It seems to me that the Finkle-Webb typology has the potential to be fruitfully applied to the range of interest groups involved in the constitutional reform process in Canada from 1980 to 1992 in order to determine their attitudinal and behavioural responses to the various proposals and agreements. For example, one might explore whether there were some important differences in the attitudes and behaviours of "public interest" groups, "charter-based" groups, and "special interest" groups towards the 1980-81 patriation package and final constitutional accord, the Meech Lake Accord, and the Charlottetown Accord. Have "public interest" groups tended to accept the "integrative agreements" involving regional and ethnic-linguistic compromises, trade-offs, linkages and "win-win" utility "satisfying" rather than "optimizing" outcomes? Or have they rejected such overall compromises as unsatisfactory in terms of their own "utility maximizing" group self-interest and adopted a "win-lose" perspective? What has been the case for the "charter-based" groups and "special interest" groups? Do the views of the interest group leaders and their constituent members appear to converge or diverge on these constitutional questions?

It is impossible to answer these questions without conducting comprehensive, systematic and detailed research on interest group attitudes and behaviour in recent Canadian constitution-making. This type of comprehensive research has not yet been done.[57] However, there are a few scattered writings on this topic in Canada that may offer some initial hints or some preliminary answers to these questions.

As Richard Simeon first pointed out in the early 1970s, interest groups have traditionally been "frozen out" of the constitutional reform process in Canada by the major actors involved in the elite negotiations of executive federalism.[58] This was the case since the search for an indigenous amending formula began in 1927, and continued during the period of unsuccessful comprehensive constitutional renewal between 1968 and 1979. It was also true, for the most part, of the intensive constitutional reform struggles and negotiations of 1980-81. The only important exceptions to this pattern were the interest group representations at the joint House-Senate committee hearings on the proposed Charter of Rights in December 1980 and January 1981, and the mobilization of women's and aboriginal groups in support of their threatened Charter rights after the first ministers' initial agreement in November 1981.

Many of the interest groups that testified before the joint parliamentary hearings of 1980-81 were part of a "rights-oriented" legal-political subculture which had been a significant presence in Canada at least since World War II, and particularly since the adoption of the Diefenbaker Bill of Rights in 1960. Those that successfully advanced their representations for a broadening of the scope of the somewhat narrow *Charter of Rights and Freedoms* originally proposed in Trudeau's unilateral package of October 1980 were able to do so largely because the federal Liberal government was strongly in need of public support and legitimacy at that time in the face of strong opposition against its unilateral action by the federal Conservatives and most provincial governments.[59] Nevertheless, it is generally acknowledged, even by those then opposed to the overall patriation package, that these successful group representations significantly improved the coherence and internal logic of the Charter, and thereby advanced the overall public interest in Canada. This is usually attributed to the superior expertise, research and information on rights issues which these groups were able to bring to these deliberations. In this sense they are viewed as acting generally in the "public interest." Yet in this case acceptance and even enlargement of the package was clearly also in the self-interest of these "rights groups." Hence it is not surprising that virtually all of these groups initially accorded the unilateral patriation package of October 1980 their strong support. The major exception in this respect were the aboriginal groups, which failed to achieve all or even most of what they sought in such a package. The role of the two other types of groups, the "public interest" and "special interest" groups, appears to have been a marginal one in these negotiations.

However, the later actions of politicians in the patriation negotiations involving inclusion or exclusion of minority group and equality rights in the Charter did not reflect the same commitment to advancing or promoting "rights group" claims. Several academic and journalistic commentators, for example, have noted that decisions concerning which particular groups should be incorporated into or excluded from the final version of the Charter were made largely on an arbitrary basis. They were shaped essentially by political "horse-trading" within the federal cabinet or between various federal and provincial first ministers and responsible ministers. In this "horse-trading," the various groups representing women and aboriginals ultimately achieved success, largely through their superior organizational and strategic skills.[60] Yet their demands were often acceded to in a begrudging and reluctant manner by elite politicians (including some provincial premiers) and many members of the general public who viewed them as politically inevitable rather than inherently desirable or in the public interest.[61]

A subsequent call by academics and others for broadening public consultative mechanisms to ensure wider group participation in constitutional reform and policy matters actually antedated the negotiation of the Meech Lake Accord in 1987,[62] but it received little attention until after the signing of the Meech Lake Accord in 1987. It was the unusually narrow, secretive and elitist style of negotiations adopted with that Accord that led to a strong political, academic and public critique of executive and summit federalism as the major structure for negotiating constitutional agreements after 1987. Throughout the entire period of negotiation and ratification of the Accord between 1987 and 1990, there was only one genuine governmental effort to consult with and accommodate interest group representations on a systematic basis; that conducted by the Manitoba Task Force on the Meech Lake Accord between April and May of 1989. As Kathy Brock notes, the representations by the anti-Meech women's and aboriginal groups (two "charter-based" groups) were far better researched and more coherently and persuasively presented than were those of the better organized and financed pro-Meech business groups (a type of "special interest" group) and the former were also more successful in achieving their demands from the essentially non-partisan Manitoba Commission.[63] Were their attitudes and actions in Manitoba against the Accord in the "public interest" or in their narrower, utility-maximizing "self-interest"? Again, this depends on one's definition of the "public interest." At any rate, the gains that these groups achieved before the Manitoba Commission had little political resonance beyond that province. The parliamentary commissions and task force hearings in

Ottawa and in some provinces such as Ontario and Quebec were not genuinely open to group representation which would substantively alter the Accord, although they did permit the various interest groups that requested permission to make representations concerning the Accord in formal briefs and recorded hearings. In short, apart from Manitoba, in the Meech Lake process interest groups of all types continued to be "frozen out" of the constitutional policy process. Some of these groups then turned to more indirect action against the Accord by attempting to influence mass attitudes in local meetings and the media. In this manner they may have contributed substantively to its demise in 1990.

Between 1990 and August 1992, governmental consultations and negotiations leading up to the signing of the Charlottetown Accord seemed to actively encourage representations and participation by organized interest groups in constitutional policymaking processes. Their substantive contribution to the final package negotiated by the first ministers at Charlottetown has yet to be assessed. Assuming, however, that they did have an impact, then a systematic examination of the attitudes and role of these groups in the numerous task forces, commissions and legislative hearings conducted at both federal and provincial levels might now prove valuable.[64] We may finally acquire some perspective on the differing views of "charter-based," "public interest" and "special interest" groups on this comprehensive and complex "integrative" Charlottetown package, and on the tension between their group orientations and that of elite negotiators within executive and summit federal structures.

In short, the evidence concerning interest group "win-lose" utility-maximizing attitudes towards the various constitutional proposals and accords presented or negotiated since 1980 is still too sparse to provide any confirmation or disconfirmation of our original hypothesis (concerning contradictions and tensions between elite negotiations and interest group behaviour in constitutional policymaking). This is primarily due to their limited role in this process, at least until 1990, in which they were largely "frozen out." It may well be that unlike the case of referendums, with interest groups there is no clear attitudinal and self-oriented "utility-maximizing" dynamic operating in a clear direction, in opposition to the "utility-satisfying" and compromising orientation of elite politicians and bureaucrats. This would have important implications for future efforts to blend and merge elite negotiations and interest group consultations in any future constitutional negotiations.

RECONCILING TENSIONS AND CONTRADICTIONS

In the preceding two sections I pointed to a fundamental tension or contradiction between the structures of elite negotiation on the one hand and those of referendums and possibly also interest group consultations on the other.

Because they have conflicting normative rationales, and because empirically they tend to operate in opposing directions, the benefits or utilities provided by each structure tend to be different. Moreover, there are important differences among individual citizens in a referendum and among types of interest groups on these questions.

One point seems certain, however: the current structural and cultural trends in Western democratic polities make it imperative that we find ways to combine both elitist structures of negotiation and structures of public consultation and mass participation in constitutional policymaking. Both types of structures are necessary for successful constitution-making, since they each contribute important but different values to the process, including efficiency, representativeness, and legitimacy. This view of the need for blending or joining these structures also appears to be shared by other specialists of Canadian constitutional process.[65]

In my view the tensions and contradictions outlined above are not *inherently* irreconcilable, provided that they are effectively managed by the political regime and its leaders, and are actively embraced or promoted by the spokespersons for mass participative and consultative structures. There are several possible ways of managing these tensions.

First, political elites involved in constitutional negotiations, leaders of interest groups and promoters of direct democracy must attempt to develop more effective appeals on those constitutional issues that emphasize common or "core" values and symbols of national patriotism. With respect to "core" values, these cannot be defined and imposed by a narrow segment of the political elite on the general population. Rather a gradual process of both elite and mass political and constitutional learning with respect to these "core" values should be fostered, which also underlines the need for regional, group and individual accommodation and compromise. Thus the idea of "two official languages" associated with the so-called two "founding peoples" must be reconciled conceptually and in political practice with the claims of aboriginal peoples and of other multicultural groups. Similarly, the concept of a "distinct society" of Quebec must be accommodated to the notion of "equality of the provinces" and the principle of "representation by population."

There is already considerable evidence in recent Canadian constitutional and political experience that constitutional learning of this kind can occur both by political elites and the broader mass citizenry. The Royal Commission on Bilingualism and Biculturalism in the 1960s and the Trudeau government in the 1970s initially promoted and subsequently implemented policies involving both "official bilingualism" and "multiculturalism." By the early 1980s there was little elite or public objection to their inclusion in the *Constitution Act, 1982* including the *Charter of Rights and Freedoms*. Similarly, the concept of a "distinct society" of Quebec involving some special legal and political rights for that province, was fiercely opposed by many Canadians from outside Quebec in the Meech Lake negotiations of 1987-90. It appears to have won a much broader degree of public acceptance in the Charlottetown Accord of 1992. This seems to be even more true of the idea of "aboriginal self-government." At the time of the 1980-81 constitutional negotiations and the first ministers' conferences involving aboriginal rights from 1983-87, there was very little elite or mass support for this notion. By 1992 it had earned wide public endorsement as indicated by analysis of voter opinion in the referendum on the Charlottetown Accord.[66]

With respect to fostering symbols of national patriotism, emphasis should be placed on promoting the positive attributes of the country, rather than arousing fears of national disintegration or economic and social collapse. In particular, the widespread perception of Canada abroad as an economically prosperous, socially humane, environmentally sensitive, politically tolerant, and internationally engaged and influential country should be propagated more widely. In past constitutional negotiations, more weight appears to have been placed on negative appeals or threats to Canada's integrity. For example, Prime Minister Mulroney resorted to such a negative appeal at one point in the 1992 referendum campaign by tearing up a list of the gains Quebec would make if the Charlottetown Accord was approved; this was supposed to indicate to his Quebec audience what the consequences would be of a "no" vote against the constitutional package. The gesture was widely criticized both for its excessive histrionics and negativism and its lack of credibility.

Second, and on the other hand, an appeal to "loss avoidance" may be an effective tension-managing or problem-solving device in some constitutional situations. "Loss avoidance" or "loss aversion" has been defined as a psychological orientation or condition felt by political actors who "are generally risk averse with respect to gains and risk acceptant with respect to losses they identify from the reference point they have chosen. They are more willing to take risks to avoid losses than to make gains, in large part because losses loom larger than gains."[67] In the constitutional area, it refers to the pre-disposition of both political elites and masses to accept a constitutional deal which they view as less than utility maximizing for themselves or their constituents, or one which may even involve some risk of long-term losses. They do so in order to avoid the certainty of an immediate loss under deteriorating status quo conditions.

Such an appeal could be quite effective in the context of a real or perceived threat of Quebec separation should the constitutional/political status quo continue to deteriorate without the achievement of some kind of promised constitutional renewal. Populations that are particularly vulnerable to immediate political and economic losses arising from separation might be most susceptible to such appeals. It is possible that both government and grass-roots leaders may have exploited such feelings of "loss aversion" to influence voters in three Atlantic provinces and among English-speaking Quebecers to "buck" the national trend and vote in favour of the Charlottetown Accord in the referendum.

Third, government and grass-roots leaders should avoid adopting the position that a constitutional accord, once negotiated, cannot be substantively amended or altered to fit the needs of particular negotiating parties. This position was adopted with respect to the Meech Lake Accord after 1987, with unfortunate consequences. As long as the major items in a package have achieved the required consensus, it is possible to introduce minor adjustments such as special parallel or side agreements or flexible opting-in or opting-out arrangements for one or several parties, which would make the overall package more palatable and "saleable" in particular jurisdictions.

A good example of this occurred in recent negotiations concerning the Maastricht Treaty providing for a single European currency and tighter political union by the end of the century. When Britain and Denmark objected to what they perceived to be real threats to their political sovereignty, they were able to negotiate special opting-out provisions for themselves on the political aspects of the Treaty, without destroying or undermining the carefully negotiated and delicately balanced compromise achieved at Maastricht. A similar attempt was made at the First Ministers' Conference on the Meech Lake Accord in June 1990, with the introduction of the so-called "companion accord." This was an initiative introduced by the federal government at the behest of dissenting provinces such as Manitoba in an effort to improve certain provisions of the agreement. The initiative might have succeeded if it had been undertaken at an earlier point in the ratification process, prior to the adoption of fixed bargaining positions by several major parties and widespread public disenchantment with the elitist negotiating and ratification process.

Fourth, leaders may make offers of "side-payments" in an effort to win broader public or mass support for a negotiated constitutional package. For example, an agreement by the federal government to allow Alberta a larger share in oil revenues early in the fall of 1981 may have helped to win its support for a compromise deal on the patriation package in the November 1981 negotiations. The Clinton administration in the United States has also recently offered such enticements to labour and environmental leaders in that country in an effort to win their support for the North American Free Trade Agreement. However, such offers of "side-payments" to political leaders and their constituents must be made with delicacy and sensitivity, or they could backfire. They may be misinterpreted or misrepresented by opponents of the negotiated package as attempts at public bribery. The federal government may have avoided linking its support of the Hibernia offshore oil project in Newfoundland to its

Meech Lake and Charlottetown constitutional proposals for precisely that reason.

Finally, elite bargaining structures in constitutional matters such as ministers' or first ministers' conferences and public input structures such as referendums and interest group consultations should be blended in a logical and coherent manner, in order to enhance the particular values of each. Thus elite structures might play the major role at the negotiation stage in constitution-making, and mass participative and consultative structures might be injected principally at the earlier (issue- and agenda-generating), and later (ratification) stages. There should be a clear consensus among governmental and grass-roots leaders about who has the right to participate in the constitutional process at each stage, and why. The rules governing public consultation and participation, whether in referendums or with interest groups, must be carefully negotiated and clearly set out. Both the political elites negotiating the agreement and the mass public should be informed that a referendum will be called well before the final package is negotiated, so that its contents can framed with that type of direct consultation in mind. There should be a greater effort to educate political elites, interest group leaders and the mass citizenry about the benefits of such a "blended" system of representative and direct democracy.

As a final point, there are several techniques that may be adopted: emphasis on "core values," loss avoidance, flexible approaches to amendment, the use of side-payments, and a clearly articulated and openly agreed blending of both elite and more directly democratic processes. By adopting these techniques, one hopes that the result will be a more effective constitutional reform process, should one arise in the near future. This may take the form of comprehensive or incremental and partial constitutional change, or even constitutional custom and convention. Judging from current trends in Quebec and in the country as a whole, it may not be long before we must address these issues once again as part of our ongoing political agenda.

NOTES

This chapter is a revised and expanded version of two earlier communications delivered to the Forum on Confederation, University of Toronto, 26 February 1993, and the Annual Meeting of the Canadian Political Science Association, Carleton University, Ottawa, 8 June 1993. I would like to thank the SSHRCC for its generous support for my research on the Meech Lake and Charlottetown constitutional negotiations, under Research Grant 410-89-0697. I am also grateful for helpful comments from Douglas Brown, Barbara Carroll, J. Stefan Dupre, Mark Sproule-Jones, Ronald Watts, Donald Wells, and two anonymous referees. Lou Pauly provided some stimulating comparative insights and ideas in his parallel paper on the Maastricht Treaty negotiations in Europe, also presented to the Forum on Confederation at the University of Toronto. Finally, I wish to thank my research assistants, Rob Jonasson and Michelle Perez, for their valuable aid in the preparation and revision of this paper.

1. Donald V. Smiley, *Canada in Question: Federalism in the Eighties*, 3d ed. (Toronto: McGraw-Hill Ryerson, 1980), p. 91.
2. Peter H. Russell, *Constitutional Odyssey: Can Canadians Become a Sovereign People?* (Toronto: University of Toronto Press, 1992), p. 10.
3. Ibid., p. 9.
4. Alan C. Cairns and Cynthia Williams (eds.), *Constitutionalism, Citizenship and Society in Canada*, Research Studies of the Royal Commission on the Economic Union and Development Prospects for Canada, vol. 33 (Toronto: University of Toronto Press, 1985), chap. 4.
5. Patrick Boyer, *Direct Democracy in Canada: The History and Future of Referendums* (Toronto: Dundurn Press, 1992), p. 236.
6. Stefan J. Dupre, "Reflections on the Workability of Executive Federalism," in Richard Simeon (ed.), *Intergovernmental Relations*, Research Studies of the Royal Commission on the Economic Union and Development Prospects for Canada, vol. 63 (Toronto: University of Toronto Press, 1985), pp. 1-33.
7. Michael B. Stein, "Canadian Constitutional Reform 1927-1982: A Comparative Case Analysis Over Time," *Publius: The Journal of Federalism*, 14 (Winter 1984): 121-39. See also Russell, *Constitutional Odyssey*, chaps. 4 and 5.
8. Michael B. Stein, *Canadian Constitutional Renewal: A Case Study in Integrative Bargaining*, Research Paper No. 27, (Kingston: Institute of Intergovernmental Relations, 1990), chap. 3; Russell, *Constitutional Odyssey*, chaps. 6-8.
9. David Milne, *The Canadian Constitution: From Patriation to Meech Lake* (Toronto: James Lorimer & Co., 1989) pp. 155-60; Keith Banting and Richard Simeon (eds.), *And No One Cheered: Federalism, Democracy & the Constitution Act* (Toronto: Methuen, 1983), chaps. 14-15; Robert Sheppard and Michael Valpy (eds.), *The National Deal: The Fight for a Canadian Constitution* (Toronto: Fleet Books, 1982), chap. 14.
10. Bryan Schwartz, *Fathoming Meech Lake* (Winnipeg: Legal Research Institute, University of Manitoba, 1987), p. 4; Andrew Cohen, *A Deal Undone: The Making and Breaking of the Meech Lake Accord* (Toronto: Douglas & McIntyre, 1990), pp. 185-86; Deborah Coyne, *Roll of the Dice* (Toronto: James Lorimer & Co., 1992), p. 1.
11. Premier Howard Pawley of Manitoba was the sole exception in this regard. There were special rules governing legislative ratification of constitutional amendments in the Manitoba Legislative Assembly which required a more careful scrutiny of any package in public hearings. For this reason, Premier Pawley did not reject the idea of a more fundamental critical examination and alteration of the Accord by provincial legislatures, and informed the other first ministers of this when he signed the deal. I am grateful to an anonymous reviewer for this point. See also Cohen, *A Deal Undone*, p. 115.
12. James Hurley, "The Canadian Constitutional Debate: From the Death of Meech Lake to the Referendum," paper presented to the 1992 Conference of the

Association of Canadian Studies in Australia and New Zealand, Wellington, New Zealand, 16 December 1992; and Brooke Jeffrey, *Strange Bedfellows, Trying Times* (Toronto: Key Porter Books Ltd., 1993), chap. 2.
13. Jeffrey, *Strange Bedfellows*, chap. 6.
14. Russell, *Constitutional Odyssey*, chap. 10; Boyer, *Direct Democracy*, pp. 235-241.
15. Smiley, *Canada in Question*, chap. 4; Ronald Watts, *Administration in Federal Systems* (London: Hutchison, 1970), chap. 2.
16. Ronald Watts, *Executive Federalism: A Comparative Analysis*, Research Paper No. 26 (Kingston: Institute of Intergovernmental Relations, 1989), pp. 6-8.
17. J. Stefan Dupre, "Reflections on the Workability of Executive Federalism," pp. 15-22.
18. In this respect the Charlottetown Accord was an exception, since it was negotiated almost entirely by Constitutional Affairs ministers until its final stage in August 1992.
19. Richard Simeon, *Federal-Provincial Diplomacy: The Making of Recent Policy in Canada* (Toronto: University of Toronto Press, 1972), chap. 13.
20. Simeon, *Federal-Provincial Diplomacy*, pp. 268-77.
21. S.J.R. Noel, "Consociational Democracy and Canadian Federalism," *Canadian Journal of Political Science*, 4 (1971): 15-18; Kenneth McRae, "Consociationalism and the Canadian Political System," in Kenneth McRae (ed.), *Consociational Democracy: Political Accommodation in Segmented Societies*, Carleton Library No. 79 (Toronto: McClelland & Stewart, 1974); Kenneth McRae, "The Meech Lake Impasse: A Theoretical Perspective," in Gagnon and Tanguay (eds.), *Democracy with Justice* (Ottawa: Carleton University Press, 1992), pp. 140-53; Arend Lijphart, *Democracy in Plural Societies: A Comparative Exploration* (New Haven and London: Yale University Press, 1977), pp. 124-27.
22. Richard Walton, and Robert B. McKersie, *A Behavioural Theory of Negotiations* (New York: McGraw-Hill, 1965), p. 5.
23. Dean G. Pruitt and Steven A. Lewis, "The Psychology of Integrative Bargaining," in Daniel Druckman (ed.), *Negotiations: Social-Psychological Perspective* (Beverly Hills and London: Sage Publications, 1977), chap. 5; D.G. Pruitt, *Negotiation Behavior* (New York: Academic Press, 1981), chaps. 5-6.
24. Oran R. Young, "The Politics of International Regime Formation: Managing International Resources and the Environment," *International Organization*, 43, 3 (Summer, 1989): 361; Oran Young, "Political Leadership and Regime Formation: On the Development of Institutions in International Society," *International Organization*, 45, 3 (Summer, 1991): 281-307.
25. Stein, *Canadian Constitutional Renewal*, pp. 37-42.
26. Ibid., pp. 40-42.
27. Young, "The Politics of International Regime Formation," p. 361.
28. David Butler and Austin Ranney (eds.), *Referendums: A Comparative Study of Practice and Theory* (Washington: American Enterprise Institute, 1978), p. 226.
29. Harlan Hahn and Sheldon Kamienicki, *Referendum Voting: Social Status and Policy Preferences* (New York: Greenwood Press, 1987), p. 21.

30. Kathy Brock, "The Politics of Process," in Douglas M. Brown (ed.), *Canada: The State of the Federation 1991* (Kingston: Institute of Intergovernmental Relations, 1991), p. 80.
31. Gordon Smith, "The Functional Properties of the Referendum," *European Journal of Political Research*, Special Issue: Referenda in Europe, 4, 1 (March 1976): 1-24.
32. Dalton Russell et al. (eds.), *Electoral Change in Advanced Industrial Democracies* (Princeton: Princeton University Press, 1984); Ronald Inglehart, *The Silent Revolution: Changing Values and Political Styles among Western Publics* (Princeton: Princeton University Press, 1977); Ian Brodie and Neil Nevitte, "Evaluating the Citizens' Constitution Theory," *Canadian Journal of Political Science*, 26 (June 1993), esp. pp. 239-42.
33. Allan Gregg and Michael Posner, *The Big Picture: What Canadians Think About Almost Everything* (Toronto: Macfarlane Walter and Ross, 1990); Harold D. Clarke et al., *Absent Mandate: Interpreting Change in Canadian Elections*, 2d ed. (Toronto: McClelland & Stewart, 1985); John Laschinger and Geoffrey Stevens, *Leaders, Lesser Mortals: Backroom Politics in Canada* (Toronto: Key Porter Books, 1992), chaps. 12-13.
34. See for example, Patrick J. Boyer, *Lawmaking by the People: Referendums and Plebiscites in Canada* (Toronto: Butterworths, 1982); Boyer, *Direct Democracy*, and Vincent Lemieux, "The Referendum and Canadian Democracy," in Peter Aucoin (ed.), *Institutional Reforms for Representative Government*, Research Studies of the Royal Commission on the Economic Union and Development Prospects for Canada, vol. 38 (Toronto: University of Toronto Press, 1985).
35. Boyer, *Direct Democracy*, p. 75.
36. Ibid., p. 239.
37. Richard Johnston, "An Inverted Logroll: The Charlottetown Accord and Referendum," *Political Science*, 26, 1 (1993): 47. Note, however, the somewhat different view of the Accord and of voter reaction to the "logroll" or overall compromise presented in a subsequent paper by Johnston et al. and his collaborators, "The People and the Charlottetown Accord" (See this volume, chap. 2). According to Johnston et al., rather than merely "embracing the logic of a logroll, which includes something for oneself," supporting the Accord for many voters would also have involved "accepting the necessity for an accommodation among strategically placed or morally advantaged others." For the most part, however, this logic "did not work" (p. 29).
38. Ibid., p. 47.
39. See for example, Butler and Ranney (eds.), *Referendums*; Philip Goodheart, *Full-Hearted Consent* (London: Davis-Poynter, 1976); Hahn and Kamienieki, *Referendum Voting*; and the Special Issue on Referenda in Europe, *European Journal of Political Research*, 4, 1 (March 1976).
40. Gordon Smith, "The Functional Properties of the Referendum," pp. 6-9.
41. Ibid., p. 13.
42. Russell, *Constitutional Odyssey*, p. 57.

43. See A. Paul Pross, *Pressure Group Behaviour in Canadian Politics* (Toronto: McGraw-Hill, 1975); Pross, *Group Politics and Public Policy* (Toronto: Oxford University Press, 1986).
44. Brodie and Nevitte, "Evaluating the Citizen's Constitution Theory," esp. pp. 235-239.
45. Alan Cairns, *Disruptions: Constitutional Struggles From the Charter to Meech Lake*, ed. Douglas Williams (Toronto: McClelland & Stewart, 1991), chap. 4.
46. Ibid., pp. 15-16.
47. Cairns does, however, make a brief reference to the expanded role of business interest associations in managing relations with the state, particularly since the 1960s, citing the research findings of William Coleman. See Alan Cairns, "The Embedded State: State-Society Relations in Canada," in Keith Banting (ed.), *State and Society: Canada in Comparative Perspective*, Research Studies of the Royal Commission on the Economic Union and Development Prospects for Canada, vol. 31 (Toronto: University of Toronto Press, 1985), p. 71.
48. Susan D. Phillips, "Democratizing Society and State in Canada: From Identity Politics to Partnerships," paper presented to the annual meeting of the Canadian Political Science Association, Charlottetown P.E.I., 1992, pp. 4-11. A partial exception to this is Cairns' reference to "citizen groups" emerging as part of broader international trends. See Cairns, *Disruptions*, pp. 19-20.
49. Peter Finkle, Kernaghan Webb, William T. Stanbury and Paul Pross, *Federal Government Relations with Interest Groups: A Reconsideration*, Draft Manuscript (Ottawa: Department of Consumer and Corporate Affairs, 1993) chaps. 2-3. The first two are the principal authors.
50. Mancur Olsen, *The Logic of Collective Action: Public Goods and the Theory of Groups* (New York: Schocken Books, 1965), pp. 14-16.
51. Finkle et al., *Federal Government Relations*, p. 19, Figure 2-1.
52. Ibid., p. 28.
53. Ibid., p. 20.
54. Ibid., p. 21.
55. Ibid., p. 22.
56. Ibid., p. 20. See, for example, the definition of "public interest groups" offered by Jeffrey M. Berry who defines a "public interest group" as "one that seeks a collective good, the achievement of which will not selectively and materially benefit the membership or activists of the organization." Jeffrey M. Berry, *Lobbying for the People* (Princeton, NJ: Princeton University Press, 1977), p. 7. This is a somewhat different definition from that of Phillips et al. cited above.
57. However, Professor Kathy Brock of the University of Manitoba has recently begun such a study, with support from the Social Sciences and Humanities Research Council of Canada. According to a recent communication, her study encompasses interest group activity in both the Meech Lake and Charlottetown constitutional negotiations. It also includes all three types of interest groups described by Finkle and Webb. The focus will be on interest groups at the federal level and in the provinces of Manitoba, Ontario, Quebec, New Brunswick, and Newfoundland. It

will involve interviews of interest group leaders as well as politicians and public servants, and will be more qualitative than quantitative in methodology and approach. For some preliminary discussion of this study, see Kathy L. Brock, "Reflections on the Constitutional Process: Does More Inclusive Mean More Effective and Representative?" unpublished paper presented to the Annual General Meeting of the Canadian Political Science Association, Carleton University, Ottawa, Ontario, 6-8 June 1993.

58. Simeon, *Federal-Provincial Diplomacy*, p. 282; see also Hugh G. Thorburn, *Interest Groups in the Canadian Federal System*, Research Studies of the Royal Commission on the Economic Union and Development Prospects for Canada, vol. 69 (Toronto: University of Toronto Press, 1985), p. 69.

59. David Milne, *The Canadian Constitution: From Patriation to Meech Lake* (Toronto: James Lorimer & Co., 1989), pp. 88-93; and Kathy Brock, "The Politics of Process," p. 59.

60. Penny Kome, *The Taking of Twenty-Eight: Women Challenge the Constitution* (Toronto: Women's Press, 1983); Chaviva Hosek, "Women and the Constitutional Process," in Richard Simeon and Keith Banting (eds.), *And No One Cheered* (Toronto: Methuen, 1983), esp. pp. 283-286; and Douglas Sanders, "The Indian Lobby," in Simeon and Banting (eds.), *And No One Cheered*, pp. 301-332.

61. Kathy Brock, "The Demand for Greater Participation," in Richard Simeon and Mary Janigan (eds.), *Toolkits and Building Blocks* (Toronto: C.D. Howe Institute, 1991), pp. 72-74.

62. See Thorburn, *Interest Groups in the Canadian Federal System*, pp. 128-132; and Cairns and Williams (eds.), *Constitutionalism, Citizenship, and Society*, pp. 40-42.

63. Kathy Brock, "Being Heard: Interest Representation in the Manitoba Constitutional Process," Paper presented to the Annual Meeting of the Canadian Political Science Association, Kingston, 1991, pp. 14-25.

64. As mentioned in note 57 above, Kathy Brock intends to conduct this kind of systematic analysis in her study of interest group consultations during the Meech Lake and Charlottetown negotiations. See also Brock, "Reflections on the Constitutional Process: Does More Inclusive Mean More Effective and Representative?"

65. See, for example, Brock, "The Politics of Process," 1991, p. 77; Russell, *Constitutional Odyssey*, p. 193; and Boyer, *Direct Democracy*, p. 224.

66. For some empirical evidence supporting these observations, see Richard Johnston et al., "The People and the Charlottetown Accord," chapter 2 in this volume.

67. Janice Gross Stein, "International co-operation and loss avoidance: framing the problem," in Janice Gross Stein and Louis W. Pauly (eds.), *Choosing to Co-operate: How States Avoid Loss* (Baltimore and London: The Johns Hopkins University Press, 1993), p. 18. I am grateful to the co-editors for bringing this concept to my attention.

6

An Experiment in Intrastate Federalism: The Cabinet Committee on Canadian Unity

Herman Bakvis and Roselle Hryciuk

On accorde généralement assez peu ou pas du tout d'attention au rôle que joue le cabinet fédéral dans le processus de renouvellement de la constitution. Pourtant, la création en avril 1991, durant la Ronde Canada, du Comité du cabinet chargé de l'unité canadienne et des négociations constitutionnelles aura fourni justement au cabinet une occasion exceptionnelle de s'illustrer dans le plus grand intérêt de la réconciliation nationale.

Ce chapitre se penche sur le rôle du Comité dans l'élaboration du document qui est devenu, en définitive, l'entente de Charlottetown. Plus précisément, les auteurs tentent d'évaluer l'efficacité de ce comité en tant que corps intraétatique ou si l'on préfère, en tant que noyau central du gouvernement au sein duquel se trouvent directement représentés les intérêts régionaux du pays.

Les quatre modèles suivants sont utilisés pour analyser les activités du Comité : 1) fédéralisme intraétatique 2) compromis au sommet 3) politique des groupes d'intérêts et 4) politique de la bureaucratie. Même si les activités du Comité furent marquées par une transparence plus grande que prévue, celui-ci s'arrangea tout de même pour ne pas avoir à subir de pression directe de la part des groupes d'intérêts. Au même moment, certains acteurs de la bureaucratie fédérale furent appelés à jouer un rôle significatif dans la préparation des propositions fédérales contenues dans le document Bâtir ensemble l'avenir du Canada, *publié en septembre 1991. Les ministres provenant de l'ouest du pays et du Québec furent ceux qui consacrèrent le plus d'efforts pour représenter les intérêts distincts de leur province ou région respective.*

L'action du Comité fut efficace à deux points de vue : d'abord, en permettant la réalisation d'un compromis global, puis en relançant le processus constitutionnel. Toutefois, l'influence du Comité aura décru presque aussitôt après le dépôt des propositions; de fait, certaines de ses recommandations clés, comme celles sur l'union économique par exemple, furent écartées ou bien modifiées au cours des phases subséquentes — parlementaire et multilatérale — de la Ronde Canada.

INTRODUCTION

In most discussions of Canadian constitution-making the role of the federal Cabinet attracts little or no attention, and for good reason. Since the 1960s the Cabinet has effectively been eclipsed by the federal-provincial conference as a body for resolving major policy issues and reconciling regional and linguistic differences within the country. As well, the federal government's constitutional proposals and negotiations with the provinces has typically been the preserve of the prime minister, a few key Cabinet ministers, and a limited number of officials in the Privy Council Office (PCO) and the Federal-Provincial Relations Office (FPRO). Furthermore, over the past decade the attention of journalists and social scientists has increasingly been captivated by the activities of special interest groups and demands for more direct citizen participation in the constitutional process. Thus in the most recent Canada round, attention was focused in good part on the innovative mechanisms that were introduced to ensure greater citizen participation, namely the five miniature citizen conventions held in the winter of 1992 and, of course, the October referendum.

While benign neglect of the federal Cabinet's role in the constitutional process may be justified in general, in the case of the Canada round it is not. For in the aftermath of the failure of Meech Lake in June 1990 and suspension of all formal first ministers' conferences, the federal Cabinet came to play a unique role in laying the ground work of the process that eventually led to the Charlottetown Accord. On 21 April 1991 the prime minister announced that Joe Clark, as minister responsible for constitutional affairs, would chair the special Cabinet Committee on Canadian Unity and Constitutional Negotiations (CCCU), and that in doing so Clark would "be responsible for the development of the Government's constitutional position and for the consultative and negotiating processes that will be followed in seeking a new national consensus."[1] In effect, the prime minister's announcement could be construed as an effort by the federal government to create what Alan Cairns, Donald Smiley and Ronald Watts have called an "intrastate" mechanism — an arena lodged within the bosom of the federal government in which regional and linguistic interests could both find expression and be reconciled.[2]

Until the Canada round, Cabinet had not played such an explicit and visible role in the constitutional process; previous constitutional crises did not appear to necessitate its participation on such a scale.[3] While certain key ministers have always been involved in constitutional negotiations, Cabinet or a committee of Cabinet has invariably played an after-the-fact role, essentially ratifying decisions reached by the key players during the course of negotiations with the provinces. It might be argued, therefore, that the striking of the CCCU represented an uncommon opportunity for the federal Cabinet to display its long dormant capacity to play an integrative, nation saving role. Alternatively, the case of the CCCU might also demonstrate that whatever capacity the Cabinet had in this regard had long been extinguished.

The specific subject under investigation in this chapter, therefore, is the role the CCCU played in shaping the document that became the Charlottetown Accord. And the primary issue is the effectiveness of the CCCU as an intrastate body: how successful was it both in bringing the diversities of interests and opinions to bear on the constitutional process and in accommodating these diverse and often strongly held views on issues such as the constitutional status of Quebec as a distinct society? Obviously its success was limited in light of the final outcome, namely the failure of the Accord in the October 1992 referendum. Nonetheless, it remains important to ask whether there was something during the CCCU phase that contributed to the ultimate failure of the Accord, for example whether serious miscalculations made by the CCCU later affected either the multilateral process or public opinion. Answers to this question are worth having, in part for the historical record, but also to help assess the role of Cabinet in dealing with constitutional issues in the future, or for that matter any issue of major import.

INTERPRETING THE PROCESS

The CCCU was struck in April 1991 and continued to play a role in the Canada round process up to and including the time of the referendum. The most critical phase for the CCCU was, however, the period from April 1991 to the delivery of Cabinet's proposals in September of 1991, embodied in the federal government's package *Shaping Canada's Future Together*. As with the constitutional process as a whole, the activities of the CCCU can be examined and interpreted from a number of different perspectives. In the existing literature, and in the public commentary on the process, there appear to be four models, none of them mutually exclusive, that can be used to help interpret developments: federalism theory, specifically that on intrastate federalism; elite accommodation theory; the interest group politics model; and the bureaucratic politics model.

INTRASTATE FEDERALISM

Given the mandate assigned to the CCCU by the prime minister, that is to help put in place the basis for "seeking a new national consensus," it is appropriate to view the CCCU as an intrastate mechanism. Briefly, intrastate federalism can be defined as the representation of provincial and regional interests directly in the central institutions of government (as distinct from *inter*state federalism, where the representation of provincial and regional interests occurs *between* federal and provincial governments) and is seen by a number of federal theorists as an important and indeed necessary hallmark of a proper federal system.[4] As

Smiley and Watts have argued: "No matter how much a federal system allows for the expression of regional differences through autonomous state or provincial governments, the federal solution is bound to disintegrate without some positive consensus among its component groups. And it is upon the structure and processes of the central institutions that the ability to generate such a consensus exists."[5]

Canada is regarded as a relatively weak intrastate federation, however, one where the regional dimension has been largely absent in the operations of central institutions. Indeed, in recent years many of the advocates of constitutional change, especially from western Canada, have pushed hard to redress this imbalance by arguing for intrastate reforms such as an elected senate.[6] Yet intrastate federalism is not a wholly unambiguous or undifferentiated concept; it can be implemented in a variety of ways and mean quite different things to different people. Alan Cairns has identified two variants of intrastate federalism — centralist and provincialist.[7] Direct provincial appointment of Senate members by the provinces along the lines of the German Bundesrat would be an example of the latter; something like the present arrangement for regional representation in the federal Cabinet, where provinces have little if any influence in selecting representatives, is an example of the former. With respect to the federal Cabinet it has been suggested that while Cabinet may once have been reasonably effective as an intrastate mechanism, during the terms in office of Prime Minister Mackenzie King, for example, when leading provincial figures routinely entered the federal Cabinet, this is no longer the case. There is debate over the issue of the present regional role of federal Cabinet ministers.[8] Certainly, however, Cabinet is not generally perceived as an arena where significant constitutional issues are debated and ultimately brokered. The task that was thrust upon the CCCU, therefore, was in many ways an unfamiliar one and it can be legitimately asked whether the ministers really had the capacity to take it on.

ELITE ACCOMMODATION

This concept, originating in the comparative politics literature, has been applied both to federal-provincial relations and to the federal Cabinet to account for the accommodation reached between the different levels of government and significant political communities in Canada.[9] It overlaps considerably with the intrastate model and can be described as the process that makes the intrastate mechanism work in an effective manner. The primary characteristics of the elite accommodation process have been the important role of the elites of competing governments or significant political communities to reach agreement on critical issues, often in the face of dissensus at the mass level, the fact that elite bargaining takes place largely in secret, that the accommodation is

An Experiment in Intrastate Federalism 121

all-encompassing (that is, representing more than a simple majority of groups or populations) and that in this process elites have the loyalty and support of their communities. In the post-Meech climate, in fact well before the Meech Lake Accord itself, the basic assumptions underpinning elite accommodation as traditionally practiced, such as the norm of secrecy, had become largely discredited.[10] There is also a question of whom the members of the CCCU, as elites, could be said to represent and the loyalties they might be able to command from significant segments of the Canadian population. Thus while the elite accommodation model might accurately portray the efforts of the CCCU to reach a consensus, there is considerable question about the overall effectiveness of the CCCU in terms of legitimacy and acceptance by the broader polity, including significant interest groups, provincial governments and citizens at large.

INTEREST GROUP POLITICS

This model concerns the manner in which a variety of groups, the special interests if you like, representing both the advantaged and disadvantaged in society, were able to successfully penetrate and influence, by various means, the CCCU's deliberations and decisions on constitutional matters. Essentially these are groups that on the whole are not well represented in governments or political parties and which operate much more in the extra-parliamentary arena. Earlier writings on interest groups and their role in the constitutional process have argued that such groups have had very limited influence.[11] On the other hand, given the changes over the past decade regarding the increasing prominence and visibility of interest groups (and especially that of public interest groups), engendered and legitimized in good part by the arrival of the *Charter of Rights and Freedoms* in 1982, more recent writings have stressed the role of these groups in shaping the constitutional process.[12] It is important to ask, therefore, to what extent the CCCU was influenced by the lobbying of such groups. At the same time the question can be cast as one concerning the degree to which the CCCU was able to transcend the pleadings of special interests and represent the broader public interest in developing its proposals.

BUREAUCRATIC POLITICS

Ever since Graham Allison's classic study of the Cuban missile crisis, political scientists have paid close attention to how major policy outcomes can be influenced by bureaucratic interests.[13] There is the question both of the influence of the bureaucracy as a whole vis-à-vis politicians and the influence of different and often competing bureaus. The thrust of the Canadian federalism literature is that under the right circumstances officials in central agencies, specifically intergovernmental affairs agencies, can have considerable influence.[14] With respect to the CCCU, the question becomes whether it is not the federal ministers, special interests or the general public, but non-elected federal government officials who were primarily responsible for the proposals tendered for consideration in September 1991. It was precisely this concern that led Newfoundland Premier Clyde Wells to state in June of 1991: "I'm bothered by the fact that a proposal for a national constitutional structure is being developed not by 11 first ministers behind closed doors, but by 11 or 21 or 25 deputy ministers with some federal advisers behind closed doors."[15]

As will be evident below, elements of all four models are useful in helping to make sense of the progress made, and not made, in achieving the broad objective set out for it by the prime minister. It will be argued that as an intrastate body, or more broadly as a deliberative forum, the CCCU had certain strengths, and in effect succeeded in its primary objective of restarting the constitutional process. It also had some distinct weaknesses, however, related in part to the nature of bureaucratic politics at the federal level, which influenced subsequent developments in the constitutional debate.

THE PROCESS

To understand the role of the CCCU it is best to begin by noting its place in the overall Canada round process, which is best visualized in five phases:

1. From June 1990 — the failure of Meech — until April 1991, a period which saw the striking of both the Joint Parliamentary Committee on the Process for Amending the Constitution of Canada (Beaudoin-Edwards) and the Citizens' Forum on Canada's Future (Spicer Commission);
2. From the striking of the CCCU in April 1991 to the tabling of the federal proposal *Shaping Canada's Future Together* in September 1991. This period also saw tabling of the Beaudoin-Edwards and Spicer reports.
3. September 1991 until 12 March 1992. This represented the public hearings process, revolving first around the Special Joint Parliamentary Committee on a Renewed Canada (Castonguay-Dobbie/Beaudoin-Dobbie Committee) and then the five public conferences.
4. March through August of 1992: The multilateral process that saw, first, negotiations between the federal government and the "rest-of-Canada" (ROC) provinces and then later involving Quebec, eventually leading to the Charlottetown agreement.
5. August 1992 until 26 October 1992 — public debate leading up to the referendum.

This chapter is concerned primarily with phase two, the series of meetings held by the CCCU and the deliberations that led to the federal proposals in

September of 1991. Nonetheless, it is important to review briefly the events and federal initiatives prior to the striking of the CCCU. The summer of 1990 in the aftermath of the failure of Meech was in many ways a long and uncomfortable hiatus. Beginning with Elijah Harper and ending with Oka, the actions of Aboriginal Peoples made the Canadian public more aware, and more accepting, of aboriginal demands. Contrary to some expectations, one development that did *not* occur in 1990 was the wholesale defection of Quebec MPs from the Conservative caucus and Cabinet following, first, the defection of Lucien Bouchard and then the failure of Meech. Prime Minister Brian Mulroney succeeded in retaining the loyalties of most of his Quebec MPs and all of his remaining Quebec ministers.[16] Benoît Bouchard replaced Lucien Bouchard as Quebec lieutenant and came to play an important role in the CCCU and subsequent constitutional negotiations.

In the intergovernmental arena, one specific and visible development was suspension of all formal first ministers' conferences, prompted by Quebec's refusal to participate in them. In the summer of 1990 Prime Minister Mulroney created an ad hoc Cabinet comittee on the constitution chaired by Deputy Prime Minister Donald Mazankowski. On 1 November 1990 the prime minister announced the creation of the Spicer Commission, largely in response to perceived demands for greater openness and transparency and, above all, greater citizen involvement. In December 1990 the Joint Parliamentary Committee on the Process for Amending the Constitution of Canada (Beaudoin-Edwards Committee) was struck. It was Quebec, however, with reports from the Quebec Liberal Party's Constitutional Committee (chaired by Jean Allaire — released 29 January 1991) and the Commission on the Political and Constitutional Future of Quebec (Bélanger-Campeau — released 27 March 1991), that set the pace and tempo. Bill 150, subsequently tabled in the Quebec National Assembly 15 May 1991, specified the deadline of 26 October 1992 for a referendum on proposals from English Canada for a new constitution or, in the absence of such proposals, on the issue of sovereignty itself.[17]

At the bureaucratic level in Ottawa there were also some important developments. Within the FPRO there was an almost complete changing of the guard. Norman Spector left as Secretary to the Cabinet for Federal Provincial Relations in August 1990 to become chief-of-staff in the Prime Minister's Office (PMO) and was replaced by Gordon Smith, who had been in External Affairs as ambassador to NATO. A number of new people, mainly from line departments, were brought in to work on different policy areas. Relatively few of them had much intergovernmental or constitutional experience, either in FPRO or other units. At the same time, given the prime minister's keen interest in matters constitutional, there was an expectation that Spector, as his chief aide and strategist, would continue to play an important role in that area. That summer of 1990 a request went out to all line departments for proposals, specifically for suggestions of areas under federal jurisdiction that could conceivably be turned over to the provinces. September 1990 saw the creation of the Deputy Ministers' Committee on Canadian Unity, with deputies from key departments such as justice and finance to oversee the process of reviewing areas under federal government jurisdiction.

Throughout the fall of 1990 activity within the FPRO was simultaneously frenetic and aimless, with analysts keeping track of developments but having only a limited sense of their import or direction, or what forms federal initiatives should take. Someone there at the time likened it to holding a finger to a bare electrical wire, standing there frozen in place feeling the current coursing through their finger tips.[18] In January 1991 deputy ministerial task forces were struck to examine and report on nine different areas, including aboriginal affairs, fiscal federalism, social policy, and the economic union. Reports were to be ready by May. Ronald Watts of Queen's University was brought on board as Assistant Secretary (Constitutional Affairs) at FPRO in April of 1991, a few weeks before the appointment of Joe Clark as Minister of Constitutional Affairs. Watts in turn recruited a number of academic consultants such as Roger Gibbins of the University of Calgary, Katherine Swinton of the University of Toronto and Douglas Purvis and Peter Leslie of Queen's University to assist in the development of the federal proposals.

In the early post-Meech period the initial emphasis of the federal government was to search for constitutional solutions amenable to being handled through existing amending procedures, that is those issues not requiring unanimity, in the main so-called "7/50" issues.[19] This low-key, pragmatic approach was exemplified in the work of the ad hoc Cabinet committee under Mazankowsi; its workings in fact were so low-key that it is almost impossible to discern its impact, at least certainly not from the public record. Joe Clark was a member of it, but apparently not an active one insofar as he missed several meetings.

Also working in relative obscurity was the Joint Parliamentary Committee on constitutional amendment (Beaudoin-Edwards). Much later, in the summer of 1991, this committee reported what most had realized earlier: if Quebec's demands were to be met, it would be virtually impossible to circumvent the political necessity of unanimous ratification, at least of certain key demands.[20] The Spicer Commission was proving, if not a vehicle for calming troubled constitutional waters, then certainly a means for a variety of groups and individual Canadians to ventilate their dissatisfaction with politicians and the political process. Thus well before the CCCU was struck, came the dawning in federal circles that any new constitutional round would require that all issues be on the table, including not only Quebec demands but also the issues of aboriginal rights, a reformed senate and so on. At the same time, within FPRO, officials used what was referred to as a split approach: attempting to focus as much as possible on 7/50 issues, while isolating issues such as Supreme Court appointments and the constitutional amending formula, which would require unanimity, into a separate package.

The creation of the CCCU and Joe Clark's appointment in April of 1991 was thus premised on a number of assumptions: in contrast to the Meech Lake round, the new Canada round would have to be much more transparent and comprehensive; some means had to be found to begin the multilateral process and, at some point, to involve Quebec in the negotiations; and finally on the federal side the process would have to be led by a figure enjoying wide respect in all parts of the country. Given Brian Mulroney's direct involvement in Meech Lake, as well as his low standing in the polls, there is little doubt that this prevented him from taking a central or visible role in restarting the process. To a large degree this also applied to others closely associated with the Meech Lake process, Lowell Murray as minister of federal-provincial relations and Norman Spector, formerly secretary of FPRO. Hence the appointment of Clark, one of the few credible senior figures within the Conservative government seen as capable of handling such an assignment.[21]

Upon Clark's appointment, organizational problems surrounding the CCCU became evident. FPRO, as the secretariat responsible for supporting the work of the CCCU, was staffed by senior people who were not necessarily ones that Clark would have chosen. Furthermore, there was a more general sense that relatively little had been accomplished in terms of policy proposals: the deputy ministerial task forces had yet to report; there was very little for the new Cabinet committee to review or discuss. Later, when the deputy ministerial task force reports began arriving and overviews and proposals in specific areas were prepared, complaints surfaced that the material was now too ponderous and academic.

Specifically on the personnel side, after working together for nearly two months Clark indicated that he wanted Gordon Smith replaced as secretary to the Cabinet for federal provincial relations. The reasons for this are not entirely clear. It is known that as minister of external affairs, Clark had not been happy in working with Smith on previous occasions. The federal government's chief civil servant, Clerk of the Privy Council Paul Tellier, was also unhappy with Smith (despite having been responsible for his recruitment earlier), blaming him for the malaise affecting FPRO. At the same time Tellier, in representing the prime minister's interests in the process, wanted more direct influence and in this he was also joined by Norman Spector. What should be stressed, therefore, was the awkward situation of having three powerful figures — Smith, Spector and Tellier — all seeking to exercise direction over the activities of the CCCU and FPRO. It was this set of circumstances that helped set the stage for Smith's departure, perhaps triggered by frictions between Smith and Clark. The solution to the vacancy caused by Smith's leaving was that Tellier himself became Smith's replacement while retaining his position as clerk of the privy council. The ambiguity of Tellier's position is noteworthy. He reported to the prime minister as clerk of the privy council and reported to Clark as secretary for FPRO. Nonetheless, it provided Tellier, and through him the prime minister, with a means of preserving and enhancing access to the deliberations of the CCCU.

Tellier also recruited other staff. During the course of the Deputy Ministers' Committee on the Constitution he had been impressed by the work of Jocelyn Bourgon, deputy minister of consumer and corporate affairs, who headed the Deputy Ministerial Task Force on Economic Union. She became the associate secretary at FPRO in mid-June and began bringing into FPRO people she felt were capable of bringing order to the perceived chaos in FPRO, in particular people she felt could present proposals based on the findings of the deputy ministerial task forces and individual line departments in a succinct and coherent fashion. These new people, including Suzanne Hurtubise and later Michael Wernick from Consumer and Corporate Affairs, essentially took over from Richard Dicerni and Ronald Watts the management of the paper flow. By late August Watts had shifted more to focusing on the background studies, many of which were later released as discussion papers at the same time as *Shaping Canada's Future Together*. During the critical final phase of the committee's work in September most of the drafting and revising of proposals was handled directly by Bourgon and Hurtubise.[22]

The role and style of Bourgon and Hurtubise were critical. Essentially, they used their experience with the economic union deputy ministerial task force as a model, that is to decentralize and consult, bringing departments much more openly into the process, farming out some of FPRO's responsibilities directly to the departments, for example, asking departments to prepare position papers. Their methodology was quite different from the closed shop approach of FPRO under Gordon Smith, that is: limited consultation and playing things close to the vest. The closed shop approach was perhaps particularly pronounced under Smith, but it has been in general a hallmark of FPRO's modus operandi vis-à-vis line departments, especially during constitutional negotiations.

The changes wrought by Bourgon and Hurtubise came into effect mainly during July and August. Preparations for the first meeting of the CCCU in Winnipeg, however, including the overview of what ought to be addressed in the federal proposals, had been undertaken by Watts and his consultants and, before being presented, were vetted by the then troika of Smith, Tellier and Spector. This troika constituted the core of the steering committee for the process. The steering committee was expanded when Joe Clark, upon his appointment as minister, decided to chair it. This soon changed, however, as scheduling problems and his overall workload made it impossible for Clark to continue in this position. Tellier became chair and Clark ceased to attend meetings of the steering committee. Fred Gorbet, Deputy Minister of Finance,

John Tait, Deputy Minister of Justice, Mary Dawson, Associate Deputy Minister of Justice, and James Judd, Clark's Chief-of-Staff became members; and later in June the steering committee was joined by Bourgon and Hurtubise, the latter becoming recording secretary. The dominant roles, however, remained those of Tellier and Spector, and the steering committee itself throughout the process played the singularly important role of framing the agenda, supervising the drafting of briefings and proposals for the CCCU, and, ultimately supervising the drafting of the final report. Rather strikingly, almost all the members of the steering committee had been brought up and educated in, or were longtime residents of, Montreal.

THE CABINET COMMITTEE

Turning to the CCCU itself, its composition did not differ radically from the Cabinet's premier committee, Priorities and Planning (P&P). The key difference was that it was chaired by Clark rather than the prime minister, and the latter was not a member. The complete membership of the CCCU is given in Figure 6.1.

Of the 18 ministers, five were from Quebec.[23] Overall the committee represented a good cross-section of the country as a whole. At the same time CCCU members shared a number of characteristics: they were not well versed on constitutional matters, most were in fact relative neophytes, and, at least at first, they embraced their task reluctantly. In the beginning Clark had to expend considerable energy cajoling CCCU members to participate; and ministers were initially unwilling to leave Ottawa for the out-of-town meetings of the committee that Clark had planned in various locations throughout Canada.[24] Secondly, at least in the eyes of some officials, CCCU members appeared to want officials and academics to present them with ready answers; they were most anxious to see specific solutions and were very reluctant to think up any of their own. Other observers were more charitable. They noted that ministers, despite an initial reluctance to leave Ottawa for the meetings, did participate wholeheartedly: attendance was remarkably good and individual ministers did bring forward some of their own ideas, such as having the provinces play a role in appointing members of the board of directors of the Bank of Canada along the lines of the German Bundesbank. In this instance Department of Finance officials persuaded ministers that the scheme could only be made to work if the Governor of the Bank was provided with greater independence and a more specific mandate. Furthermore, the ministers' lack of schooling in constitutional matters did mean that their views, beliefs and sensibilities were closer to that of ordinary Canadians. One additional factor accounting for the inability of at least some ministers to rise to the occasion was that they were cut off from their normal support staff. In virtually all other settings ministers could expect to be briefed

Figure 6.1: Members of the Cabinet Committee on Canadian Unity (CCCU)

Member	Province	Portfolio
The Rt. Hon. Joe Clark	Alberta	Constitutional Affairs, President of Privy Council
The Hon. John Crosbie	Newfoundland	Fisheries & Oceans, Minister for Atlantic Canada Opportunities Agency (ACOA)
The Hon. Don Mazankowski	Alberta	Deputy Prime Minister, Finance
The Hon. Elmer MacKay	Nova Scotia	Public Works
The Hon. Jake Epp	Manitoba	Energy, Mines and Resources
The Hon. Robert De Cotret	Quebec	Secretary of State
The Hon. Perrin Beatty	Quebec	Communications
The Hon. Michael Wilson	Ontario	Trade and Industry, Science and Technology
The Hon. Bill McKnight	Saskatchewan	Agriculture
The Hon. Benoît Bouchard	Quebec	Health and Welfare
The Hon. Marcel Masse	Quebec	Defence
The Hon. Barbara McDougall	Ontario	External Affairs
The Hon. Lowell Murray	Ontario	Government Leader in the Senate
The Hon. Jean Charest	Quebec	Environment
The Hon. Bernard Valcourt	New Brunswick	Employment and Immigration
The Hon. Doug Lewis	Ontario	Solicitor-General
The Hon. Kim Campbell	British Columbia	Justice Minister and Attorney-General
The Hon. Gilles Loiselle	Quebec	President of the Treasury Board, Minister of State (Finance)

Source: Office of the Prime Minister, *News Release*, 21 April 1991.

by both departmental civil servants and their own political staff. This was not the case here. There was little or no advance briefing material given to the ministers beforehand; and all material, discussions and decisions were to be kept strictly within the confines of the CCCU.

There was variation among ministers in their interest and degree of participation: John Crosbie was relatively inactive, as was Elmer MacKay; Mazankowski, while active, did not have strong views, except possibly on the distinct society issue; Kim Campbell and Perrin Beatty of the anglophone ministers were among the more dynamic and vocal members of the committee and had distinct views on most issues. Michael Wilson was most interested in the economic union issue. Among the Quebec ministers, while Bouchard did most of the talking, Loiselle was perceived to carry more weight; certainly the other Quebec ministers deferred to him. Jean Charest tended to speak during the closing phases of meetings and was regarded as particularly adept in perceiving common ground and integrating the often disparate views in the discussion. His views tended to carry less weight, however, certainly among Quebec ministers largely because of his junior status. While there were shadings of opinion, all Quebec ministers felt strongly about the distinct society principle. And, given the Quebec government's formal abstention from the constitutional process, the five ministers were acutely aware of the burden they carried in representing Quebec interests.

As noted, part of Clark's strategy for handling the committee involved a series of meetings taking place in different locations in Canada. A list of these meetings over the summer of 1991 is shown in Figure 6.2. These sessions would last two days on average and, clearly, were intended to wrest ministers away from the pressures and obligations of their portfolios in Ottawa so that they could devote their full attention to the constitutional matters at hand. These meetings were also intended to give them an opportunity to meet with groups and individuals in the different locales and to give them a feel for the different regions of the country.[25] In between these major sessions there were also shorter meetings in Ottawa, typically lasting an afternoon. The out-of-Ottawa meetings concentrated on broader issues while the briefer Ottawa meetings focused on resolving specific questions. Early on the CCCU adopted a self-imposed deadline of September 1991 for readying the federal proposals. As indicated in Figure 6.2, the CCCU met for major sessions approximately every two weeks until the middle of August. Then two sessions of the Cabinet's P&P committee, which included the prime minister, reviewed the CCCU's handiwork and resolved outstanding issues. After public release of the proposals the role of the CCCU changed considerably. It was reduced effectively to a working group of approximately eight ministers, a number that crept back up to 12 by March of 1992, and was used mainly as a sounding board. In effect, when the constitutional proposals moved to the parliamentary and later multilateral arenas

Figure 6.2: Meetings of the Cabinet Committee on Canadian Unity Held Outside Ottawa

Date	Location
10-11 May 1991	Winnipeg, Manitoba
25-26 June 1991	Niagara-on-the-Lake, Ontario
3-4 July 1991	Quebec City, Quebec
9-10 July 1991*	Meech Lake, Quebec
1-2 August 1991	Charlottetown, P.E.I.
14-16 August 1991	Iqaluit, N.W.T.
27-28 August 1991**	Kelowna, British Columbia
12-13 September 1991**	Sherbrooke, Quebec

*This meeting was with the prime minister.
**Meetings of the Priorities and Planning Committe (P&P) to deal with the federal constitutional proposals.

(phases 3 and 4 of the Canada round process as noted earlier) the CCCU ceased to have much influence.

The CCCU did not meet formally with groups or individuals, nor did it hold open hearings. It was only during luncheon sessions or receptions at the out-of-town meetings that groups might have an opportunity to interact with individual ministers, but these sessions were not well advertized and invitations were available mainly through local Conservative MPs. At one point in July, shortly after the Quebec City meeting of the CCCU, Clark by himself had a well publicized meeting with Grand Chief Ovide Mercredi of the Assembly of First Nations (AFN). An agreement was struck between the two that would see the Aboriginal Peoples organize their own consultative forums on the constitution and exchange ideas and information regularly with the CCCU.[26] While there may have been informal contacts subsequently between Clark and Mercredi, beyond this initial meeting there is no evidence of regular meetings between the AFN and Clark or the CCCU. Direct participation of the AFN in the constitutional process came later during the multilateral phase.

There were links between CCCU members, remaining members of Cabinet and the Conservative caucus. These were mainly individual links — there is no evidence of systematic efforts to brief caucus during the course of the summer — although items were included in the final package to appeal to some of the more vocal elements in the caucus. The proposal for a Charter amendment to guarantee property rights was seen as one such item. As noted, on the whole efforts were made to keep a tight lid on the process. Usually, ministers only saw the most recent proposals upon entering the room and after discussing them would be asked to leave the drafts behind.[27] After the meeting at Meech Lake on 9-10 July, the only one attended by the prime minister until the P&P meeting late August, Mulroney explicitly warned ministers and instructed them not to discuss CCCU deliberations outside the confines of the meeting room.[28] This constrained Benoît Bouchard, by far the most voluble minister, but only somewhat. During the course of the summer a number of ministers, including Clark, continued to provide at least hints as to progress or lack of it within the committee. At other times actions were louder than words, for example, when four of the five Quebec ministers appeared to walk out for a short period during the meeting in Iqaluit.[29]

For the first major session, 10 and 11 May 1991, in Winnipeg FPRO staff had prepared an overview of the seven major issues: distinct society, economic union, central institutions, the Charter, language rights, Aboriginal Peoples, and the distribution of powers. Separate presentations were made on each of these issues at subsequent meetings. The preparatory work for this was done mainly by Watts under the guidance of the steering committee; subsequently experts in particular areas developed these issues and made more detailed presentations, such as those by Purvis and Leslie on the economic union, Gibbins on central institutions and Swinton on the distribution of powers. Later in August and September Bourgon and her officials took on responsibility for drafting specific proposals in light of CCCU discussions and again under the eye of the steering committee.

The sequence in which issues were discussed by the CCCU was determined in part by the format of the present constitution and the ill-fated Meech Lake document; these presented items in a primary order, for example, basic values were followed by central institutions and so on. The Canada clause and distinct society, therefore, came first in the discussion; then in late May the committee began tackling central institutions. Aboriginal issues came next, followed by the economic union. The distribution of powers issue was not discussed until near the very end of the process. The order in which these items were handled was of more than minor import. Considerable time was devoted to the distinct society clause and central institutions, for example; the economic union issue also proved contentious. Later at the end of the summer, when the committee ran up against its self-imposed deadline of September, distribution of powers, an issue of crucial importance to Quebec, was finally discussed in detail but in very rushed fashion. The term "tackling issues" is used advisedly and does not imply that agreements were always reached. At any given meeting a frequent outcome was stalemate, with perhaps the only agreement being that the issue would be revisited later. This was especially true with regard to central institutions and the distinct society clause, about which the Quebec ministers felt strongly but where there were often equally strong opposing views from the non-Quebec ministers. In a statement to the press during an apparently tempestuous session in Quebec City, Benoît Bouchard, vice-chair of the CCCU, told reporters: "We have to get over walls 75 feet high, established by different cultures over 200 years."[30] And later Bouchard noted, "I have to admit that in terms of explaining or trying to convince that Quebec is different, it's a lot of frustration."[31]

The question, however, was not on whether a distinct society clause ought to be included; that was never an issue. As Clark noted at one stage during the summer, "It's accepted by the ministers as a fundamental concept that there is a distinct society here."[32] The debate was essentially over its form and its reach. Furthermore, it appears that the Quebec ministers were in some respects playing a double game, that is intimating to the media the presence of major rifts between themselves and the rest of the committee that in reality did not exist. This posturing was no doubt related to the difficult position in which the Quebec ministers found themselves, of the need to present themselves to their Quebec constituency as strong representatives aggressively pursuing Quebec interests in the face of anglophone opposition.[33] To be sure there were differences over the distinct society clause but again they related more to form and its placement in the proposed document.

In other areas, such as central institutions, there was perhaps more common ground. Western ministers, while favouring an elected Senate, were not strongly wedded to a Senate with equal representation, not even the ministers from Alberta. At one point the committee favoured a Pepin-Robarts type solution, that is an appointed Senate where both levels of government would be able to select members, until it was pointed out by officials that this proposal had received very little support when it had been made in earlier constitutional rounds. Here the committee was clearly struggling with the problem of finding ways to meet public expectations for a properly elected Senate, whetted in part by the federal government having committed itself to this concept in the parallel agreements of 1990 intended to help save the Meech Lake Accord, while at the same time providing some kind of institutional mechanism allowing for the direct representation of provincial government interests. The end result was the proposal for both an elected Senate and a Council of the Federation that appeared in the September package. Progress on central institutions, however, did tend to undermine progress made in other areas, such as distinct society.

The subject of the Canadian economic union was also cause of much debate and pre-occupied several sessions. And like the distinct society clause, while there was no objection to the basic principle of economic union there was disagreement over its concrete conceptualization. Some ministers felt that the objective of economic union was best realized through the reinforcement of section 121, that is that the prohibition of barriers to interprovincial trade be extended to services, people and capital. Others put greater emphasis on harmonization in areas such as interprovincial transport. As well, debate centred around the means to be used to enforce the economic union and whether new provisions were best placed under section 91 (federal powers) or section 95 (concurrent powers). At a later stage there was discussion over an opting-out provision, both on its desirability and, if there was one, whether it should be renewable.[34]

Much of the debate within the CCCU cut across the Quebec-ROC divide, at least in the sense that Quebec ministers as a whole were neither more nor less opposed to the notion of a strong economic union compared to the others, which in some respects was surprising in light of the controversies that arose later after the release of the proposals. In the view of Quebec ministers on the committee, Quebec favoured a strong economic union; after all this was one of the major themes of the Allaire Report! This was also the position of Department of Finance officials, who played a key role on briefing ministers on the issue. With the benefit of hindsight, it was clear that Quebec ministers on the committee, and all members for that matter, had not anticipated the variety of interpretations that could be placed on the economic union proposals and that perhaps insufficient attention had been paid to alternative means for ensuring adherance to a set of proper and effective economic union provisions.

On other issues, however, little progress was made. The emotive question of distinct society, where the debate and misunderstandings tended to mirror in part those in Canadian society at large, was intrinsically difficult to resolve. Part of the blame, however can also be placed on the manner in which the chair of the CCCU, Joe Clark, conducted the meetings. His style was to let people talk as much as they wished, with little direction, in the hope of eventually reaching a consensus. While this approach did serve to help members educate each other, unfortunately it also hindered the committee in being able to bring matters to a conclusion, particularly on contentious issues. As will be noted below, Clark's manner of chairing meetings of the CCCU had further implications with regard to the role and influence of officials.

Throughout the process, ministers were acutely concerned with how the proposals would fly with the general public, and to this end detailed polling information was provided on all of the issues, and much of the discussion centred on what the public reaction might be, or whether public expectations would be satisfied, with regard to specific recommendations.[35] This presumably was one of the strengths of the CCCU, acting as the political antenna of the government, as a political reality check on proposals generated by officials, for example. On certain issues public opinion was reasonably clear cut. A strong majority of Canadians favoured affirming or extending aboriginal rights. On Senate reform a plurality of Canadians favoured not an equal and elected Senate but simply outright abolition of the Senate. The dilemma was, however, that public opinion on a number of issues, on economic union, for example, was ill-formed at best, non-existent at worst. As is often the case, it is only when proposals are spelled out, and after discussion in the media by other political actors and the like, that the opinions of citizens begin to gel, and these opinions may be quite different from those held at an earlier stage.[36] Thus in September 1991 a Decima report to FPRO indicated that non-Quebecers' willingness to make compromises had actually lessened over the course of the summer.[37]

Overall, in terms of regional representation, the voices heard most forcefully within the CCCU were those of ministers from Quebec and western Canada. One common refrain was, "how would this particular proposal play in Alberta? Or in Quebec City?" Very rarely, if ever, was the question asked, "how would this play in Atlantic Canada?" Neither Crosbie nor MacKay were energetic participants. Bernard Valcourt, the third minister from the Atlantic region, was concerned primarily with the interests of francophones outside Quebec, an issue that often put him at odds with Quebec ministers, and those of his portfolio of Employment and Immigration. The views of Perrin Beatty, the most active participant among the Ontario ministers, represented a blend of sectoral and national concerns. Simply on the basis of his stated beliefs, it was difficult to discern he was from Ontario. Quebec ministers were clearly committed to positions important to their province. Non-Quebec ministers, to the extent that they were regional advocates, appeared to be more grudging in arguing their case and were more likely to justify their position in pragmatic or strategic terms.

THE STEERING COMMITTEE AND BUREAUCRATIC INFLUENCE

Prior to each meeting of the CCCU, proposals would be drafted by the steering committee. The ministers would discuss them at length; the steering committee and officials would then revise them in light of the discussion in the CCCU. The process was largely one of narrowing the options; while the CCCU was frequently unable to give specific directions or indications of specific proposals to the steering committee, it was nonetheless able to say what it did not like. Proposals often went through several iterations, and in this fashion progress was gradually made. At the end of many of the marathon sessions of the CCCU, however, because little had been accomplished by the ministers themselves, the steering committee draft proposals would often become decisions by default.

The steering committee, therefore, became the cockpit in which the direction of the CCCU's deliberations were set. And it was the prime minister's two key officials, Tellier and Spector, who effectively dominated the steering committee.[38] In a room, on the walls of which were sometimes posted some of Spector's decision tree charts depicting the possible outcomes of different roads taken, steering committee officials would deal not only with proposals to be readied for next day CCCU deliberations but also longer term strategic considerations. It was also here where the influence of other officials, and through them certain agencies, could be felt. The two officials from Justice, John Tait and Mary Dawson, played a crucial role in drafting and redrafting the key sections on distinct society and aboriginal rights. Their role, however, was primarily one of facilitating, bringing some coherence to the sentiments of the CCCU in relation to the substance of these important issues, as distinct from asserting a particular agency interest.

If there was a discrete agency interest at work within the steering committee it was most likely that of Finance. The deputy minister of finance, Fred Gorbet, was both the main source of expertise on the topic of economic union for the steering committee and the CCCU and felt strongly about the issue of reducing interprovincial barriers. The Department of Finance had a special working group on the constitution that prepared much of the background material and helped draft the section on the economic union that ultimately appeared in *Shaping Canada's Future Together*.[39] The approach and philosophy of the special working group and of the Department of Finance as a whole can be discerned in the background paper, *Canadian Federalism and Economic Union*, released in September 1991 at the same time as the federal proposals.[40] An equally critical factor, however, was that the report of the Deputy Ministerial Task Force on Economic Union, chaired by Gorbet and Bourgon, was considered by far to be the most coherent and plausible of those submitted by the nine task forces.[41] As such the report on economic union had considerable impact on the drafting of the initial proposals considered by the CCCU; further it was the quality of the report that drew the attention of Tellier and resulted in Bourgon's move to FPRO and a position on the steering committee.

Beyond this, one must recognize the political context that gave impetus to the position of officials from Finance. During the initial post-Meech phase in 1990 and in the May 1991 speech-from-the-throne, where constitutional reform was twinned with the theme of rendering the Canadian economy more competitive, the government had indicated that the elimination of interprovincial barriers to trade and mobility would be an important goal for the federal government in any future round of constitutional negotiations.[42] Within Finance the issue of ensuring the integrity of a genuine Canadian economic union had been a long-standing concern; it was promoted by the long serving minister of finance, Michael Wilson, and it appeared to have the strong endorsement of the prime minister himself. For Gorbet a major goal, therefore, was to ensure that the government's position on economic union would be high on the agenda of the CCCU and become a major plank in the federal government's constitutional proposals. Within the steering committee he had the opportunity to see that this was accomplished.

Gorbet was not alone in arguing strongly on behalf of an effective economic union proposal. Most officials within FPRO were sympathetic. And for strategic reasons it could be argued that the proposals on economic union would help impart a strong Canadian identity to the overall package. Where there was disagreement was on how the economic union proposal should be cast, particularly with respect to the active management of the economic union. Some officials thought it best that management powers be brought under section 95 of the *Constitution Act* as a concurrent power along with immigration and agriculture, indicating that it was not solely a federal power and thereby ensure greater likelihood of acceptance by the provinces. Those from Finance, however, were fearful that this might weaken the provisions and that it should, instead be placed under section 91, as a new head entitled "91A," the section normally reserved for federal powers.[43] The end result was a recommendation in *Shaping Canada's Future* that the "Power to Manage the Economic Union" provision "be added ... immediately after section 91."[44] Mazankowski, as minister of finance, endorsed the economic union proposal; but it is interesting that within the CCCU he did not give the impression of necessarily being the strongest proponent or promoter of this issue. This role clearly appeared to belong to Minister of Trade Michael Wilson with support from External Affairs Minister Barbara McDougall.

Evidence of departmental interests, as articulated through ministers, can also be discerned with respect to the distribution of powers issue, which as noted was not addressed until the end of the summer. In fact the prime minister in one of his briefings with Joe Clark in early August expressed considerable alarm that so little had been accomplished in this area. And when the issue was discussed a number of the ministers dug in their heels with the view to protecting departmental interests. Perrin Beatty, for example, as minister of communication was highly resistant to seeing the federal government give up significant powers in this field. And the reports of the nine deputy ministerial task forces, which were supposed to provide indications of areas that could be turned over to the provinces, contained very few actual candidate areas for decentralization other than important elements of language policy. This helps explain in part why the federal proposals ultimately proved disappointing to those who were expecting the federal government to yield more in the way of powers to the provinces.[45] With respect to language policy, after some initial forays the CCCU decided to leave this sensitive topic alone, a sentiment shared by the prime minister, Joe Clark and outsiders such as Robert Bourassa and former Alberta premier Peter Lougheed who indirectly advised the committee at various stages.[46]

Ministers such as Beatty, however, were not simply representing departmental interests. A number, including Beatty and Wilson, felt strongly about maintaining a strong federal government and not only with respect to their own portfolio interests. The case for decentralization was carried in the main by the Quebec ministers. The only area where they had much success, however, was in the field of labour market development and training. Jurisdiction over this area was something that the Quebec governments had long pressed for; within the CCCU the Quebec ministers took up the case, led by Bouchard who as a former college principal had a personal interest in the issue. The proposal for yielding labour market training to the provinces was first discussed at the Charlottetown meeting in early August and was not resolved until after the Sherbrooke meeting.

THE FINAL STAGES AND BEYOND

Several points, some of them quite substantial, remained unresolved when the results of the CCCU's deliberations were presented to the P&P committee of Cabinet first in Kelowna 27-28 August 1991 and then in Sherbrooke. The significance of the shift from the CCCU to P&P was that the prime minister himself was now in the chair, providing an opportunity for him to apply his considerable skills in bringing people together and reconciling their interests. This period also saw direct consultations with Quebec. According to an article in the *Montreal Gazette*, on 17 August after the Iqaluit meeting, Paul Tellier travelled to Bourassa's summer home in Sorel, Quebec, where Bourassa appeared to express satisfaction with the developing package.[47] Matters seemed to be progressing satisfactorily at the Kelowna meeting. Two weeks later, however, Bourassa's right hand-man, Jean-Claude Rivest, arrived in Ottawa to inform officials that Bourassa, upon reflection, was far from happy with the document and wanted changes. The distinct society clause, and in particular its placement in the constitutional document, remained a source of contention as well as the economic union provisions, among other issues. News of Bourassa's unhappiness led the Quebec ministers to increase their resolve to protect their province's interests. Two days before the scheduled Sherbrooke meeting of P&P, Mulroney called a "crunch meeting" of Joe Clark, his senior Quebec ministers — Loiselle, Masse and Bouchard — as well as Lowell Murray and Perrin Beatty who apparently still had major difficulties with the distinct society provision. Also in attendance were Tellier and Spector.[48] According to officials, "excellent progress was made."[49] The distinct society issue was largely resolved at the Sherbrooke meeting and, as well, "western ministers Don Mazankowski, Kim Campbell and Harvie Andre finally convinced their Ontario colleagues to accept an elected Senate with a limited veto."[50]

After the Sherbrooke meeting on 12-13 September differences still remained. At this stage it appears the CCCU was willing to entrust the prime minister to impose a solution on outstanding differences. As Bouchard explained it: "Those questions are for the Prime Minister: the co-ordination, the moment it will come out, what will be in it ... There are moments when all that depends on the Prime Minister himself. That's where we are."[51] Between this last combined P&P-CCCU meeting and the public release of the proposals on 24 September the prime minister made the final decisions on both labour market training and the economic union.[52]

The main highlights of *Shaping Canada's Future Together* were as follows:[53]

- A Canada clause acknowledging the core values of the Canadian identity;
- Recognition of Canada's linguistic duality and of Quebec's distinctiveness;
- A constitutional amendment to entrench a right to aboriginal self-government within the Canadian federation;
- A directly elected Senate providing more equitable provincial and territorial representation as well as aboriginal representation;
- An economic union managed by the federal government to guarantee the free movement of persons, goods, services, and capital within Canada;
- More control for provinces in immigration, culture and job-training;
- Creation of a Council of the Federation to determine shared-cost programs and national standards, composed of federal, provincial and territorial appointees; and,
- Charter amendments to guarantee property rights.

Upon release of these proposals the federal government concentrated most of its communication efforts on stressing that the package was not cast in stone; that the intent was to provide some basis for re-opening discussion of constitutional issues; and that in certain areas such as Senate reform important details still needed to be resolved. Some of the elements of the federal government's longer term strategy could be discerned, however. With the exception of the amending formula and procedures for Supreme Court appointments, the package was designed to circumvent the unanimity rule so as to avoid the case, as with Meech Lake, of one or two provinces being able to veto a final package. The proposals broke ground by affirming in principle a process to allow Aboriginal Peoples to attain self-government. Clearly the government wished to avoid a situation of eliciting negative reactions to its proposals right at the outset; it certainly did not want the aboriginal community to become an immediate opponent and thereby trigger negative public sentiment. Also, in citing the need to entrench aboriginal rights and not just the need to recognize Quebec's distinctive nature among the "compelling reasons for constitutional renewal," Ottawa was sending a signal that this was not just a package for Quebec.[54]

Upon their release it was planned for the proposals to be turned over almost immediately to a special Joint Parliamentary Committee. Thereafter, it was hoped, the multilateral process would begin. Even before the Joint Committee began its hearings, however, the prime minister began intimating that certain features in the proposals, mainly those relating to the economic provisions, would likely be altered. For a time in October-November 1991 it appeared the whole endeavour would sink in the morass of the ill-fated Castonguay-Dobbie Committee. Revival of the Committee through the appointment of Gérald Beaudoin as the new co-chair and a parallel series of mini-conferences helped restart the process and resulted in significant changes to the *Shaping Canada's Future Together* proposals. Thus even before the start of the multilateral process in March, provisions such as the property rights amendment, the Council of the Federation and some of the more central components of the economic union proposal had been dropped.

At the time *Shaping Canada's Future Together* was released the understanding within the CCCU was that the Cabinet would have an opportunity to revisit the proposals, essentially to have a final say over the package, most likely before the start of multilateral negotiations. This was not to be, however. What started out as preliminary feelers to the provinces in early March 1992 very quickly blossomed into fullscale negotiations on 12 March. There was no longer an opportunity for the CCCU to participate in any significant manner. As noted, after release of the proposals in September 1991 the CCCU became little more than a sounding board. Clark continued to consult with key ministers such as Mazankowski and Wilson, but Norman Spector who left as Chief of Staff of the PMO in January 1992 and his replacement, Hugh Segal, made it clear to officials in FPRO that they did not wish to involve further the CCCU in the delicate process of dealing with the provinces and, ultimately, of enticing Quebec to the negotiating table.

Some ministers, especially those who felt they had particular interests at stake, were distinctly unhappy with the course of events and from being excluded from the process. Thus by July 1992 longtime Mulroney loyalist Michael Wilson publicly voiced his displeasure over what he saw as the gutting of the economic union proposal: "I have to say that I have some problems with the proposal as it stands now.... The results of the federal- provincial agreement last week are not good enough. We've got to do better."[55] Clearly, during the more critical phases of constitutional negotiations federal ministers, other than those directly involved in the negotiations such as Clark and Bouchard, were reduced to the role of bystanders, and Cabinet as a whole had reverted to its more traditional role of non-involvement.

ANALYSIS

To better understand what transpired and to draw lessons it is best to return to the four categories introduced at the beginning, although in the following discussion it makes sense to pair the categories, as will be seen.

INTEREST GROUP AND BUREAUCRATIC POLITICS

It is clear that interest groups had little in the way of direct access to the CCCU process. In many ways the strategy of having the CCCU meet in different locations across the country was a clever one. It imparted a sense of the ministers breaking out of their cloistered Ottawa surroundings meeting with ordinary Canadians (selected ordinary Canadians to be sure). At the same time newspaper reports indicated that the logistics of this hectic travel schedule made it exceedingly difficult for various organizations to meet with the minister of constitutional affairs or to have him speak to their members.[56] Some of the proposals in the September package were clearly designed to cater to certain special interests, the proposals concerning aboriginal rights, for example. But these propositions were in response to long-standing and well-known claims by the Aboriginal Peoples, reinforced by the events of the summer of 1990, and not a result of specific lobbying during the summer of 1991. To the degree that there was a specific minister arguing on behalf of natives, it was Joe Clark who had definite sympathy for their position. And to the extent that the aboriginal community had a particular influence, it was the realization by the committee that given the general sympathy for aboriginal rights among the public at large the government simply could not afford to incur the enmity of this significant group, especially not at the beginning stages of the Canada round process.

In brief, while the CCCU was aware of the position of different interest groups and cast its proposals in part in response to the perceived significance of those groups, the CCCU managed to keep itself well insulated from direct lobbying pressures and, even more importantly, did not at any stage become involved in debate or direct negotiations with groups.

In assessing the influence of the bureaucracy one has to keep in mind that it was not simply a matter of the bureaucrats versus the politicians. There were differences between officials in central agencies and line departments; and there were differences within central agencies, in FPRO for instance where the approach of officials recruited under Gordon Smith was quite different from that of officials brought in under Jocelyn Bourgon. The interests of the different officials also varied. For Norman Spector, the goal was largely strategic — getting a deal. For Fred Gorbet of Finance, the goal was in some sense both narrower and more substantive. For him preserving and enhancing the economic union was most critical. It should also be stressed that in many instances there were alliances that crossed the administrative-political divide. Thus the positions articulated by officials from Finance were strongly supported within the CCCU by ministers such as Michael Wilson and Barbara McDougall. Furthermore, there was support for the economic proposals among both ministers and officials simply on the basis of strategy: the federal government could not be seen as giving away too much to the provinces; there had to be something over which Ottawa was seen to have influence if not outright control; and subsequent bargaining in the parliamentary arena and with the provinces would likely see the initial federal position being eroded.

At the same time there were definite differences of opinion between officials and ministers. Clark, for example, was opposed to the idea of a national referendum, while Spector was of the view that this was a weapon that the federal government would be wise to have in its arsenal and for that reason should be taken into account in designing the package, if only for strategic reasons.

The approach of FPRO under Bourgon, of consulting more extensively with line departments and other agencies than had hitherto been the case, had the effect of giving those departments more say in the process. The impact here can be found in the rather limited number of powers that the federal government appeared willing to yield to the provinces, much less than was initially expected in the spring of 1991. The exception was labour market training, and this was only the result of strenuous argument by the Quebec ministers. Among bureaucratic interests, Finance can be seen as the biggest winner on the economic union issue, although in this instance it was a largely Pyrrhic victory as most of the economic union provisions were stripped away or radically weakened during the Joint Parliamentary Committee and multilateral stages. Some have argued that it was largely a matter of packaging, that rather than a section 91A there should have been a section 95A, and that a "federal power grab" was never the intention by either Finance or the CCCU. Outside observers, however, have noted that the provisions in the September document could legitimately be seen to centralize federal powers in economic matters, in part because the proposed sections 121(3) and 91A would not bind Ottawa.[57] At a minimum the federal economic union proposals helped trigger negative comments about the document as a whole, especially in Quebec, in a way that a milder set of proposals might not have done.

In short, bureaucratic interests had an important role in shaping the September package: less was yielded to the provinces in terms of the distribution of powers and the economic union provisions were more forceful than they might have been. Again, however, the broader strategic elements at play facilitated bureaucratic interests in generating support for their position. In addition, it should be stressed that the influence of officials, and the steering committee in particular, was in part a result of stalemate within the CCCU itself. It would not be unfair to say that at times ministers simply invited officials to fill a vacuum that existed within the CCCU. Furthermore, simply from a process point of view, the steering committee played a critical role in keeping the CCCU on track and in refining the various proposals and the collective thoughts of the CCCU into a coherent document ready for release in September. This was no small achievement. Finally, it should be noted that the consultative-cooperative approach fostered by Bourgon and her officials within FPRO and vis-à-vis line departments may have served the federal government less well in the post CCCU phase. That is, in dealing with provincial governments during the multilateral phase, an arena where governments are much more used to playing things close to the vest and less willing to concede points, the cooperative and decentralized style of negotiating agreements favoured by Bourgon may have put the federal government at a disadvantage in making trade-offs or extracting concessions and more generally in influencing the overall course of events.

INTRASTATE FEDERALISM AND ELITE ACCOMMODATION

To what extent did the CCCU succeed in bringing differing regional and provincial interests to bear on the constitutional issue and to what extent were they reflected in the outcome? And to what degree did the ministers succeed in overcoming long-standing enmities over language and the like? According to one observer, *Shaping Canada's Future Together* reflected all too much the regional particularisms inherent in the country:

> Mulroney ministers tend to be deeply rooted in their regions. Few have an over-arching sense of the whole country. Fewer still can speak both languages. In the end, what emerged was a brokered deal in which each region seemed to be offered something of interest.[58]

This would suggest that the CCCU, in reconciling competing regional interests, acted as an intrastate institution. One might wish to quarrel with this characterization, at least in part. Certain regional interests, Quebec and the west, likely had more influence than other regions. As well, it can be argued that inclusion of the economic union and aboriginal rights provisions both broke new ground and to a degree transcended regional differences. Recognition of Quebec as a distinct society, while designed to meet demands from the Quebec ministers, can also be seen as representing a broader spirit of compromise. Furthermore, items such as the property rights amendment reflected more internal Conservative party ideology than any particular regional dimension.

To the degree, however, that the brokered deal represented primarily the interests of the regions two points ought to be made. While ministers may have reflected in their arguments distinct regional views, these views were not necessarily those of provincial governments. Nor is there evidence that ministers saw themselves as representing those governments. For example, western ministers, while favouring an elected Senate, did not support equal representation within that body. Furthermore, "provincial governments were told only in general terms about the outlines of the emerging package."[59] As one provincial official put it: "Our principal sources of information were the CBC and *The Globe and Mail*."[60] The exception may be Quebec. More so than the others, Quebec ministers (and in a sense the whole committee) did attempt to anticipate, and to a degree cater to, Quebec government views. Throughout there was a feeling that Quebec was constantly "at the table." Marcel Masse had at least two meetings with Bourassa. The Quebec government and premier were from time to time kept abreast of developments within the CCCU and efforts were made to elicit from Bourassa his reactions to possible proposals. If there was a flaw in the consultative process it resided with the Quebec government and with Bourassa's unwillingness to reveal his hand until near the very end of the CCCU process in September. Bourassa's hand, in turn, was likely constrained by conflicts and machinations within the Quebec government and the Quebec Liberal party.

In short, ministers were not primarily seeking to represent provincial government interests, with the possible exception of Quebec, and this was both a strength and a weakness. In not taking more explicit account of provincial government interests, this likely made the multilateral phase more difficult later on. On the other hand, it did mean that ministers were able to capture a wider range of views, and while *Shaping Canada's Future Together* may have had in the eyes of some a provincial flavour to it, at least it was a more broadly grounded provincialism based on more than just provincial government views.

The second point is that the CCCU never pretended to be a full-scale intrastate body. That is, it did not see itself as representing expressly the interests of the regions from which the ministers were drawn. Nor did it make any claims to be the final arbiter of what kind of constitution Canadians should have. Its pretensions were more modest: to act as a forum in which a set of initial proposals were to be developed for purposes of further discussion and negotiation. And in this the CCCU succeeded reasonably well, if success here is measured by the fact that the federal proposals did restart the constitutional process. When released in September the package drew grudging praise from Premier Wells who, while expressing doubts about the ultimate fate of the package did praise Joe Clark for his "tremendous effort."[61] And Robert Bourassa, while describing the economic union proposal as unacceptable to Quebec, nonetheless indicated a willingness to negotiate on the constitutional package as a whole.[62] Overall, assessments must be tempered by the fact that the CCCU represented the opening phase of the Canada round. The committee had to be careful not to give too much away in what would constitute the government's initial bargaining position. Yet there needed to be enough in the package to get the bargaining started.

During the course of the CCCU deliberations, charges were made that the process was too closed, charges given credibility by Mulroney's injunction that "I never, ever, discuss anything that goes on in cabinet, nor will any of my ministers in the future,"[63] in response to alleged leaks to reporters by CCCU members. The saving grace here was that ministers felt only partially constrained by the prime minister's injunction and Bouchard in particular continued to let his feelings be known about what transpired within the committee room. In combination with close media scrutiny, this ensured that the main lines of conflict were made known. Further, it helped convey to the public that the CCCU ministers, like many other Canadians, were struggling hard with questions such as Quebec's position within the Canadian confederation and were seeking to come up with honest answers. These impressions as relayed through the media, however, may not have been wholly accurate, in part because of the efforts by some of the Quebec ministers to present their labours in a particular light before the Quebec public.

Nonetheless, precisely because the CCCU did not fit the mould of the traditional elite accommodation model, this allowed it to play a more constructive role. Along with Joe Clark's association with the proposals, the CCCU's semi-transparency helped impart a legitimacy to *Shaping Canada's Future Together* that a document emanating directly from the prime minister and the FPRO probably would have lacked. At the same time, elite accommodation customs were not absent. The master practitioner of the art, Brian Mulroney, applied his skills and succeeded in forging a consensus at the culmination of the process. Without his direct intervention there would not have been a package.

LESSONS

What lessons can be drawn? At one level one can ask whether, in light of the ultimate failure of the Charlottetown Accord, Cabinet should have been used at all. Perhaps the federal government should have moved immediately to something like a constituent assembly or more generally adopted a process that was much more transparent. Whether the time frame, in large part dictated by the Quebec government, would have allowed for a much more open process or whether the end results would have been appreciably different is almost impossible to answer here.

Accepting the CCCU more on the terms that the prime minister initially set out for it, and with the inestimable benefit of hindsight, one can argue, for example, that ministers might have been better schooled in constitutional matters, that FPRO officials might have used more of a closed shop approach in dealing with other agencies and departments, and that within the CCCU Clark should have been more effective in controlling discussion. Had it been done a little differently, the proposals might have drawn less negative comment from certain quarters. But applying these lessons to some unspecified future constitutional round is much more difficult. In effect, the CCCU and the Canada round as a whole was a one-shot affair. And even if Cabinet or a Cabinet committee were to be assigned a similar function in some future round, it may be impossible to recreate the conditions that helped make the CCCU at least a partial success, that is protection from direct lobbying by groups and other governments yet still allowing some public insight into its deliberations. The next time round there will be much greater awareness of its role in setting the constitutional agenda. A variety of interested parties, including special interest organizations, would seek to have access and be heard. Demands for such access will be difficult to resist on the one hand, given the contemporary stress on transparency, but difficult to meet on the other without transforming Cabinet or a Cabinet committee into something other than an executive body.

Nevertheless, it would be difficult to visualize any new constitutional round taking place without some direct involvement by Cabinet. To this end one specific recommendation might be for the prime minister to create a committee, or at least a core group of ministers, with responsibility for the constitution, at a stage well before the restarting of the constitutional process. This would allow ministers to be brought up to speed on constitutional issues so that they would be more effectively informed and engaged for the time when the prime minister and Cabinet confront the exigencies and crises invariably thrown up by any new constitutional round. In a similar vein, there is something to be said for letting ministers have access to advice on constitutional matters from sources other than FPRO. At a minimum they should be allowed to consult their own political staff during the course of Cabinet deliberations on the constitution with the view of making ministers more confident of their capacity to participate in the constitutional process.

To the extent that the role of the CCCU, or something like it, will be retained in some future round, one additional point is worth stressing. Although analysis of the role of the Joint Parliamentary Committee and the five mini conferences is beyond the scope of this chapter,[64] it is worth noting that many of the changes made in the September 1991 proposals, for good or ill — dropping property rights, the Council of the Federation, and key economic union provisions — occurred *before* the start of the multilateral process on 12 March 1992. In effect, there were checks in the system to counter at least portions of whatever interests, bureaucratic and political, influenced the September 1991 outcome. In other words, in setting the stage for any future constitutional round, the capacity of central governing institutions as a whole, and not just Cabinet, to play a meaningful role in the process should not be ignored.

NOTES

Research for this chapter was based on documentary evidence, newspaper records and interviews with a number of officials in the Federal Provincial Relations Office (FPRO), and two separate line departments carried out by the first author. These did not include members of the Prime Minister's Office (PMO). The number interviewed totalled nine in all. While some were willing to have their name put on the record, others requested that the interview be confidential and not for attribution, or, when offered confidentiality, accepted. Given the limited number interviewed and to ensure confidentiality it was decided to keep all names of interviewees confidential. The initial ideas upon which the chapter is based were presented by the first author, and subjected to helpful criticism, at a seminar hosted by the Political Science Department of The University of British Columbia in February 1993. Peter Aucoin, David Milne, Robert Young, two anonymous reviewers and the editors of this volume kindly provided detailed comments on subsequent drafts. The research was made possible through the generous financial support of the Social Science and Humanities Research Council of Canada. We would like to thank all those who provided assistance, comments and ideas. Above all we would like to thank those who agreed to be interviewed. Errors of fact or interpretation remain the responsibility of the authors.

1. Office of the Prime Minister, *Release* (Ottawa, 21 April 1991).
2. Alan C. Cairns, *Charter versus Federalism: The Dilemmas of Constitutional Reform* (Montreal: McGill-Queen's University Press, 1992); Donald V. Smiley and R.L. Watts, *Intrastate Federalism in Canada* (Toronto: University of Toronto Press, 1985).
3. It would be misleading to say that the federal Cabinet has played only a limited role in previous constitutional rounds. For example, during the period 1980-81, especially when Ottawa was developing its unilateral proposals, it appears Cabinet was used extensively; see David Milne, *The New Canadian Constitution* (Toronto: Lorimer, 1982), pp. 76-83. Overall, however, relatively little has been written on Cabinet's role in the constitutional process.
4. See, for example, Preston King, *Federalism and Federation* (Baltimore: John Hopkins University Press, 1982).
5. Smiley and Watts, *Intrastate Federalism in Canada*, p. 38.
6. Cairns, *Charter versus Federalism*, pp. 44-45.
7. Ibid., pp. 45-47.
8. Herman Bakvis, *Regional Ministers: Power and Influence in the Canadian Cabinet* (Toronto: University of Toronto Press, 1991), chap. 1.
9. See S.J.R. Noel, "Consociational Democracy and Canadian Federalism," in K.D. McRae (ed.), *Consociational Democracy: Political Accommodation in Segmented Societies* (Toronto: McClelland & Stewart, 1974), pp. 262-68; Arend Lijphart, *Democracy in Plural Societies* (New Haven: Yale University Press, 1977)
10. The discrediting of the elite accommodation process can be attributed to a change in the nature of citizen participation, which is driven in part by value changes in society at large (the so-called post-materialist generational change) and in part by certain features of the *Constitution Act, 1982*, such as the *Charter of Rights and*

Freedoms and the amending formula, which required legislative approval of constitutional amendments at both levels of government. For different views on the relative importance of the Charter and broader societal changes see Ian Brodie and Neil Nevitte, "Evaluating the Citizens' Constitution Theory," *Canadian Journal of Political Science*, 26 (June 1993): 235-59; Alan C. Cairns, "A Defence of the Citizens' Constitution Theory," *Canadian Journal of Political Science*, 26 (June 1993): 261-67.

11. See, for example, Richard Simeon, *Federal-Provincial Diplomacy: The Making of Recent Policy in Canada* (Toronto: University of Toronto Press, 1972), pp. 144, 280-83.

12. See Alan C. Cairns, "Constitutional Minoritarianism in Canada," in R.L. Watts and D.M. Brown (eds.), *Canada: The State of the Federation 1990* (Kingston: Institute of Intergovernmental Relations, 1990), pp. 71-96; R. Knopff and F.L. Morton, *Charter Politics* (Scarborough: Nelson, 1992).

13. Graham T. Allison, *Essence of Decision: Explaining the Cuban Missile Crisis* (Boston: Little, Brown, 1971).

14. See J.S. Dupré, "The Workability of Executive Federalism in Canada," in H. Bakvis and W.M. Chandler (eds.), *Federalism and the Role of the State* (Toronto: University of Toronto Press, 1987), pp. 236-58.

15. Robert Russo, "Public must have a say, Wells declares," *Montreal Gazette*, 6 June 1991, p. A8.

16. For a discussion of this period see Bakvis, *Regional Ministers*, pp. 270-72.

17. On these developments see Kathy L. Brock, "The Politics of Process," in D. Brown (ed.), *Canada: The State of the Federation 1991* (Kingston: Institute of Intergovernmental Relations, Queen's University, 1991), pp. 57-87. For a most useful discussion of the significance of the two Quebec reports see Mollie Dunsmuir, *The Bélanger-Campeau and Allaire Reports* (Ottawa: Minister of Supply and Services, 1991).

18. Interview, November 1990.

19. These are those that could be amended using the general amending formula in i.e., section 38, *Constitution Act, 1982*, which specifies that a resolution is to be passed by the Parliament of Canada plus two-thirds (7) of the (10) provincial legislatures which combined represent 50 percent of the Canadian population.

20. See Robert Young and Douglas Brown, "Overview," in D. Brown and R. Young (eds.) *Canada: The State of the Federation 1992* (Kingston: Institute of Intergovernmental Relations, Queen's University, 1992), p. 6.

21. On the role and standing of these personalities in relation to restarting the constitutional process see Donna Greschner, "Closings, Cynics and Cheerfulness," in D. Brown, R. Young and D. Herperger (eds.), *Constitutional Commentaries: An Assessment of the 1991 Federal Proposals* (Kingston: Institute of Intergovernmental Relations, 1992), pp. 109-110.

22. On personnel changes and shifts in power see Anthony Wilson-Smith (with E. Kaye Fulton), "All the PM's Men," *Maclean's*, 25 March 1991, p. A16; Graham Fraser, "The Constitutional Backroom Gang," *The Globe and Mail*, 5 October 1991, p. D2.

23. The membership of the CCCU included all "political" or regional ministers, that is the senior Cabinet ministers from each province. Elmer MacKay was responsible for two provinces — P.E.I. as well as Nova Scotia — insofar as the former had no minister of its own after failing to elect any government MPs in 1988. As Mulroney announced in 1986, "These men and women will have primary responsibility of improving the Government's direct consultations with the people, with the party, with ordinary voters, to bring to our attention in a political way those concerns that can best be addressed most effectively at the federal level." Quoted in Bakvis, *Regional Ministers*, p. 246.
24. See Geoffrey Stevens, "Why Joe Clark had to throw a temper tantrum," *Toronto Star*, 12 May 1991, p. B3.
25. In each city at least one meal time was set aside for a reception with community leaders. Each table would have three or four local residents, one minister and one official. Ministers and officials were told "to listen, not too preach," an instruction apparently based on lessons from the Spicer Commission. See Robert Lee Mason, "Politicians seem to learn more with mouths closed, ears open," *Ottawa Citizen*, 4 August 1991, p. B1.
26. Anthony Wilson-Smith, "The Hard Road to Unity," *Maclean's*, 15 July 1991, p. A19.
27. Simpson, "Package filled with last-minute compromises," *The Globe and Mail*, 28 September 1991, p. A5.
28. Huguette Young, "Mulroney impose le silence au lac Meech," *Le Devoir*, 9 July 1991, A1.
29. This walkout was widely reported in the press, but there is some question about what triggered this action and secondly whether it was in fact a walkout at all. One report (Graham Fraser, "PM in charge of constitutional proposal," *The Globe and Mail*, 14 September 1991, p. A2) claims that the four Quebec ministers were unhappy with the proposal for the Council of the Federation, seeing it as simply one more central institution in which Quebec would be outvoted. Another report (Helen Branswell, "Les Canadiens sont plus sensibles aux demandes du Québec, estime Clark," *Le Devoir*, 17 août 1991, p. A4), however, claims that the walkout was precipitated by discussion over opting out and compensation provisions in future federal-provincial programs. On the other hand two officials described the event more as a "trickle out" as the four ministers left separately at different times, and, further, that there was nothing in the discussion or temper of the meeting at the time that would precipitate a sudden walkout. Media representatives saw the four Quebec ministers gathered together outside and reached the conclusion that the ministers had walked out simultaneously in response to some issue.
30. Quoted in Carol Goar, "On unity, PM should swing open cabinet doors," *Toronto Star*, 11 July 1991, p. A21.
31. Quoted in Anthony Wilson-Smith, "The Hard Road to Unity," *Maclean's*, 15 July 1991, p. A19.
32. Quoted in Wilson-Smith, "The Hard Road to Unity," p. A19.
33. This double-game in constitutional politics is not new. Simeon notes "the phenomenon of Quebec participants being more vehement and forceful outside the

conference room than inside it" during federal-provincial negotiations over the constitution in the 1960s. *Federal-Provincial Diplomacy*, p. 235.

34. See Graham Fraser, "Contentious opting-out clause was late addition, strategist says," *The Globe and Mail*, 1 October 1991, p. A4.

35. The federal government spent more than $1.4 million on polls on the constitutional issue over a period of less than two years during 1991-92, including $576,223 in 1991 while preparing the constitutional proposals. See Geoffrey York, "Pollsters profit from unity issue," *The Globe and Mail*, 3 October 1992, pp. A1, A2. Most of the details of the polling conducted for the government were released in response to a suit brought by the Access to Information Commissioner in the federal court after the federal government had originally denied requests for access by *The Globe and Mail*, Southam News and others. See Hugh Winsor and Graham Fraser, "Tories ignored own polls: Public warned in 1991 that constitutional issue unpopular," *The Globe and Mail*, 19 November 1992, pp. A1, A4.

36. Elizabeth Gidengil and Neil Nevitte, "'Know More': Information, Interest, and the Constitutional Proposals," paper presented to the Annual Meeting of the Canadian Political Science Association, Ottawa, June 1993.

37. Winsor and Fraser, "Tories ignored their own polls," p. A4.

38. Jeffrey Simpson, "Package filled with last-minute compromises," *The Globe and Mail*, 28 September 1991, A5.

39. *Shaping Canada's Future Together*, pp. 28-32, 43-44, 55-56.

40. Canada, *Canadian Federalism and Economic Union: Partnership for Prosperity* (Ottawa: Minister of Supply and Services, 1991)

41. The only other report that drew praise was the one submitted by External Affairs, which apparently presented quite a compelling argument on the need to preserve a single Canadian identity in Canada's representation abroad. This topic, however, did not figure prominently in CCCU discussions.

42. Anthony Wilson-Smith, "Fighting for Favor: high hopes and shrunken budgets mark the Tory plan for a new session of Parliament," *Maclean's*, 27 May 1991, p. A16.

43. Some of the division of opinions among the officials can be inferred from comments subsequently made by one of the academic advisers to the CCCU, Douglas Purvis, who clearly favoured using section 95 and stated, "Even if one accepts the principles behind and the substance of the s.91A proposal, it is clear that the optics are unacceptable." D. Purvis, "The Federal Proposals and the Economic Union," in R. Boadway and D. Purvis, *Economic Aspects of the Federal Government's Constitutional Proposals* (Kingston: John Deutsch Institute for the Study of Economic Policy, Queen's University, 1991), p. 9.

44. *Shaping Canada's Future Together*, p. 56.

45. These reports varied considerably in quality and some in fact were never completed, or at least were not in a condition to be considered by the CCCU. According to Jeffrey Simpson, in explaining the limited number of powers to be yielded to the provinces: "In part, that reflected the work last spring of committees of deputy ministers who reviewed federal proposals and concluded, as committed defenders

of federal turf, that Ottawa should not give away very much." "Package filled with last minute compromises," *The Globe and Mail,* 28 September 1991, p. A5.
46. Ibid., p. A5.
47. Robert Russo, "Cabinet deal didn't come easily," *Montreal Gazette,* 25 September 1991, p. A9.
48. Ibid., p. A9; Chantal Hébert, "La proposition constitutionnelle d'Ottawa aura été le fruit de profonds déchirements," *Le Devoir,* 24 September 1991, p. A1.
49. Quoted in Russo, "Cabinet deal didn't come easy," p. A9.
50. Ibid., p. A9.
51. Graham Fraser, "PM in charge of constitutional proposal," *Globe and Mail,* 14 September 1991, p. A1.
52. Ibid., p. A9; Fraser, "Contentious opting-out clause was late addition, strategist says," p. A4; Chantal Hébert, "Le cabinet reste divisé sur la proposition constitutionnelle," *Le Devoir,* 12 September 1991; Chantal Hébert, "Mulroney devra seul trouver un compromis: Pas de consensus au cabinet sur le projet constitutionnel," *Le Devoir,* 13 September 1991, pp. 1, 4.
53. Based on *Shaping Canada's Future Together* and "Proposal Highlights," *The Globe and Mail,* 25 September 1991, p. A1.
54. In the order of "compelling reasons" the need to entrench aboriginal rights to self-government is listed first followed by "Quebec's desire for recognition of its distinct nature." *Shaping Canada's Future Together,* p. vi.
55. Quoted in "Wilson calls economic plan ineffectual," *The Globe and Mail,* 15 July 1992, p. A4.
56. See Paul Gessell, "We're sitting on a constitutional time bomb," *Ottawa Citizen,* 9 November 1991, p. B1. Clark did, however, manage to meet with a number of groups.
57. Thomas J. Courchene, "The Economic Union and Other Aspects of the Federal Proposals," in D. Brown, R. Young and D. Herperger (eds.) *Constitutional Commentaries: An Assessment of the 1991 Federal Proposals* (Kingston: Institute of Intergovernmental Relations, Queen's University, 1992), p. 39.
58. Simpson, "Package filled with last-minute compromises," p. A5.
59. Ibid.
60. Ibid.
61. Susan Delacourt, "The buying: It doesn't totally fulfil the giant Canadian wish list — but it's a start," *The Globe and Mail,* 28 September 1991, pp. A1, A5.
62. Rhéal Séguin and Patricia Poirer, "Bourassa rejects economic plan," *The Globe and Mail,* 26 September 1991, pp. A1, A2.
63. Quoted in Carol Goar, "On unity, PM should swing open cabinet doors," *Toronto Star,* 11 July 1991, p. A21.
64. On the five public conferences see the the excellent analysis of David Milne, "Innovative Constitutional Processes," in *Canada: The State of the Federation 1992,* pp. 27-51.

III

Immediate Issues

7

Aboriginal Policy and Politics: The Charlottetown Accord and Beyond

J. Anthony Long and Katherine Beaty Chiste

En 1992, l'ordre du jour du dossier autochtone fut dominé par l'entente de Charlottetown. La participation des peuples indien, inuit et métis au processus de la réforme constitutionnelle aura atteint un degré sans précédent. Par ailleurs, si les leaders de toutes les organisations autochtones à l'échelle nationale endossèrent les dispositions de l'accord les concernant, on assista en revanche, au sein même des communautés indiennes, à un vaste mouvement de rejet à l'égard de l'entente.

L'échec de l'accord, le 26 octobre 1992, aura eu pour conséquence de perpétuer jusqu'à ce jour la situation ambigue des peuples autochtones au Canada. Néanmoins, le processus de négociations tripartite conjugué aux dispositions substantielles de l'accord, détermineront à la fois les demandes autochtones et la réponse des gouvernements. On peut d'ores et déjà prévoir une intensification des initiatives à caractère non-constitutionnel telles que les négociations autour des revendications territoriales et l'autonomie gouvernementale. Mais il est possible aussi qu'à défaut d'un cadre précis de référence, semblable à celui fourni par l'entente de Charlottetown, l'union sacrée des groupes autochtones du Canada ne fasse pas long feu. De fait, en l'absence d'une solution prochaine sur le plan constitutionnel, les communautés autochtones pourraient être amenées à exercer leur action en fonction d'abord de leurs aspirations, cultures et capacités spécifiques.

Dans ce contexte, la Commission royale sur les peuples autochtones s'avérera peut-être un facteur de cohésion pour l'ensemble des groupes autochtones. Plus que jamais, cette Commission — dont le mandat vise à une amélioration radicale des conditions de vie des Canadiens d'origine autochtone — apparaît-elle comme l'instrument de la dernière chance, compte tenu de l'échec patent, jusqu'à présent, de toutes les autres tentatives faites au regard de cette question.

During 1992, the aboriginal public policy agenda was dominated by the Charlottetown Accord. Aboriginal Peoples became involved in the process of constitutional reform on an unprecedented scale when they were given extensive opportunities to articulate their demands in both the public and constitutional forums.[1] Throughout the pre-Accord stage Aboriginal Peoples, as well as the political organizations representing them, formed an integral part of the public consultation process during the Renewal of Canada Conferences and the hearings of federal and provincial committees established to formulate recommendations on constitutional reform. Four national aboriginal organizations were funded to carry out a parallel consultation process with their respective memberships, so that the grass-roots opinions of Aboriginal Peoples would be reflected in the constitutional positions of organizations representing them. The Assembly of First Nations (AFN), the Native Council of Canada (NCC), the Métis National Council (MNC) and the Inuit Tapirisat of Canada (ITC) were allowed full participant status over the entire range of constitutional issues with the federal and provincial government delegations during the tripartite negotiations leading up to the Accord. In the end, the aboriginal political organizations involved in the negotiations became an active part of the "Yes" side during the referendum campaign.

On the governmental side, as the negotiations over the substance of the Accord developed, changes from previous positions on crucial aboriginal constitutional demands found expression in the final draft of the Accord. The shift in governmental positions was strongly endorsed by the Métis and the Inuit, and both groups looked forward to the type of constitutional recognition of their peoples and cultures that they had been seeking for over a decade. Within the status Indian community, however, major splits developed over the Accord. While negotiated and strongly endorsed by the leadership of the AFN, the agreement was vehemently denounced by a number of native women's associations and by many chiefs and band councils whose reserve communities have treaty relationships with the Canadian government. In the end, nearly two-thirds of the residents voting on these reserves rejected the Accord.

The defeat of the Accord on 26 October 1992 in effect reconfirmed the existing, albeit ambiguous, constitutional status of Aboriginal Peoples, leaving their basic position within the federal system unchanged. However, not only the outcome of the referendum but also the tripartite negotiating process and the substantive provisions of the Accord itself will leave their marks on future aboriginal demands as well as on federal and provincial approaches towards aboriginal policy. Moreover, the events of 1992 promise to influence significantly the future of politics both between and within the respective aboriginal communities.

THE CHARLOTTETOWN ACCORD: PROCESS AND SUBSTANCE

The failure of the Accord to achieve constitutional status has tended to overshadow the achievements made by Aboriginal Peoples in the process of constitutional reform and the implications those gains hold for the future of Aboriginal Peoples within the dynamics of Canadian federalism. From 12 March 1992 until the final agreement was concluded in August four national aboriginal organizations were afforded formal participant status over the entire gamut of constitutional issues. Even though their primary involvement in the negotiations occurred within the aboriginal working subgroup they were not precluded from participating in the dealings over the entire constitutional package. Although the aboriginal associations chose to participate only minimally on a number of the other constitutional issues under negotiation, the principle of full participation remained and aboriginal political organizations became integrated into executive federalism. Arguably, the elevation of the aboriginal organizations to the level of equal status within the tripartite negotiations finally afforded these groups the recognition they had previously fought so hard to achieve.

The incorporation of aboriginal political organizations into the model of executive federalism has been a gradual evolution from previous attempts to define a constitutional status for Aboriginal Peoples. This process has been influenced by the personalities and politics of sitting premiers, prime ministers and aboriginal leaders. The AFN, the NCC, the MNC and the ITC were originally invited to be representatives of their respective constituencies by Prime Minister Trudeau during the constitutional conferences from 1983 to 1987. Four years later, aboriginal leaders were invited to the Premiers' Conference at Whistler, B.C. in August 1991. The press, perhaps presaging future events, even declared Ovide Mercredi as Canada's "eleventh premier" following his election as National Chief of the AFN. Governments were sensitive to aboriginal demands for expanded participation in the constitutional revision process, particularly after the abortive Meech Lake episode. The ability of Aboriginal Peoples to influence constitutional change, as demonstrated by the Member of the Manitoba Legislative Assembly, Elijah Harper, and his supporters, was not lost on either federal or provincial politicians.

It is difficult to judge the full effect that the Charlottetown Accord process has had on the position of Aboriginal Peoples within federalism. The most obvious effect is that it elevated the benchmark for the role of aboriginal political organizations within the constitutional forum, at least if the constitutional revision process continues to be characterized by executive federalism. Whether aboriginal political associations will be invited to attend future premiers' or first ministers' meetings that focus on general public policy concerns depends upon the residual strength of the Charlottetown Accord process. It is possible that the participation achieved by Aboriginal People in 1992 will turn out to have been, for some time to come, a *sui generis* event. Such aboriginal participation in the first ministers' process, however, as Menno Boldt has argued, might serve to undermine the position of more sovereigntist First Nations, who see such participation as incorporating them within the constitutional framework of the Canadian state and thereby diminishing their claim of nationhood.[2]

Like Meech Lake, the Charlottetown Accord is now part of the constitutional history of Canada. While its relative place within that history will be decided by scholars in the future, it is important to consider what might have been for two significant reasons. First, the elements of the Accord intended for constitutional entrenchment as well as their associated political accords established a new baseline for future demands by aboriginal leaders at both the constitutional and legislative policy levels, whether aboriginal leaders act singly or in concert. It is likely, moreover, that the Accord will drive some of the future recommendations of the Royal Commission on Aboriginal Peoples, which endorsed the general thrust of the Accord's aboriginal provisions during the negotiation process.[3] And second, the Accord stands as an indicator of how far both the federal and provincial governments are capable of moving in their thinking about the place of aboriginal governments within the federal system. While it remains an open question whether the final federal and provincial positions represented a basic shift in principle or were rather a pragmatic, politically motivated response to the demands of aboriginal leaders or a combination of both, these positions were nevertheless crystallized in the Accord. An overview of some of the major features of the Accord will illustrate the extent of this movement.

The elements of the Charlottetown Accord that held the greatest potential impact for the place of aboriginal governments within the Canadian federal scheme were the recognition of the "inherent right of self-government within Canada" for Aboriginal Peoples, the description of aboriginal governments as a third order of government, the future relationship of those governments to the *Charter of Rights and Freedoms* and the inclusion of the Métis under section 91(24) of the *Constitution Act, 1867*.

Aboriginal leaders had fought vigorously since the constitutional conferences of the 1980s for constitutional recognition of their inherent right of self-government — a battle that has until recently been resisted with equal vigor by most provincial premiers. Paragraph 41 of the August 1992 *Consensus Report on the Constitution* provided that the inherent right of self-government within Canada should be placed in section 35.1 of the *Constitution Act, 1982*. Furthermore, the inherent right of self-government should be interpreted within the context of aboriginal self-government as a third order of government within

Canada. While the concept of inherency attempted to acknowledge the historical self-governing status of Aboriginal Peoples, the qualifying phase "within Canada" effectively precluded recognition of that status outside the Canadian constitutional framework, thus delegitimizing any claim to sovereignty in the international sense by aboriginal governments. That is, any independent legal status for aboriginal societies and their governments outside the jurisdiction of Canada was rejected. Still, the provision would have had the effect of establishing a "stand-alone" constitutional footing for aboriginal government thus elevating it from its current legislative base, as exemplified by the band government provisions of the *Indian Act*.

The authority of aboriginal governments as a third order of government was to be described in the constitution, but not defined. Essentially, paragraph 45 provided that definitions of self-government with respect to jurisdiction, lands and resources, and economic and fiscal arrangements would emerge through negotiations among the federal government, provincial governments and aboriginal leaders. The process and parameters of these negotiations would have been spelled out in a political accord to be developed subsequently. Should the respective parties have failed to reach self-government agreements, the Accord provided that judicial definition of the right of self-government could occur after a five-year period. Delaying the justiciability of the right for five years, however, would not have made the right of self-government "contingent" on the results of the negotiations. A "contingent" right had been vigorously opposed by aboriginal leaders not only during the Charlottetown negotiations but also during the 1980s FMCs when several provinces insisted that they would have to see the details of aboriginal self-government fleshed out before they would agree to give it constitutional status. Once negotiations over the specifics of aboriginal governments had been completed, paragraph 45 provided that they would acquire constitutional status as "treaties" protected by section 35 of the *Constitution Act, 1982*.

While ultimately the exact nature of aboriginal governments as a third order of government within Canadian federalism would not have been known until the various self-government agreements had been finalized or judicial definition of the right to self-government had occurred, the Accord provided some general parameters. Paragraph 41 stipulated that a contextual statement be inserted in the constitution, specifying that the right of self-government includes the authority of aboriginal governments: "(a) to safeguard and develop their languages, cultures, economies, identities, institutions and traditions; and (b) to develop, maintain and strengthen their relationship with their lands, waters and environment so as to determine and control their development as peoples according to their own values and priorities and ensure the integrity of their societies." Paragraph 47 provided that a constitutional provision would ensure that federal and provincial laws applied until they were displaced by the laws of aboriginal governments. Also, as Sanders suggests, paragraph 41 indicated that aboriginal legislative powers would overlap with federal and provincial ones and that in case of conflict the laws of aboriginal governments would have paramountcy over the laws of both other orders of governments.[4] As to the role of aboriginal governments in future constitutional reform, paragraph 60 provided that there should be aboriginal consent to future constitutional changes that directly affect Aboriginal Peoples. This represented a substantial change from the earlier constitutional conferences on aboriginal rights which, organized under section 37 of the *Constitution Act, 1982* were essentially first ministers' conferences to which the representatives of Aboriginal Peoples were invited to discuss constitutional matters that affected them. Moreover, the reference in paragraph 60 is to aboriginal consent only, not to aboriginal governments, leaving open the question of what mechanism would be used to express that consent. The right of aboriginal governments to participate in constitutional negotiations on a level with the federal and provincial governments in the future was thus left problematic in the Accord.

On the restrictive side, paragraph 47 would have required that laws passed by aboriginal governments could not be inconsistent with those laws that are essential to "the preservation of peace, order and good government in Canada." This provision, along with paragraph 44's statement that the constitutional provision on inherency and the commitment to negotiate land claims should not create new aboriginal rights to land, was put in to placate provincial concerns, in particular that of Quebec, over the protection of provincial territorial integrity.

Another limitation on the authority of aboriginal governments rested on the application to them of the *Charter of Rights and Freedoms*. The issue of Charter exclusion was one of the most heated and divisive issues within the native community during the Accord negotiations. Indian leaders have argued consistently since the late 1970s that First Nation governments should not be subject to the unqualified application of the Charter. Although often cast in legal terms, this argument rests on cultural grounds. Indian leaders argue that the belief systems and many of the governance processes of Indian societies are fundamentally antithetical to the Western liberal ideas that Indian leaders believe underlie the Charter; therefore, Indian societies and cultures cannot survive and traditional forms of governance, such as matriarchal or patriarchal kinship forms, cannot be revitalized under such an ideological regime.[5] On the opposite side of the issue, the Native Women's Association of Canada (NWAC), claiming to represent a large constituency of aboriginal women, argued that First Nation governments must be subject to the Charter.[6] In particular, NWAC leadership argued that the equality guarantee in section 15 is a universal human right which should not be violated by aboriginal governments. Failing this, native women will continue to face gender discrimination from male-dominated band councils by being denied an equal voice in community affairs and will have little protection against oppression and family violence in their communities.

The division between the NWAC and the AFN has its roots in what the NWAC leaders conceive to be the AFN's opposition to their efforts to end sexual discrimination as evidenced by the AFN's opposition to Bill C-31 as an unwarranted intrusion on band government authority. Bill C-31, mandated by the equality provision of the Charter, was enacted into law in 1985. The Bill contained several major provisions.[7] First, it removed sex discrimination clauses from the *Indian Act*. Second, it abolished the concept of enfranchisement. Third, it provided for the restoration of Indian status and band membership to persons who had lost them because of provisions in the *Indian Act*. And finally, it enabled Indian bands to establish their own membership codes, presumabbly constituting a major step in their evolution towards self-government. The AFN leadership's opposition at the time to Bill C-31 left a legacy of mistrust on the part of many aboriginal women. During the course of the Charlottetown Accord process, the NWAC, claiming that the AFN does not speak for the interests of Indian women, launched separate legal actions in the Federal Court of Canada, initially to achieve participant status in the constitutional negotiations over aboriginal self-government and later to get the referendum declared invalid. Given the Accord's defeat, it remains to be seen if the NWAC argument for participant status alongside the other national aboriginal political associations will be resurrected in any future round of constitutional negotiations.

In the final analysis, the Accord went a considerable distance in meeting the demands of the AFN. Section 25 of the *Constitution Act, 1982* would have been buttressed by a paragraph to "ensure that nothing in the Charter abrogates or derogates from the Aboriginal, treaty or other rights of Aboriginal peoples, and in particular any rights or freedoms relating to the exercise of their languages, cultures or traditions." This section, in combination with section 24 of the Draft Legal Text, which would have limited the democratic rights provisions of the Charter to federal and provincial legislative assemblies rather than to legislative assemblies in general, arguably could have permitted traditional forms of aboriginal government that do not conform with the democratic or other rights guaranteed in the Charter. And last, paragraph 43 would have allowed aboriginal governments access to the opt-out provisions in section 33 of the Charter, previously available only to federal and provincial governments. The net effect of these provisions is that as a third order of government aboriginal governments would have enjoyed a unique status in relationship to the Charter. That is, aboriginal governments would have had the opportunity to depart from the Canadian constitutional tradition of democratic rights and representative government, creating the potential for a significant anomoly within the structure of Canadian federalism.

Finally, paragraph 54 of the Accord suggested that a new provision be added to the *Constitution Act, 1867* to ensure that section 91(24) which gives the federal government authority over "Indians and Lands reserved for the Indians" would apply to all three aboriginal groups, in effect bringing the generally landless Métis under federal jurisdiction along with the Indians and Inuit. This provision would have gone a long way towards satisfying Métis demands to be put on a legal par with Indians and Inuit, and eliminating their ambivalent historic legal and political status. Moreover, it would have opened the door for Métis claims to federal financial resources as well as federal participation in dealing with Métis land claims. This was certainly an important consideration for the Métis in light of paragraph 50 which, through a separate political accord, would have committed the federal and provincial governments to the principle of providing the governments of Aboriginal Peoples with fiscal and other resources, such as land. Moreover, paragraph 49 provided that all Aboriginal Peoples should have access to those aboriginal and treaty rights recognized and affirmed in section 35 of the *Constitution Act, 1982* that apply to them, respectively. However, while endorsing the general idea of incorporating the Métis under section 91(24), the Accord recognized the unique status of the Métis settlements in Alberta; paragraph 55 called for a constitutional amendment to safeguard the legislative authority of the Alberta government for Métis and Métis Settlement Lands.

THE FAILURE OF THE ACCORD: THE ABORIGINAL REACTION

The leaders of the national aboriginal associations that had participated in the negotiation process leading up to the Accord reacted with disappointment and frustration to its rejection, even though post-referendum polls revealed that over 60 percent of Canadians agreed with the constitutional changes proposed for Aboriginal Peoples.[8] Ron George, head of the NCC, angrily denounced non-aboriginal Canadians for betraying Aboriginal Peoples by refusing to recognize their demands for a just place within Canadian society. He rejected the status quo as acceptable, and added, "I'd like to see those people who are celebrating the No victory come and see what it's like to live on the streets."[9] Ovide Mercredi, Grand Chief of the AFN, reacted to the Accord's defeat by promising a "quiet revolution" among Indian peoples and a "campaign of creative disobedience" to challenge federal and provincial laws.[10] The quiet revolution would see Indian peoples taking control of their affairs by passing their own laws in areas such as child welfare, education, gambling and economic development. This action would flow from the inherent right of Indians of self-government which, according to Mercredi, was given *de facto* recognition by the federal and provincial governments during the negotiations over the Charlottetown

Accord.[11] Rosemarie Kuptana, President of the Inuit Tapirisat, whose constituency overwhelmingly supported the Accord, expressed the hope that self-government provisions would not die with the Accord.[12] Likewise, Yvon Dumont, the leader of the MNC, while admitting that the Accord's failure signified a major setback for the Métis, called on the federal and provincial governments to maintain their political will and implement the Métis Nation Accord, negotiated as part of the Charlottetown package.[13] This political accord committed governments to negotiate self-rule agreements for the Métis, the transfer and ownership of lands and resources and cost-sharing agreements. Failing this, Dumont indicated that the Métis would accelerate a huge land claim in the Manitoba courts, thus using the judicial route to force governments to talk to them.

While the disappointment over the failure of the Accord expressed by the Métis and Inuit leadership appeared to mirror the views of their constituents, the same could not necessarily be said for Mercredi's reaction. Referendum results indicated that status Indians voting at more than 750 polling stations on reserves across Canada rejected the Accord by nearly a two-thirds margin.[14] The AFN, unlike the other national aboriginal associations, had requested that its constituents be polled separately. The extent to which "off-reserve" Indian voters may have mirrored the "on-reserve" position cannot be ascertained, because the referendum results were not broken down to reveal the off-reserve vote. However, the self-proclaimed representative of urban Indians, the NCC, certainly did endorse the Accord.

The rejection of the Charlottetown Accord by a significant segment of the status Indian community was not a complete surprise. A number of events that occurred during the previous months provided clear warning signals that the agreement was in trouble. In May, the Indian Association of Alberta withdrew its support from the AFN, objecting to provincial involvement in constitutional discussions, particularly over treaty rights. Many of the chiefs in Alberta wanted to develop their own constitutional positions and establish a bilateral process with the federal government. In August, Mohawk leader Billy Two Rivers publicly disagreed with Mercredi, making it clear that the AFN did not represent Mohawk interests. In a full page advertisement in *The Globe and Mail* on 24 September, chiefs from reserves in the Treaty 6 and Treaty 7 areas disassociated themselves from the position of the AFN and stated that they would not support the unity package nor would they participate in the ratifying process.[15] Perhaps the greatest indicator of status Indian feelings towards the Accord occurred in mid-October, when nearly 400 Indian leaders from across Canada failed to endorse the constitutional package at an AFN general meeting on the Squamish reserve in North Vancouver. Finally, the chiefs and councils on several reserves, including the Mohawks in the east and the Bloods of southern Alberta refused to allow enumerators to cross their reserve boundaries or set up polling stations.

Reserve residents who wanted to participate in the referendum had to go to neighbouring non-Indian communities to be enumerated and vote. As Chief Peter Yellowquill of Manitoba commented, "If they wish to vote, they can vote in Canada."[16]

The split that occurred within the status Indian community over the Charlottetown Accord reflected both long-standing divisions and tensions as well as circumstances unique to the process itself. In the first place, the difference between the AFN and the NWAC over application of the Charter to aboriginal governments undoubtedly resulted in some Indian women voting against the Accord. It is difficult to tell just how many voted negatively, because some aboriginal women's groups supported the Accord as it stood, including the Inuit Women's Association of Canada, the Métis National Council of Women and the Ontario Native Women's Association. In the second place, the rift between some of the leaders of treaty-based Indian reserves and the leadership of the AFN took a significant amount of Indian support away from the Accord. The opposition of treaty-based Indian leadership to the Accord consisted of several interrelated arguments. In its basic form, this position held that constitutional recognition of the inherent right of self-government proposed in the Accord incorrectly implied that the right was created by the Canadian state. Instead, many treaty Indians hold that the inherent right to self-government is already possessed by First Nations and was recognized in the treaties which they argue were negotiated on a "nation to nation" basis and thus have the legal status of international agreements. Following this, some treaty-based Indian leaders claimed that since treaties are in essence international agreements, any negotiations concerning the content of and rights under treaties must be conducted exclusively on a bilateral nation-to-nation basis. Consequently, they refused to be part of a tripartite process of treaty negotiation that involved the provinces. At another level, they objected to the inclusion of the Métis under section 91(24). This objection was based on the belief that inclusion of the Métis would intrude upon the traditional trust obligation of the Crown to status Indians grounded in this section. In a more pragmatic vein, these Indian leaders envisaged a siphoning off of federal financial resources to other aboriginal groups and a consequent dwindling piece of the financial pie for status Indians.

Finally, not only the vagueness of a number of the aboriginal provisions of the unity package, but also the presence of political accords leading to unspecified future negotiations on such critical matters as the financing of aboriginal governments left many Indian voters unsure as to what they were voting upon. The legacy of distrust that has characterized Indian-government relationships in Canada for decades inhibited many Indians from giving the federal and provincial governments the benefit of the doubt. Moreover, it became apparent after the referendum that the leadership of the AFN had not done an effective job of either explaining or selling the Accord to the grass-roots Indian community.

The divisions within the Indian community that occurred over the Accord are symptomatic of a larger problem that confronts both First Nations and governments in their relationship with each other. Despite the AFN being accepted by the federal and provincial governments as representative of status Indians on constitutional matters, that association, like its predecessor the National Indian Brotherhood, has never enjoyed hegemony over First Nations. First Nations in Canada exhibit a great deal of cultural diversity, significant differences in levels of economic development, varying ideological stances and differing legal relationships with the Canadian state. Furthermore, the leadership of the AFN is hardly immune to the mistrust and hostility facing many elected politicians at all levels of Canadian government. The experience of the status Indian community with the Charlottetown Accord process may force both governments and Indian peoples to rethink how they want to approach the question of Indian participation in future constitutional discussions. The divisions within the status Indian community underscore a larger problem that governments have in developing aboriginal policy at the constitutional level, namely the difficulty of constructing provisions that encompass the entire aboriginal community in general while at the same time accommodating the historical differences between, and present aspirations unique to Indians, Métis and Inuit.

In retrospect, the Accord offered a mixture of substance and promises to Aboriginal Peoples. It is unfortunate that the agenda for aboriginal constitutional reform was linked so closely to the Quebec agenda. When the Assembly of First Nations released its report on the Accord package — after six months of hearings — one of the major concerns was the "artificial deadlines" imposed by Quebec. Ovide Mercredi observed that the fast-paced process was not designed to take care and caution with constitutional reform.[17] In fact, the speed and pressure of the negotiations into which Aboriginal Peoples were drawn were antithetical to the consensual and thoughtful nature of many aboriginal political traditions. Given more time, Aboriginal Peoples might have been able to sort out the differences both between and within their respective communities and emerge with accommodating and meaningful constitutional reform.

LOOKING TO THE FUTURE

Both aboriginal governments and the federal and provincial governments face challenges as they adjust to the reality of finding non-constitutional solutions to the pressing social and economic needs of Aboriginal Peoples. While constitutional negotiations on aboriginal issues are likely to be reinitiated at some future date, governments are gun-shy about restarting any constitutional reform process in the immediate future, given the message sent by the Canadian electorate in its decisive rejection of the Accord that it was fed up with constitutional haggling and that governments should redirect their attention to economic and other concerns.

Within the aboriginal community, this adjustment will vary with the level of political organization. The rejection of the Accord will probably necessitate the greatest adjustment on the part of aboriginal political associations. These groups are confronted with problems not only of maintaining organizational momentum but also of retaining their constituencies as members of those constituencies seek to find individual remedies for their specific needs. In March 1993, the AFN released a draft version of a strategic plan for 1993-94.[18] This strategic plan was a response to a Chiefs-in-Assembly Resolution adopted by the AFN in November 1992 that directed the AFN to review its structure, role, mandates and priorities. This draft plan is to be reviewed by the AFN membership at a future date. In essence the plan seeks to retain the original mandate of the AFN, while suggesting, among other things, reforms in the area of internal procedures; the development of a more formalized and focused bilateral process between the AFN and the government of Canada; the development and operation of national institutions such as a First Nations Land Registry, a National Citizenship Registry and a network of First Nation financial institutions; as well as the extension of AFN activities in the international forum through a strengthened international unit.

It remains uncertain if the AFN's strategy proposal can surmount the centrifugal forces within its membership. The sovereignist-oriented First Nations, exemplified by the Mohawks, have made it clear that only their own leadership represents them. Moreover, the legacy of perceived "backroom" negotiations by Mercredi and his advisors over the Charlottetown Accord will continue to affect the representational legitimacy of the AFN with a number of chiefs. Also, in April 1993 a group of treaty chiefs meeting on the Tsuu T'ina reserve near Calgary announced the formation of the United Treaty First Nations Council (UTFNC), declaring that they were dissatisfied with the manner in which they were represented by the AFN.[19] The focus of the UTFNC will be on treaty rights, with a mandate to speak for treaty Indians in any bilateral treaty discussions with the Crown.

In late March 1993, the Métis National Council formalized and staffed a new internal governing structure in order for the leadership to serve their constituents more effectively as well as to better represent them to departments of other governments.[20] The overall result is the creation of an umbrella type of Métis First Nation government that transcends provincial boundaries. At the apex of the new governing body is the Métis Nation Cabinet, consisting of seven portfolios ranging from Justice and Social Development to Environment and Northern Development. The Cabinet is headed by the president, Gerald Morin, who is also Minister of National Affairs responsible, among other things, for developing and implementing a national political strategy relating to intergovernmental affairs. A Métis National Council Secretariat and a Métis Nations Secretariat will complete the government organization. The effectiveness of this new structural approach in articulating and representing Métis interests remains to be seen; in particular how this governmental level might relate to the Alberta Métis Settlements, which recently concluded agreements with the Alberta government involving their land base, a form of self-government and economic development matters.

In contrast to the AFN and MNC, the Native Council of Canada does not appear to be eager to begin any major organizational reforms but rather will focus on defining the relationships it has with other organizations such as the AFN and the NWAC, as well as its recent alliances with several non-Aboriginal organizations and lobby groups. Moreover, the NCC is a leading participant in governmental negotiations aimed at maintaining the momentum gained during the Charlottetown process. One principal outcome of these efforts was a meeting of federal, provincial and territorial ministers and senior officials, with representatives of the national aboriginal organizations, which took place in Inuvik in July 1993. A working group from that meeting is scheduled to report to the annual premiers' conference to be held in August 1993 in Nova Scotia, where aboriginal issues have been placed on the agenda.

Formal organizational change is also less urgent for the Inuit. Representing the least numerous of Canada's Aboriginal Peoples, their leadership is a small and flexible group which moves between various organizations as circumstances warrant. With Canadian constitutional reform on hold the ITC is likely to refocus on its international role as a stakeholder in the Arctic on such issues as the moratorium on whaling. Moreover, the preparations for governance of the new Territory of Nunavut will take on increasing urgency as the millenium approaches.

Regardless of organizational change and mandate redefinition, the bottom line for aboriginal political associations is financial support, and the prospect of continued financial support related to their role in the constitutional process is not promising. The budget cutting strategies of both the federal and provincial governments will undoubtedly affect all First Nations' governments and other aboriginal organizations, leaving levels of financial support emanating from these sources unpredictable. Even the ITC, which probably faces the most secure future of any aboriginal political association, must worry whether the federal government can come up with the estimated one billion to cover the cost of establishing Nunavut.

At the individual community and tribal group level, most First Nations will likely resume their previous efforts to achieve a greater degree of self-government, resolve land claims and move forward with economic development, efforts that were either put on hold or pushed to the background during the Charlottetown Accord process. First, treaty First Nations will continue to push for revitalization of treaties, not only from the viewpoint of enforcing current Crown obligations, but also as a base for the evolution of future Indian-Crown relationships. Second, the absence of a constitutional option for self-government is likely to accelerate the entry of still more Indian bands, both non-treaty and treaty-based, into the federal Department of Indian Affairs "Alternative Funding Arrangement" initiative and the negotiated community-based self-government process, designed to allow Indian communities a legislative base for self-government outside the *Indian Act*. Both of these initiatives are major instruments for achieving the federal policy goal of devolution. This development will follow a trend that has been occurring for a number of years. While in 1988-89 only 3.7 percent of Indian bands were participating in the Alternative Funding Arrangement program, by 1991-92 this figure had increased to over 37 percent.[21] Similarly, the interest expressed in the community-based negotiations has increased. Currently, 15 Indian communities including the Gitksan Nation, the Siksika Nation and the Kahnawake Mohawk Nation have signed framework agreements within which substantive negotiations over jurisdiction and Indian government political structures will take place.[22]

Third, Indian bands, both individually and collectively, will undoubtedly increase pressure in both the political and judicial forums for the resolution of specific and comprehensive land claims. Indians may find a more receptive audience for their claims in the political forum since the federal government has moved to an accelerated claims process and provinces appear more willing to compromise. The government of British Columbia, for example, has reversed the province's historical opposition to the concept of aboriginal title by withdrawing from the position that a blanket extinguishment of aboriginal rights occurred throughout British Columbia. Moreover the province became involved in the British Columbia Claims Task Force and has now appointed its representative to the British Columbia Treaty Commission, an arms-length agency established from a recommendation of the Task Force. A recent (June 1993) British Columbia Court of Appeal decision in the Gitksan/Wet'suwet'en land claim appeared to encourage this kind of development, criticizing the Gitksan and Wet'suwet'en for taking an "all or nothing" approach and calling instead for negotiation and "co-existence."[23]

Fourth, a number of the more entrepreneurially oriented bands will push Indian Affairs to develop new legislation in the areas of band taxation, financial control and land and resource development to escape the strictures of the *Indian Act*. A prominent example of this type of legislation is the *First Nations Chartered Lands Act* now being developed by chiefs from several of these kinds of bands sitting on a board funded by Indian Affairs. All of these initiatives promise to be highly controversial and divisive, since many Indian leaders view them as threats to First Nations' treaty rights, bilateral relationships with the federal government and communal land bases.[24] Finally, some of the more adventuresome band governments will attempt to enter the financially lucrative gambling industry by establishing casinos and installing other gambling devices on their reserves. Bands in Quebec, New Brunswick, Manitoba and Saskatchewan have already put forward proposals to the respective provincial governments for the establishment of Indian gaming commissions. The provinces, however, have remained cool to such intrusion on their perceived jurisdiction, and Manitoba and Saskatchewan have authorized police action to stop the bands that have established gambling casinos on their reserves without provincial authorization.

The demise of the Charlottetown Accord will have the greatest effect at the community level on the Métis. Métis leaders were hopeful that their peoples would be incorporated under section 91(24) *Constitution Act, 1867* and that their communities would be subsumed under federal financial responsibility. They also looked forward to the finalization of the Métis Nation Accord, which would have committed the federal government and the governments of Ontario, Manitoba, Saskatchewan, Alberta, British Columbia and the Northwest Territories to negotiate agreements in the areas of self-government, lands and resources and cost-sharing arrangements for the Métis, among other things. However, both the federal government and the provinces appear to take the position that both the principle of equal footing for all aboriginal peoples and the Métis Nation Accord died with the Charlottetown Accord.

The microcircumstances of various Métis communities differ, and some face a more favourable geopolitical environment than do others. The eight Alberta Métis settlements, for example, are currently undergoing a devolution of authority from the province overseen by the Métis Settlements Transition Commission. Having reached agreement with the province in 1991 for $310 million for land settlement, their opportunities for self-determination at the community level are favourable. In the Northwest Territories, where land claims are being negotiated region by region, the Métis have traditionally allied themselves with Indians in the negotiations process and can expect a mutual increase in community autonomy and control of resources. In Manitoba, a lawsuit is before the courts in which Manitoba Métis are seeking constitutional recognition of their rights, including those to land lost a century ago; however, this case has been dragging on since the early 1980s. A number of non-status Indians, formerly grouped with the Métis for policy purposes, have also regained status as registered Indians under the provisions of Bill C-31, although reacquired status does not translate automatically into socio-economic advantage nor to participation in an established Indian community. In the end, Métis aspirations to self-government as a "Nation" are linked to their acquisition of a community land base, and in many cases this seems a remote possibility.

The Inuit, meanwhile, are least affected at the community level since the new Territory of Nunavut fits within the current federal system and constitutional amendment is not necessary to achieve Inuit aspirations. Two votes were held in 1992 on the Inuit land claim settlement which would establish Nunavut. In May, the proposal was narrowly passed by voters in the Northwest Territories, although opposition to the deal was strong among some western Arctic communities. In the west there was concern both about the location of the territorial boundary and about the demographic changes to government in the west which territorial division would bring. In November, an Inuit vote on ratification of the agreement passed overwhelmingly, and the territory of Nunavut is scheduled to be formally established in 1999. It has been estimated that 1,000 new jobs will be created to administer the government of Nunavut, and in preparation a non-profit Inuit agency is conducting an experimental management training course by satellite to reach students in the remote communities.[25]

The defeat of the Accord has eliminated, at least for the near future, the constitutionally based third order of aboriginal government upon which the federal and provincial governments were predicating their future relationships. On the federal level, it is unrealistic to expect anything beyond incremental tinkering with existing policies and programs until after the next federal election. Moreover, it is unlikely that the Department of Indian Affairs and Northern Development (DIAND) will attempt any major reformulation of its relationship to Aboriginal Peoples until the recommendations of the Royal Commission on Aboriginal Peoples, now expected in l995, can be reviewed and incorporated into policy. Until then, federal policy will continue to reflect the basic principles of Prime Minister Mulroney's Native Agenda, announced in September 1990.[26] Under this statement, the federal government committed itself to addressing issues arising from social and economic conditions on reserves, the relationship between Indians and government, land claims and the place of Aboriginal Peoples within Canada. Apart from seeking a constitutional basis for aboriginal government, the federal government has pursued this agenda through the instruments of devolution, the settlement of specific and comprehensive land claims[27] and the shifting of an increasing level of responsibility for aboriginal programs and services to other federal departments such as Justice, Employment and Immigration, National Health and Welfare and the Solicitor General.[28]

The commitment of the federal government to the native agenda resulted in a number of organizational changes made to DIAND in 1992.[29] The major reorganization occurred at the regional level, where the traditional regional delivery function has been replaced by a funding service approach and by the addition of an explicit intergovernmental affairs role. The shift from service delivery to funding service at the regional level follows DIAND's emphasis on devolution, with the result that the lion's share of program delivery formerly done by DIAND now will be carried out at the band level. The creation of intergovernmental affairs offices at the regional level reflected both an incremental approach by the federal government to developing a more government-to-government oriented relationship with First Nations as well as the anticipation that the Charlottetown Accord would pass and that DIAND would be intricately involved with not only band governments, but also with the provinces in developing aboriginal governments as a third order of government. With the rejection of the Accord, the intergovernmental affairs role is likely to evolve on an incremental, pragmatically oriented basis.

The devolution policy also underpins a continuing emphasis on the downsizing of DIAND. In a November 1992 interview, Indian Affairs Minister Tom Siddon reiterated the federal government's commitment to reducing the department and eliminating its historic policy of paternalism.[30] Moreover, it is likely that the trend of shifting aspects of its responsibilities to other federal departments and the provinces picking up still other functions will continue as aboriginal governments develop more capacity to interact directly with other levels of government. The failure of the Accord is likely to intensify the pressure on provinces to become more involved in aboriginal policy and programs, continuing a trend that has been in existence for some time. This is somewhat ironic, because provincial involvement in the negotiations over the Accord as well as in its implementation, had it passed, constituted a significant source of opposition to the Accord by treaty-based Indians.

Although circumstances vary among provinces with respect to their relationships with Aboriginal Peoples, the pressure for greater provincial activity in aboriginal policy and programs is likely to occur on several closely related fronts. First, the devolution policy of the federal government aimed at providing more control over finances and service delivery at the community level is forcing bands to develop arrangements with the provinces for the delivery of social and educational services, among others. Second, provinces will have to respond to the demands of band governments for more authority in areas of provincial jurisdiction such as policing, corrections and child welfare, either under community-based self-government negotiations or through separate agreements with the provinces. In the case of the Métis, provinces will face pressure to develop structures that allow for community level self-control. The Saskatchewan government, for example, has recently signed an agreement with the Métis Society of Saskatchewan to work together on social and economic issues.[31] Third, provinces will have to come up with creative ways to deal with the growing number of urban Aboriginal People, who draw heavily on provincial welfare resources and municipal government infrastructures and have little voice in either municipal or their native community governments. And finally, provinces will be expected to move ahead on both specific and comprehensive land claim negotiations, including the establishment of new mechanisms for negotiations, where necessary.

Faced with the necessity of stringent budget cuts over the next several years, provinces will be forced to take a cautious approach towards enlarging their policymaking role in aboriginal matters and devoting increased financial and other resources to this area. Their most likely course of action will be to assess agreements already in place or committed to before entering into new ones that require additional financial resources. Provincial monies allocated to programs dealing with native alcohol and drug abuse, native friendship centres and education, among others, may suffer cutbacks. Moreover, outside participation in community-based self-government negotiations or self-government arrangements tied to land claims, provinces are likely to restrict negotiations over the transfer of authority with First Nations to existing political accords such as the Ontario "Statement of Political Relationship" signed in August 1991, and the recently agreed upon memorandum of understanding between the Grand Council of Treaty No. 8 and the Alberta government, a process-type agreement for the discussion of issues of mutual concern. Unfortunately, whatever political goodwill developed between the provinces and Aboriginal Peoples during the Charlottetown Accord process may be lost on the grounds of financial expediency.

Without question, the spotlight within the aboriginal policymaking arena over the next year will be focused on the Royal Commission on Aboriginal Peoples. Established in August 1991, the Commission was originally scheduled to make its report in 1994, although the report is now likely to be delayed until sometime in 1995. The Commission was given a mandate to examine a broad range of issues concerning Aboriginal Peoples and furnished with a generous budget. In fact, the Commission may turn out to be one of the most costly of any royal commission; early estimates suggest $50 million will be required to cover its costs.[32] The first two rounds of public hearings were held in 1992, described by the Commission respectively as the "listening phase" and the "discussion phase" of its consultations. Testimony during the first phase crystallized around anger and frustration about the basic relationship between Aboriginal and non-Aboriginal People in Canada.[33] Fundamental concerns expressed included increasing the autonomy and self-sufficiency of Aboriginal Peoples, maintaining a strong sense of aboriginal identity and improving the living conditions of individuals in aboriginal communities.[34] As the Commission went into the second phase of hearings in October, it sought to focus the dialogue around four "touchstones for change," issues that had been raised repeatedly by its witnesses: a new relationship between Aboriginal and non-Aboriginal People, self-determination for Aboriginal Peoples within Canada through self-government, economic self-sufficiency for Aboriginal peoples and personal and collective healing for Aboriginal People and communities.[35] The third and fourth phases of hearings, scheduled for 1993, were intended to identify solutions leading to "lasting change" in the four touchstone areas.[36]

In 1992, the Commission made an impressive effort to canvass aboriginal opinions, holding hearings in 72 communities across the country and commissioning $8 million worth of research; yet its work has already come under harsh criticism. In February the commissioners inserted themselves into the debate over the Charlottetown Accord by issuing a position paper listing the criteria they felt a constitutional amendment on self-government should meet. While Indian representatives declined to comment on the paper, Inuit and Métis leaders responded with anger, accusing the Commission of arrogantly meddling and overstepping its mandate.[37] The co-chairs, René Dussault and Georges Erasmus, defended their action as an attempt to "smooth the path" of constitutional reform,[38] but the potential for political entanglements was already apparent. The Commission has also been attacked for ignoring the voices of aboriginal women, for failing to identify concrete solutions to well-known problems and for tiptoeing around the question of government accountability.

With the failure of the Charlottetown Accord the day before the second round of hearings commenced, the Commission's work has come under even greater scrutiny and pressure to produce results. The problems the Commission faces in meeting those expectations were brought to the forefront in April 1993 when Commissioner Allan Blakeney suddenly resigned, quoted as saying that the Commission was still settling for statements of generalities rather than moving to come up with concrete solutions to aboriginal problems.[39] How a task force of seven — despite its extensive resources — is to come up with answers that will not only satisfy the diverse aboriginal constituency but will be capable of being acted upon by governments remains an open question. It may be that the contextual focus provided by the aboriginal sections of the Charlottetown Accord will make some of the obstacles faced by the Commission surmountable. On the other hand, the Commission may have to distance itself from those elements of the Accord that proved to be unacceptable to segments of the aboriginal community.

In retrospect, the year 1992 had the potential of being a major watershed in the history of Aboriginal Peoples in Canada. A combination of forces and events occurred that resulted in a constitutional proposal that went a long way to meeting the demands that many aboriginal leaders had been making since the early 1970s. While the Charlottetown Accord was rejected by a segment of the status Indian community, its failure during the 26 October 1992 referendum was due to factors within the Canadian electorate largely beyond the control of aboriginal leaders. The challenge now facing the Canadian federation is accommodating the demands of Aboriginal Peoples through legislative and administrative solutions until Canadians are willing to accept a resurrection of the constitutional reform process.

NOTES

1. Section 35.2 of the *Constitution Act, 1982* identifies Aboriginal Peoples in Canada as the Indian, Métis and Inuit. Indians have been traditionally divided into three groups, status, non-status and treaty Indians. A status Indian is a person registered or entitled to be registered as an Indian for purposes of the *Indian Act*. Non-status Indians are those persons of Indian ancestry and cultural affiliation who have lost their right to be registered under the *Indian Act*. Non-status Indians do not have a distinct constitutional standing, but are grouped with the Métis for jurisdictional and public policy purposes. Since 1985, however, over 90,000 non-status Indians have been reinstated as status Indians under the provisions of Bill C-31. Treaty Indians are those who are registered members of, or who can prove descent from, a band that signed a treaty. Most status Indians are treaty Indians, except those living in areas not covered by treaties, such as most of British Columbia. The Métis are people of mixed Indian and non-Indian ancestry. The term Métis originally referred to people of mixed blood living on the prairies, but Statistics Canada now includes in the category of Métis all people living in any part of Canada who claim mixed Indian and non-Indian ancestry. Finally, the Inuit are those Aboriginal People who inhabit the Northwest Territories and northern parts of Quebec and Labrador. In 1939, they were brought under the jurisdiction and responsibilility of the federal government in a Supreme Court decision.

   The term "First Nations" is now commonly used by Indian leaders to identify their societies and to emphasize their distinctiveness from the English and French founding nations. The term, however, is conceptually vague because it is used in both a legal and cultural sense by treaty and non-treaty Indians. The Métis also refer to themselves as a "nation" on a more general cultural level. In this chapter, however, "First Nations" will only refer to Indian societies.

2. Menno Boldt, *Surviving as Indians* (Toronto: University of Toronto Press, 1993), pp. 94-108.

3. Royal Commission on Aboriginal Peoples, *The Right of Aboriginal Self-Government and the Constitution: A Commentary* (Ottawa: Royal Commission on Aboriginal Peoples, 13 February 1992).

4. Douglas Sanders, "Aboriginal Self-Government: Elements of the Accord," *Network on the Constitution*, Analysis no. 4, 2.

5. The Assembly of First Nations, "Resolution Adopted at the Special Chiefs Assembly on the Constitution Resolution," Ottawa, 23 April 1992, no. 6/92 and Assembly of First Nations, "Restoring the Path, Renewing our Nations: A First Nations' Guide to the Charlottetown Agreement," Ottawa, 1992.

6. Native Women's Association of Canada, "Statement on the Canada Package," Ottawa, 1992 and Native Women's Association of Canada, "The Future Will Live with the Choices We Make Today," Oshweken, Ontario, October 1992.

7. Indian and Northern Affairs Canada, *Report to Parliament: Implementation of the 1985 Changes to the Indian Act* (Ottawa: Indian and Northern Affairs Canada, June 1987).
8. For example, an Angus Reid poll, commissioned by the NCC and conducted shortly after the referendum, revealed that 61 percent of those polled said that they supported the aboriginal package in the Charlottetown Accord.
9. "What Does It Mean?" *The Globe and Mail*, 27 October 1992.
10. "Mercredi Serves Notice 'Quiet Revolution' to Begin," *The Globe and Mail*, 20 November 1992.
11. "Natives Set to Move Ahead with Own Laws," *The Globe and Mail*, 20 November 1992
12. "Inuit Referendum Results Differ from Reserve Indians," *The Vancouver Sun*, 29 October 1992.
13. "Métis Demand Talks on Self-Rule," *The Globe and Mail*, 29 October 1992.
14. "Most Indians on reserves voted No, results show," *Toronto Star*, 28 October 1992.
15. "A Message to all Canadians from First Nations of Treaty 6 and 7, " *The Globe and Mail*, 24 September 1992, p. A11.
16. "Can't Take the Leap of Faith, Fontaine Says," *The Vancouver Sun*, 26 October 1992.
17. "Fast-Paced Unity Talks Alarm Natives," *The Globe and Mail*, 26 October 1992.
18. Assembly of First Nations, "A New Direction: Strategic Plan, 1993-1994," Ottawa, 19 March 1993.
19. "Treaty Chiefs Want to Replace AFN," *Windspeaker*, vol. 11, 12 April 1993.
20. Métis National Council, "Métis Nation Cabinet Meeting — Briefing Documents," Regina, 29 March 1993.
21. Indian and Northern Affairs Canada, *Basic Departmental Data — 1992* (Ottawa: DIAND, December 1992), p. 69.
22. Source: First Nations Relations, Department of Indian Affairs and Northern Development, 20 May 1993.
23. Frank Cassidy, "On the Road to Recognition of Canadian Native Rights," *The Globe and Mail*, 9 July 1993.
24. See, for example, some of the literature on these intiatives circulated by the Coalition Against First Nations Genocide and the Aboriginal and Treaty Rights Defence Fund.
25. "Bridging the Arctic with Classroom TV," *The Globe and Mail*, 13 May 1993.
26. Indian and Northern Affairs Canada, "The Native Agenda," *Information Sheet No. 33*, Ottawa, March 1991. This policy was reiterated in the federal government's 1991 position paper on Aboriginal Peoples and constitutional reform. See Government of Canada, "Aboriginal Peoples, Self-Government and Constitutional Reform," (Ottawa: Minister of Supply and Services, 1991), p. 12.
27. See Indian and Northern Affairs Canada, *Federal Policy for the Settlement of Native Claims* (Ottawa: DIAND, March 1993).

28. Indian and Northern Affairs Canada, *Growth in Federal Expenditures on Aboriginal Peoples* (Ottawa: DIAND, February 1993), pp. 2-4.
29. "DIAND Reorganization Reflects Wishes of First Nations," *Transition*, 5, 3 (Ottawa: Indian and Northern Affairs Canada, March 1992): 1-2. See also Indian and Northern Affairs Canada, *Towards a Working Relationship with Indian First Nations in Alberta: A New Organizational Structure for the Alberta Region of Indian and Northern Affairs Canada* (Ottawa: DIAND, 4 March 1992).
30. "Powers Shift to Aboriginals, Government Says," *The Globe and Mail*, 20 November 1992.
31. "Métis Sign Deal," *Windspeaker*, 5 July 1993.
32. "Panel on Natives May Run Up Record Tab," *The Globe and Mail*, 14 July 1993.
33. Royal Commission on Aboriginal Peoples, *Discussion Paper 1: Framing the Issues* (Ottawa: Royal Commission on Aboriginal Peoples, October 1992), p. 1.
34. Ibid., p. 2.
35. Royal Commission on Aboriginal Peoples, *Discussion Paper 2: Focusing the Dialogue* (Ottawa: Royal Commission on Aboriginal Peoples, April 1993), p. 2.
36. Ibid., p. 63.
37. "Panel Sparks Royal Debate," *Winnipeg Free Press*, 14 February 1992.
38. Ibid.
39. "Inaction by Panel Prompted Resignation," *The Globe and Mail*, 6 April 1993.

8

Current Issues in Federal-Provincial Fiscal Relations

Paul A.R. Hobson

En continuant d'affirmer sa prépondérance dans le champ d'impôt sur le revenu des particuliers, le gouvernement fédéral est parvenu à réaliser une importante harmonisation au sein du système fiscal canadien. En tout premier lieu, Ottawa a fourni une base pour le financement du programme de péréquation fiscale. De plus, par l'entremise du Financement des programmes établis, le gouvernement fédéral a été en mesure de remettre aux provinces, en respectant scrupuleusement les règles de la péréquation, l'espace fiscal réservé à l'impôt sur le revenu des particuliers; l'objectif étant ici d'améliorer le fonctionnement du programme de péréquation fiscale. Enfin, Ottawa a pu poursuivre l'octroi de transferts aux provinces, au titre des dépenses en matière d'aide sociale, en vertu du Régime d'assistance publique du Canada. Pour l'heure, le souci du gouvernement fédéral de s'attaquer à la réduction du déficit compromet, dans sa forme actuelle, le système de paiements de transfert; on s'interroge présentement sur la nécessité, pour le gouvernement fédéral, de maintenir son engagement en faveur du partage des revenus entre les provinces. Ottawa réfléchit également à la possibilité de renouveler les accords actuels de perception fiscale.

INTRODUCTION

Federal-provincial fiscal relations have resurfaced as a major policy issue in the Canadian federation. While much of the political rhetoric has focused on budget deficits and how the federal government has downloaded its deficit problem to the provinces through unilateral actions, the issues involved are, in fact, quite fundamental to the future of Canada as an economic and social union. In part, these issues found some expression in the debate and negotiations leading up to the Charlottetown Accord.[1] In addition, a major review of federal-provincial fiscal arrangements is underway at the intergovernmental level, scheduled for completion by April 1994.

The existing system of federal-provincial fiscal arrangements is a reflection of the postwar devolution of income tax room to the provinces. This process has been characterized by a continued federal dominance in the income tax field through which a substantial degree of fiscal harmonization has been achieved within what is widely recognized as being an otherwise highly decentralized federation. Fiscal harmonization is manifested to the extent that provinces with widely different own-source fiscal capacities[2] are, in the presence of intergovernmental transfers, able to provide "reasonably comparable levels of public services at reasonably comparable levels of taxation"[3] — a principle that was enshrined in the *Constitution Act, 1982*. In addition, it is manifested through a highly coordinated personal income tax system as a consequence of the tax collection agreements.

For 1992-93, the federal Department of Finance estimates that some 27.2 percent of provincial gross revenues may be attributed to the three major transfer programs[4] — fiscal equalization, Established Programs Financing (EPF) and the Canada Assistance Plan (CAP). This represents a total of $35.5 billion. Of this figure, $24.2 billion is in the form of cash transfers, representing almost 22 percent of federal program expenditures. The significance of these transfers varies by province — between 27 percent of provincial revenues in Saskatchewan and 44 percent of provincial revenues in Newfoundland among the have-not provinces,[5] and 20-21 percent of provincial revenues among the have provinces.

Under the fiscal equalization program the federal government makes unconditional revenue transfers to the have-not provinces, designed to raise provincial per capita revenues, based on the Representative Tax System[6] (RTS), to the corresponding average yield for Quebec, Ontario, Manitoba, Saskatchewan and British Columbia.[7] This program is subject to review at five-year intervals. Traditionally, this review has also provided an opportunity to assess the two other major federal-provincial transfer programs — EPF, under which the federal government provides equal per capita transfers to the provinces in respect of health care and post-secondary education expenditures, and CAP, under which the federal government shares equally with the provinces in the cost of eligible provincial expenditures in respect of social assistance and social services.

The major federal-provincial transfer programs result in a significant redistribution of federal tax revenues across provinces.[8] Each program has a distinct role to play in this process. Fiscal equalization raises per capita revenues in the have-not provinces to the standard, thereby clearly redistributing in favour of those provinces with fiscal capacities that are below the standard for equalization. Layered on top of this, EPF is a "fully equalized" revenue transfer. While the total per capita amount is independent of provincial fiscal capacities, the tax effort required to generate equivalent revenues in the have-not provinces would exceed that in the have provinces, even in the presence of fiscal equalization. This program therefore redistributes in favour of those provinces with below average fiscal capacities, particularly the have-not provinces. Finally, eligible per capita provincial welfare expenditures made from (equalized) own-source revenues receive a 50 percent subsidy under CAP. By the same token, then, the tax effort required to replace per capita revenues received under CAP would be greater in those provinces with below average fiscal capacities than in those with above average fiscal capacities, again resulting in a net redistribution in favour of the have-not provinces.

A similar pattern of net redistribution would occur if all revenue and expenditure functions were fully centralized. For example, equal per capita expenditures across the country financed through uniform taxes, assuming different fiscal capacities in different parts of the country, would result in redistribution in favour of those parts of the country with below average fiscal capacities. While the extent of net redistribution relative to the *status quo* may be somewhat greater or somewhat less, in practice it is unlikely that it would differ significantly. The relevance of decentralized expenditure and tax authority is that it allows decisionmaking to better reflect differences in preferences or needs across provinces while maintaining some element of accountability. The "costs" associated with the loss in accountability resulting from transfers must then be weighed against the "benefits" resulting from decentralized decisionmaking.

There is, therefore, some level of net redistribution that is, in principle, consistent with attaining the same standard of fiscal equity[9] in a decentralized federation as would exist under a fully centralized system. Moreover, fiscal equity will ensure the efficient allocation of individuals across provinces; that is, there will be no incentive to migrate for fiscal reasons alone. The system of federal-provincial transfers is therefore integral to the functioning of the economic and social union.

Either directly or indirectly, each of these programs have been affected by the strained fiscal environment of the 1990s. Per capita entitlements under EPF have been subject to a five-year freeze since 1990-91. Also for a five-year period beginning in 1990-91, annual growth in entitlements under CAP in each of the three have provinces have been subjected to a 5 percent ceiling. Growth in entitlements under fiscal equalization has also been restrained under a growth ceiling provision put in place in 1982. This provision, which limits the cumulative rate of growth in entitlements to the cumulative rate of growth of GDP over a designated base year, first became effective in 1988-89 and has impacted in each year since then (other than the 1992-93 fiscal year as a result of a change in the designated base year to 1992).

The province of Ontario has estimated that, since 1982-83, the cumulative loss in revenues to all provinces resulting from federal expenditure controls affecting the major transfer programs amounts to $40.8 billion. In 1992-93 alone they estimate that transfers will be 21 percent less than they would have been in the absence of federal expenditure controls, amounting to a $9.4 billion revenue shortfall.[10]

The end result of all this is a situation in which all provinces — the haves and the have-nots — are financing an increasing share of their expenditures out of own-source revenues. This has seriously compromised the application of the principle of fiscal equity in the Canadian federation. It has also had consequences for provincial expenditure decisions: in all provinces the marginal cost of expenditures has risen, but, perhaps more importantly, these increases have been uneven across provinces. Uniformity in essential public services across the provinces is in serious jeopardy.

The provinces, of course, have not been unaware of the fiscal consequences of federal expenditure control programs. In part, this was manifested in the various elements of the Charlottetown Accord which pertained to federal-provincial fiscal relations. Included among these were the possibility of constitutionally enshrining intergovernmental agreements to prevent the sort of unilateral actions on the part of the federal government that have characterized fiscal relations in recent years. Also, there was an attempt to strengthen the federal commitment to making equalization payments as currently contained in section 36, the *Constitution Act, 1982*. More generally, concerns over the maintenance of Canada as a social union as well as an economic union gave rise to the proposed clause enshrining the social union, committing governments to

> providing adequate social services and benefits to ensure that all individuals resident in Canada have reasonable access to housing, food and other basic necessities; [and] providing high quality primary and secondary education to all individuals resident in Canada and ensuring reasonable access to post-secondary education[11]

as well as enshrining the five principles of medicare — comprehensiveness, universality, portability, public administration and accessibility.

The issues remain unresolved. The scheduled review of the fiscal arrangements in 1992 resulted in only relatively minor modifications to the fiscal equalization program, with the intent that, over the next two years, a major review of the fiscal arrangements would be undertaken. Necessarily, this must involve a redefinition of the role and level of transfers under EPF as well as a new approach to the federal-provincial dimension of income security programs.

The remainder of this chapter will review in greater detail the issues associated with the federal-provincial fiscal arrangements. First, there is a brief review of the evolution of federal-provincial fiscal arrangements in Canada, as reflected in the evolution of the division of income tax room between the federal government and the provinces. This is followed by a more detailed review of the issues associated with EPF and CAP and some proposals for reform of these programs. Next, proposals for modifying the income tax collection agreements are reviewed. Finally, the consequences of the growth ceiling on equalization entitlements are examined. The final section of the chapter provides some concluding remarks.

ISSUES AND ALTERNATIVES

THE POSTWAR DEVOLUTION OF INCOME TAX ROOM

The division of income tax room between the federal and provincial governments has been central to the evolution of federal-provincial fiscal relations in the period since World War II. Both levels of government were assigned the power to levy income taxes under the *Constitution Act, 1867*. However, the federal government became the sole occupant of the income tax field during the war years, in return for agreed upon levels of compensation to each of the provinces (the, so-called, tax rentals) and has maintained a dominant position in the income tax field since that time while gradually devolving income tax room to the provinces.

Federal dominance in the income tax field has resulted in a highly coordinated income tax system. It has also permitted the federal government to make redistributive transfers to provincial governments. These redistributive transfers have taken different forms over time. Prior to 1957, the federal government transferred revenues to the provinces in the form of tax abatements[12] supplemented by equal per capita transfers. In addition, minimum total and per capita revenue yields were guaranteed. This system involved a significant degree of implicit redistribution through the equal per capita component and the minimum yield provisions. Specifically, those provinces in which federal per capita revenue collections were below (above) the amount of per capita transfer were equalized up (down). Additional "equalization" was paid under the minimum yield provisions. It is also significant that the value of the tax abatement was tied to a particular base year rather than to current year revenues. Thus, in effect, total rental payments made to any province were unrelated to current federal revenue collections by province.

In 1957, the tax rentals were restructured such that each province was provided with an abatement tied directly to current year federal tax collections within its borders. In addition, an explicit equalization formula was introduced under which per capita revenues from the tax abatements were to be equalized up to the average per capita yield in Ontario and British Columbia. Thus, per capita yields under the tax abatements were "fully equalized" — up to the "top-two-province" standard.

Since 1947, Quebec had chosen to opt out of these arrangements (initially, Ontario had opted out also) and had instead received standard abatements tied to federal revenue collections within the province. In 1954, Quebec introduced its own personal income tax (throughout, it had levied its own corporate income tax) and, in lieu of the federal tax abatement, was granted equivalent personal income tax room.[13] Significantly, Quebec's personal income tax revenues were eligible for equalization payments under the 1957 arrangements.

The 1962 *Federal-Provincial Fiscal Arrangements Act* replaced the system of tax rentals with the tax collection agreements that continue under the present system. Under the 1962 arrangements, the federal government transferred personal income tax room to all provinces, allowing them to levy their own income taxes to fill the gap as they wished. Per capita revenues were still to be equalized to a "top-two-province" standard. The federal government undertook to collect personal income taxes on behalf of those provinces that wished it. Participating provinces were bound to accept the federal definition of the tax base as well as the federal rate structure. Provincial income taxes, under the tax collection agreements, were to be levied as a single rate of tax applied to basic federal tax (the tax-on-tax method). Each province had discretion over setting its own tax rate. Quebec was (and continues to be) the only province that chose not to participate.

Since that time, the practice of transferring income tax room to the provinces has been an integral part of the evolution of federal-provincial fiscal relations. In 1967, additional tax points were transferred as part of a combined cash-tax point transfer in lieu of previous cash transfers for post-secondary education. The process culminated in 1977 with regard to the, so-called, established programs financing, or EPF (discussed in more detail below). Under EPF, provincial accountability was to be increased through the transfer of additional tax room to the provinces in lieu of health-care grants. The intent was that, for 1977, 50 percent of the federal transfer for post-secondary education, health care and hospital insurance (the established programs) would be derived from the value of the associated 13.5 EPF tax points[14] (plus the value of 1 corporate tax point transferred as part of the 1967 post-secondary education arrangements). EPF tax points were eligible for equalization. The balance was to be made up through cash transfers.

Also in 1967, the equalization standard was changed from a "top-two-province" standard to a national average standard (along with other important changes to the program). Those provinces with below average per capita yields under the representative tax system would be equalized up to the standard; those with above average yields, however, would not be equalized downwards. A significant implication of this was that provincial per capita income tax yields would no longer be "fully equalized" (to the average per capita value in the two wealthiest provinces); rather, while they would be equalized up to the national average in those provinces with per capita yields below the national average, they would be of greater value (per capita) in those provinces with above average yields.

Prior to 1967, the transfer of tax room to the provinces in lieu of federal cash transfers, when equalized to the "top-two-province" standard, produced equal per capita yields across provinces. The adoption of a national average standard for fiscal equalization in 1967, however, rendered the matter of transferring income tax room to the provinces more complex. In order to preserve the principle of equal per capita yields, a variable cash component was required in addition to the transfer of tax room. In a sense, the cash component would provide a form of supplementary equalization, raising the per capita yield associated with the transferred tax points from a national average standard to a top-province standard.

ESTABLISHED PROGRAMS FINANCING

EPF transfers are made on an equal per capita basis. The transfer is largely unconditional, although the provinces must adhere to the five principles of medicare. The total transfer consists of a cash component and the value of the EPF tax points. Since 1982, each province's per capita cash transfer under EPF has been calculated as a residual — the difference between total per capita entitlement and the per capita value of the EPF tax transfer (computed as the per capita value of the EPF tax points, inclusive of associated fiscal equalization).[15]

Total per capita EPF entitlements were to be escalated annually according to a three-year compound moving average of GNP growth per capita. The escalator has, however, been modified under successive federal austerity programs. For 1983-84 and 1984-85 growth was limited to 6 and 5 percent, respectively, for the post-secondary education component as part of the federal government's "6&5" program. For 1986-87 through 1989-90 it was reduced to growth of per capita GNP less 2 percentage points. This was scheduled to be scaled down further to growth of GNP per capita less 3 percentage points for 1990-91, but this was preempted by the two-year freeze on total per capita entitlements announced in the 1990 budget. The 1991 budget extended the freeze through to the end of 1994-95 at which point the growth in per capita GNP less 3 percentage points escalator is scheduled to kick back in. Thus, a growth rate on per capita entitlements of 14 percent in 1977-78 fell to 5.8 percent in 1986-87, to just under 5 percent in 1989-90 and has been held at 0 percent since then.

The province of Ontario estimates that the total revenue loss to all provinces resulting from these modifications to the EPF escalator amounts to $33.6 billion. They estimate that all provinces combined will lose $7.3 billion in 1992-93 alone as a result of these modifications. In Ontario alone, they estimate that the cumulative loss since 1982-83 amounts to $12.3 billion, projected to be just under $2.7 billion in 1992-93.[16] The province of Quebec estimates that its loss in revenues for 1992-93 will be just under $2 billion.[17]

The inclusion of a cash component as part of the EPF transfer as well as the interplay with the fiscal equalization program made it possible to provide an effective transfer of tax room that was equal per capita across provinces. The effective transfer of tax room to the provinces in any year is the implicit number of tax points associated with the total EPF transfer for that year. The cash component of EPF serves the role of ensuring that the revenue yield associated with this effective transfer of tax room accrues to provinces on an equal per capita basis; that is, the effective transfer of tax room is "fully equalized."

It might be argued that the federal government has, in various ways, been unilaterally pre-empting tax room earmarked for provincial finance of the established programs since the inception of EPF in 1977. Modifications to the EPF escalator have simply hastened this process. The basis for this argument is that the rate of growth of per capita revenues from the implicit number of tax points transferred in 1977 has exceeded the rate of growth of per capita GNP in view of the progressivity of income taxation. Put another way, the implicit number of EPF tax points has been declining since 1977 because of what amounts to a per capita GNP ceiling (as variously modified) on growth in total entitlements. This is entirely inconsistent with previous transfers of tax room. Moreover, it has produced a confusion between federal and provincial budget deficits and policies aimed at deficit reduction; and finally, it has been to the detriment of promoting accountability at the provincial level.

Thus, there is an important sense in which the devolution of income tax room to the provinces with respect to the established programs remains as incomplete business on the federal-provincial fiscal relations agenda. In order to finally effect a complete disentanglement, tax room should be devolved to the provinces once and for all with respect to the established programs. This would be consistent with the call for disentanglement in program delivery and funding that appears to be receiving such popular support at present. It would also be consistent with earlier transfers of tax room.

One way of achieving this within the existing EPF framework, as outlined in research which the author has conducted with France St-Hilaire,[18] would be for the federal government to cede the value of the cash component of EPF to the provinces as an income tax abatement rather than as a direct transfer of tax room. That is, a fixed percentage of federal income tax revenues would be earmarked for the established programs. The revenue yield from this abatement would then form a pool from which cash transfers could be made to provinces on a similar basis to the existing cash component of EPF. In this way, the federal role in funding social programs would simply be that of coordinating inter-provincial revenue pooling through centralized collection and redistribution.

A significant aspect of this proposal is the notion of a federal role in coordinating interprovincial revenue pooling. The proposed tax abatement would earmark for the provinces a fixed percentage of federal income tax revenues. These revenues would not, however, be distributed in proportion to collections by province; rather they would be pooled for purposes of "topping up" the per capita value of the existing EPF tax transfer by province. This would seem to lend some definition to the notion of a transfer of "fully equalized tax room" in lieu of EPF cash transfers contained in a recent proposal by the western finance ministers.[19] Here, full equalization is achieved through revenue pooling. Revenue pooling is, however, achieved indirectly through formula-driven disbursements of a federal tax abatement to the provinces.

OTHER EPF SCENARIOS

Other scenarios are, of course possible. Recent analyses by Peter Leslie[20] and Ken Norrie[21] both consider the possibility of simply allowing EPF cash payments to continue to wind down. This could be effected more or less rapidly through modifications to the GDP escalator on per capita total entitlements (currently set at zero). The end result of this would, *de facto*, be a federal withdrawal from the health care and post-secondary education fields. The provinces would not acknowledge the value of the EPF tax points as a "transfer"from the federal government. Also, the per capita value of the EPF tax points would differ between the have and have-not provinces, and, indeed, among the have provinces, purely on the basis of fiscal capacities. The degree of fiscal disparity across provinces would be increased.

Norrie also considers the possibility of federal withdrawal accompanied by a transfer of tax room. This would occur in two stages. First, the other nine provinces would receive additional EPF tax points such as to place them on an equal footing with Quebec.[22] Next, additional tax points would be transferred to all provinces, sufficient to yield the desired total transfer of tax room. Since the value of any tax transfer would vary by province based on fiscal capacity, transitional cash payments may be required to raise all provinces, for example, to a "top-two-province" standard. His concern is that the additional pressures placed on the fiscal equalization program would jeopardize its future — place the sharing community in jeopardy.

Both Norrie and Leslie propose that preservation of the sharing community will require a commitment to direct interprovincial revenue sharing. There is, however, a legitimate concern that such a scheme would not be sustainable; that, in hard times, the richer provinces may simply withdraw from such revenue sharing arrangements. The advantage of the Hobson and St-Hilaire proposal is that it provides a mechanism whereby there can be further disentanglement without placing the sharing community in jeopardy.

Proposals by Robin Boadway and this author go further than this.[23] They argue that one way of attaining fully equalized fiscal capacities would be to compute EPF entitlement as a net entitlement; that is, actual entitlement plus equalization entitlement. For those provinces with negative equalization entitlement (the have provinces), then, their net EPF entitlement would be less than for the have-not provinces. Under such a scheme, the net effect would be to fully equalize the per capita revenues of the provinces. While this would be consistent with the equity and efficiency arguments first presented over ten years ago by the Economic Council of Canada,[24] it would involve a significantly expanded federal presence in cash transfers.

THE CANADA ASSISTANCE PLAN

Under the original terms of CAP, the federal government agreed to pay 50 percent of eligible provincial and municipal government expenditures on social assistance and welfare services. The imposition of the cap on CAP in 1990 has resulted in a reduction in the federal share in eligible program expenditures to 28 percent in Ontario, 47 percent in Alberta and 37 percent in British Columbia.[25] Moreover, the effect of the growth ceiling has been to convert what was a matching grant to a lump sum grant, no longer tied to actual program expenditures. The result is that additional expenditures on social assistance in the three have provinces are not cost-shared at all; costs must be met entirely from own-source revenues.

Estimates made by the province of Ontario suggest that the cumulative loss to the three have provinces since 1990 will exceed $4.0 billion of which $3.4 billion can be attributed to Ontario. For 1992-93, the loss to Ontario is estimated at $1.8 billion.[26] Moreover, it is evident that a return to open-ended cost sharing would result in a significant increase in the share of total transfers going to Ontario.

The cap on CAP has not only had serious budgetary consequences, especially in Ontario, it has also strained the commitment in the have provinces to the principles of Canadian federalism. In particular, the discriminatory nature of the cap — applied only to the have provinces — has created the perception of a departure from the tradition of the equal treatment of provinces. Moreover, some have argued that a return to 50 percent cost sharing at the end of the five-year period is now impossible; the implied magnitude of the increase in transfers to Ontario is simply too great. From the perspective of the federal government a return to open-ended cost sharing runs counter to any deficit control objectives, also suggesting that CAP will not return to its previous form. Finally, a renewed interest in reviewing income security programs in Canada carries with it the implication that federal-provincial cost-sharing arrangements too will be reviewed.

The discriminatory aspect of the cap on CAP needs to be viewed in the context of overall program restraints. The growth ceiling on equalization entitlements has impacted severely on the have-not provinces. Replacing revenues lost because of the freeze on per capita EPF entitlements has had to be done through own-sources, requiring significantly greater tax effort relative to national averages. Their ability to fund rising welfare payments has been equally constrained. In particular, their ability to keep up with welfare reforms elsewhere, especially Ontario, has been more constrained than ever. To the extent that the cap on CAP has slowed the pace of welfare reform, some uniformity has been preserved across provinces.

Traditionally, the provinces, especially Quebec, have complained that cost-sharing arrangements distort provincial priorities and inhibit innovation in the delivery of services. In addition, the provinces, especially the Atlantic provinces, have argued that provinces with relatively greater fiscal capacities have greater ability to spend in these areas. The argument that it is the role of fiscal equalization to account for differences in fiscal capacities seems somewhat hollow in this respect, since its goal is to raise fiscal capacities in the recipient provinces to a standard that is somewhat below the national average.

During the 1970s, there was a proposal to replace the portion of the CAP tied to welfare services with a block grant similar in structure to EPF.[27] Social assistance (income maintenance) programs would, however, have continued to be cost-shared. The block grant would have been structured as an equal per capita payment to be escalated annually in accordance with the rate of growth of per capita GNP.

More recently, Ken Norrie[28] has considered the possibility of complete federal withdrawal from cost sharing under CAP, accompanied by a transfer of tax room to the provinces. One difficulty with such a proposal is establishing the amount of tax room to be transferred since federal liabilities under CAP tend to be cyclical. In addition, since the associated tax points would be eligible for equalization, this would further strain the fiscal equalization program.[29]

As argued by Boadway and Hobson,[30] social assistance liabilities ought to be viewed as negative tax liabilities and treated symmetrically with personal income taxes under fiscal equalization. This is not done, however, and it can be argued that cost sharing of social assistance provides some offset to this defect in the design of the fiscal equalization program.

If negative tax liabilities were incorporated directly into fiscal equalization, those provinces with per capita social assistance liabilities above the standard for equalization would receive additional positive entitlements.[31] Hence, those provinces with positive net entitlements under the existing program would have their entitlements increased accordingly. Those provinces with negative net entitlements under the existing program, however, would only receive equalization if these were outweighed by positive entitlements with respect to social assistance liabilities.

An alternative proposal of Hobson and St-Hilaire[32] would maintain a federal presence in social assistance through a system of differential cost sharing. Those provinces with above average social assistance liabilities would be eligible for a differentially higher level of cost sharing and *vice versa*. The scheme would involve implicit equalization of social assistance liabilities across provinces but maintain the spirit of existing CAP arrangements.

The federal government has made the argument that it has no control over additional liabilities resulting from the enrichment of provincial programs. That is, a given province can shift 50 percent of the cost of program enrichment to the federal government. Moreover, it is the richer provinces that are best able to contemplate such enrichment schemes. At the least, then, it seems likely that CAP will be redesigned along block grant lines rather than reverting to open-ended cost sharing. What seems even more likely is that a review of income security programs will result in substantially more social assistance being delivered through the personal income tax, resulting in less reliance on cash transfers to the needy. This could substantially reduce the levels of transfers under CAP even if it reverted to its original cost-sharing design.

REFORM OF THE TAX COLLECTION AGREEMENTS

The federal and provincial governments have been exploring alternative models for the tax collection agreements, designed to give the provinces greater flexibility in tax policy, to promote transparency while at the same time maintaining the desirable features of a harmonized system.[33] A common aspect of these alternative models is that provincial tax would be levied against taxable income. This would obviate the need for the myriad of tax credits and the like which the provinces have introduced over time in order to affect their own redistributive and/or economic development goals within the constraints of the tax-on-tax system.

Rather, there would be a common set of non-refundable credits and associated eligibility criteria, but provinces would be able to set values for these and establish their own income thresholds and reduction rates. These would be broken down into two major categories — personal credits and expense credits. Personal credits would include basic, married or equivalent, child, disability and age credits. Expense credits would include credits for Canada/Quebec pension plan contributions, unemployment insurance premiums, tuition fees, education expenses, and medical expenses. In addition there would be credits for charitable donations and pension income.

One important issue for consideration in reforming the income tax collection agreements is providing the provinces with sufficient flexibility to better integrate the delivery of social assistance with the personal income tax system. Quebec, because it does not participate in the tax collection agreements, has already been able to move significantly in that direction.[34]

FISCAL EQUALIZATION

It has been estimated that, between 1988-89 and 1991-92, the growth ceiling on equalization has resulted in a shortfall in transfers to the have-not provinces of $3.3 billion.[35] While this is a significant amount, what is even more important is that the presence of the growth ceiling has increased the extent of fiscal disparity among the provinces.

In the absence of fiscal equalization, fiscal capacities vary significantly across provinces. For example, Newfoundland's fiscal capacity in 1990-91 was just over 62 percent of the national average compared with 133 percent in Alberta. What this means is that, based on the RTS, the tax effort required to generate $1 in revenues in Newfoundland is approximately twice that required in Alberta. Such differentials are significantly reduced through the operation of the fiscal equalization program; in the absence of the ceiling, fiscal capacities in the have-not provinces would have been raised to almost 93 percent of the national average in 1990-91.

With regard to EPF, the equalization ceiling has two effects. First, it lowers the effective equalized value of the EPF tax points. At present this is compensated by an offsetting adjustment in the cash transfer. Such an adjustment would not be possible if the federal government were to withdraw from EPF.

Second, to the extent that the provinces respond to reductions in EPF cash entitlements through offsetting tax increases, the additional tax effort required in the have-not provinces will be significantly greater than in the have provinces. The province of Quebec estimates that the tax effort required to replace $1 per capita in reduced EPF cash transfers is 39 percent greater in the have-not provinces than in the have provinces. These figures vary significantly by province. Relative to the average for the three have provinces, the index (relative to the have provinces) is 170 in Newfoundland, 168 in Prince Edward Island, 148 in Nova Scotia, 156 in New Brunswick, 134 in Quebec, 102 in Ontario, 142 in Manitoba, 133 in Saskatchewan, 85 in Alberta and 108 in British Columbia. If there were no growth ceiling on equalization entitlements, the index of tax effort required to compensate for each $1 shortfall in EPF cash transfers would be only 17 points higher than for the have provinces.[36]

As an example, Quebec has estimated that its loss in revenues resulting from the various modifications to the EPF escalator was $1.7 billion in 1991-92. In order to maintain service levels (i.e., compensate for the loss in transfers through a provincial tax increase), they estimate the resulting increase in the provincial tax burden to be $285 million more than it would have been had the province exhibited the average fiscal capacity among the have provinces. This figure would have been substantially lower in the absence of the growth ceiling on equalization entitlements.

In order to partially alleviate this latter effect, the base year against which the growth ceiling is applied has been altered to 1992-93. While this had the effect of restoring equalization flows for that fiscal year, the growth ceiling is again expected to bite in 1993-94.[37]

It seems clear that of the three major transfer programs, the fiscal equalization program has an overarching role in compensating for differences in fiscal capacities among provinces. Inevitably, federal withdrawal from funding social programs places pressure on the fiscal equalization program which further increases the likelihood of the growth ceiling continuing to have effect. If the sharing community is to survive, it seems imperative that the growth ceiling be removed.

CONCLUSIONS

There is a crisis in federal-provincial fiscal arrangements in Canada: the system is unravelling. By maintaining a dominant position in the personal income tax field, the federal government has been able to achieve a substantial degree of fiscal harmonization in the Canadian system through federal-provincial transfers. First and foremost among these has been the fiscal equalization program. In addition, through Established Programs Financing, the federal government has been able to effectively devolve personal income tax room to the provinces on a fully equalized basis, supplementing and enhancing the functioning of the fiscal equalization program. Finally, the federal government has been able to provide transfers in respect of provincial social assistance expenditures through cost-sharing arrangements under the Canada Assistance Plan. Now, the federal government's preoccupation with deficit reduction has compromised the effectiveness of the transfer system as an instrument of fiscal equity in the federation.

The growth ceiling on equalization entitlements has had the effect of widening disparities in fiscal capacities across provinces. Differing fiscal capacities across provinces render them unequal in their ability to meet the rising costs of delivering social programs. In addition, the federal government has been eroding the total number of income tax points implicitly transferred to the provinces in respect of programs in health care and post-secondary education with the introduction of EPF in 1977. This erosion has resulted both from the use of per capita GNP growth as the basis for escalating per capita entitlements and from a series of modifications to the growth formula itself (including the current freeze on total per capita entitlements). Inevitably, this has resulted in a serious fiscal imbalance at the provincial level. Moreover, EPF has itself been significant in reducing disparities in fiscal capacities across provinces, thereby supplementing and enhancing the functioning of the fiscal equalization program. In the presence of the growth ceiling on equalization entitlements, the tax effort required to compensate for each dollar per capita in scaled-back EPF cash entitlements is significantly greater among the have-not provinces than among the have provinces. In other words, the have-not provinces are further disadvantaged by the shortfall in EPF transfers, because the deficiencies must be made up entirely by (unequalized) own-source revenues.

Had the EPF cash transfer originally been structured as a tax abatement to the provinces, it would have been possible to implement a system of direct revenue sharing among the provinces, coordinated by the federal government, thereby rendering the total EPF transfer (cash plus tax) equivalent to a fully equalized transfer of tax room. Not only would this have forced further accountability on the provinces, it would have transferred the cost of equalization pertaining to the tax-room transfer directly to the provinces as a whole and further restrained federal spending in the designated program areas. There is yet sufficient cash associated with EPF to undertake a scheme of this type. There would, however, be the additional issue of determining the appropriate division of income tax room between the federal government and the provinces in light of the existing fiscal imbalance at the provincial level.

The issues surrounding cost-sharing arrangements under CAP are somewhat different. First, in the have provinces there is no longer cost sharing beyond the 5 percent annual growth ceiling on transfers. In the have-not provinces, widening disparities in fiscal capacities make it increasingly difficult to participate in cost-sharing arrangements. Second, existing restrictions on the eligibility of programs for cost sharing, especially programs that deliver income security through the income tax code, limit the incentive for provinces to experiment with alternative delivery mechanisms. Moreover, the tax collection agreements limit participating provinces in their ability to integrate income security programs with the tax code. Third, any review of CAP must be undertaken in conjunction with a review of the entire income security network.

One area that ought to receive more attention, however, is the impact of provincial income security liabilities (negative taxes) on fiscal capacities. A deficiency of the fiscal equalization program is precisely that it does not take such differences into account. One way of doing this, parallel to the fiscal equalization program, would be to implement a system of differential cost sharing based on differences in per capita liabilities. One significant aspect of such a scheme, appropriately designed, would be that the implicit equalization associated with it would be borne by provinces rather than by the federal government.

It seems clear that the current state of federal-provincial fiscal arrangements has seriously compromised the important redistributive function of the federal government to the detriment of both fiscal equity and economic efficiency in the federation. Yet it may be that there has been too much reliance on the federal government as the vehicle for interprovincial redistribution. Rather, there appears to be some scope for developing a greater degree of interprovincial revenue sharing within the framework of the existing federal-provincial fiscal arrangements.

NOTES

This paper draws heavily on work I have done with each of Robin Boadway and France St-Hilaire. I wish to acknowledge their contributions to my thinking on the themes I have chosen to pick up on in the paper, without in any way implicating either of them in my interpretations. The paper has also benefited from the comments of two anonymous referees, as well as those of Doug Brown and Ron Watts.

1. See Canada, *Consensus Report on the Constitution* (the Charlottetown Accord) agreed to at Charlottetown, 28 August 1992.
2. Own-source fiscal capacity is defined to be a province's ability to generate revenues when national average tax rates are applied to a standardized set of provincial revenue bases.
3. Part III of the *Constitution Act, 1982*, section 36(2).
4. In part as a result of the impact of federal expenditure controls, this figure is down somewhat from 30.8 percent in 1982-83.
5. The designated "have-not" provinces are those that are eligible for transfers under the fiscal equalization program — Newfoundland, Prince Edward Island, Nova Scotia, New Brunswick, Quebec, Manitoba and Saskatchewan. The non-recipient provinces — Ontario, Alberta and British Columbia — are designated as "have" provinces.
6. The Representative Tax System (RTS) provides a standardized measure of provincial fiscal capacities. The RTS estimates for each of 32 revenue sources the potential yield, by province, if a common rate were applied to a commonly defined base. The common rate is simply a national average tax rate.
7. Prior to 1982, the equalization standard was the national average revenue yield. In practice, the five-province standard is only slightly less than the national average.
8. See Robin W. Boadway and Paul A. R. Hobson, *Intergovernmental Fiscal Relations in Canada* (Toronto: Canadian Tax Foundation, 1993), p.128, for a discussion of the extent of redistribution involved.
9. Fiscal equity requires that otherwise identical individuals be treated in a similar manner in the presence of provincial fiscal programs regardless of province of residence.
10. See Ontario, *1992 Budget Paper D*, "Federal-Provincial Programs: The Need for Change."
11. See *Consensus Report on the Constitution*.

12. A tax abatement involves the payment to a provincial government of a fixed proportion of taxes collected within the province by the federal government.
13. A transfer of tax room involves the federal government reducing its tax rates (and revenues), creating tax room which can be filled through provinces raising their rates with no net change in total (federal + provincial) yield.
14. A tax point is simply 1 percent of basic federal tax.
15. In 1977, the cash component of EPF was set up as an equal per capita amount to be escalated annually in accordance with growth in per capita GNP. Growth in the per capita value of the tax transfer varied with provincial fiscal capacities, however, necessitating supplementary cash transfers to ensure that total per capita entitlements remained equal. The 1982 modifications to EPF obviated the need for such supplementary payments.
16. See Ontario, *1992 Budget*.
17. See Quebec, *Budget 1991-92, Annex E*, "Federal Transfers to the Provinces: Quebec's Point of View."
18. See Paul A.R. Hobson and France St-Hilaire, *Rearranging Federal-Provincial Fiscal Arrangements: Toward Sustainable Federalism*, Institute for Research on Public Policy (forthcoming).
19. Western Finance Ministers, *Report of the Western Finance Ministers: Economic and Fiscal Developments and Federal-Provincial Fiscal Relations in Canada*, submitted to Western Premiers' Conference, Lloydminster, Saskatchewan, 26-27 July 1990 (unpublished).
20. Peter M. Leslie, "The Fiscal Crisis of Canadian Federalism," in Peter M. Leslie, Kenneth Norrie and Irene K. Ip, *A Partnership in Trouble: Renegotiating Fiscal Federalism* (Toronto: C.D. Howe Institute, 1993).
21. Kenneth Norrie, "Intergovernmental Transfers in Canada: An Historical Perspective on Some Current Policy Choices," in ibid..
22. In addition to the standard 13.5 EPF tax points, Quebec receives an additional 8.5 point abatement in respect of earlier opting-out arrangements.
23. See Boadway and Hobson, *Intergovernmental Fiscal Arrangements*.
24. Economic Council of Canada, *Financing Confederation: Today and Tomorrow* (Ottawa: Minister of Supply and Services, 1982).
25. See Ontario, *1992 Budget*.
26. Ibid.
27. See Canada, *Fiscal Federalism in Canada: Report of the Parliamentary Task Force on Federal-Provincial Fiscal Arrangements* (The Breau Report) (Ottawa: Minister of Supply and Services, 1981).
28. See Norrie, "Intergovernmental Transfers."
29. Norrie also argues that, if responsibility for funding social assistance were devolved wholly to the provinces, it would be logical to also devolve responsibility for unemployment insurance. As discussed in Boadway and Hobson, *Intergovernmental Fiscal Arrangements*, if unemployment insurance were devolved to the provinces, it would be necessary to provide for associated equalization payments. The arguments here are symmetric with those for equalization of social assistance.

30. Ibid.
31. For a proposal as to how to incorporate negative tax liabilities into the representative tax system (RTS), see Hobson and St-Hilaire, *Rearranging Federal-Provincial Arrangements*.
32. Ibid.
33. See Canada, *Personal Income Tax Coordination: The Federal-Provincial Tax Collection Agreements* (Ottawa: Department of Finance, 1991).
34. See Hobson and St-Hilaire, *Rearranging Federal-Provincial Arrangements*, for a fuller discussion of the importance of undertaking reform of the tax collection agreements in conjunction with reform of delivery of social assistance and the federal role therein.
35. See Ontario, *1992 Budget*.
36. See Quebec, *Budget 1991-92*.
37. See Ontario, *1992 Budget*.

9

The NAFTA, the Side-Deals, and Canadian Federalism: Constitutional Reform by Other Means?

Ian Robinson

Cet article identifie les principaux domaines où l'ALÉNA empiète sur la juridiction provinciale, ainsi que les moyens dont dispose le gouvernement fédéral pour instituer ces chevauchements. L'article analyse dans quelle mesure ces ententes viendront accroître les contraintes commerciales par rapport aux initiatives politiques provinciales. Robinson se demande aussi si le rejet ou l'abrogation des ententes en question se traduira par la survie du volet social que comporte le fédéralisme canadien. L'auteur soutient que la mise en oeuvre de l'entente de libre-échange entre le Canada et les États-Unis a marqué le début d'une nouvelle ère dans l'histoire du fédéralisme canadien, une réalité que sont venus conforter d'ailleurs l'ALÉNA et l'«ébauche Dunkell».

La mobilité accrue du capital international, qu'encouragent ces ententes, a pour effet d'augmenter aussi les pressions commerciales à l'endroit de tous les paliers de gouvernement, en particulier, sur les gouvernements provinciaux. Du coup ces derniers seront moins en mesure de répondre efficacement aux attentes de leurs commettants, y compris dans les secteurs où leur juridiction n'est pas remise en cause par suite des obligations nouvelles contractées par ces ententes internationales.

INTRODUCTION

The North American Free Trade Agreement (NAFTA) and its labour and environmental "side-deals" are part of a growing number of international agreements that seek to regulate the global economy. Like the FTA and the Dunkel draft of the Uruguay round of the General Agreement on Trade and Tariffs (hereafter, Dunkel GATT), the NAFTA is dubbed a "free trade" agreement. However, it applies to much more than the border measures (e.g., tariffs and quotas) that impede trade (i.e., the international flow of goods and services).

Indeed, the most important element of these agreements are the new international property rights that they grant to investors, and the new restrictions that they impose on government regulatory powers. In this light, this genre of international economic agreement may be more accurately labelled a "free capital" agreement. At the same time, as the NAFTA's side-deals and the rapid expansion of the "social dimension" of the European Community in the 1980s suggest, pressures are also mounting to develop international agreements on environmental protection and labour rights and standards backed by economic sanctions.

In the past, important changes in the structure of the international economy and the role of the state have precipitated major changes in the powers possessed by the federal and provincial governments of Canada, in the ends to which those powers are used, and in the relationships between federal and provincial governments. This chapter asks what kinds of changes in the character of Canadian federalism are likely to result from the NAFTA and the labour and environmental side-deals that accompany it. Each of these agreements represents a particular case of a more general phenomenon: ever more comprehensive free capital agreements, and increasing pressures for an enforceable international social dimension. The chapter also asks what these more general trends imply for Canadian federalism, whether or not the NAFTA and its side-deals are implemented in their current form.

In seeking answers to these questions, it is important not to become obsessed with the formal constitution. Changes in the character of Canadian federalism have occasionally been facilitated by constitutional amendments (e.g., the transfer of exclusive jurisdiction over unemployment insurance to the federal government in 1940). But most such changes — notably, the dramatic expansion of the federal government's activities after World War II, under the rubric of the "spending power" — were not the result of a formal constitutional amendment or a landmark court decision.[1] It is therefore important to distinguish between impacts on government roles and policy instruments and impacts (if any) on the constitutional division of powers. Either can profoundly affect the character of federalism. The former is more common and often more important.

This chapter argues that the NAFTA, especially if reinforced by the Dunkel GATT, is likely to produce a change in the character of Canadian federalism on the same order of magnitude as the changes that launched the postwar era of "modern" or "social" federalism. So, too, would a substantial international social dimension, whether taken alone or in conjunction with such free capital agreements. Whether such changes someday receive the official imprimatur of a formal constitutional amendment or a ringing Supreme Court declaration is a secondary issue.

The chapter considers mainly how the NAFTA and its side-deals are likely to affect the policy options and the policy instruments available to the federal and provincial governments of Canada. The analysis in this chapter is part of broader work examining the impact of and response to economic globalization on Canadian federalism.[2]

How will the NAFTA and its "side-deals" affect the balance of political power between federal and provincial governments, and between governments in general and private investors? Two causal routes from the NAFTA to these power balances can be traced. The first runs from the NAFTA's impact on capital mobility to the market constraints faced by governments. Such impacts would be felt even if Canada did not sign the NAFTA, provided that Mexico and the United States did. The second route runs from the NAFTA's new international obligations, through the federal government's duty to enforce (some of) these obligations against provincial governments, to the loss of provincial policy instruments.

The discussion below has three sections. The first considers how the NAFTA increases capital mobility, and to what effect. The second asks whether the side-deals offset or otherwise affect the NAFTA's impact on distribution of economic power. The last section considers the legal restrictions that both sets of agreements impose on provincial governments.

CAPITAL MOBILITY AND GOVERNMENT POLICY CAPACITY

International capital mobility is affected by many things that governments can influence: transportation costs, communications technologies, the extent of tariff and "non-tariff barriers" (NTBs) to the movement of goods, services and capital, and the scope and strength of private property rights. By reducing tariff and non-tariff barriers, governments make it easier for private investors to produce goods in countries other than those that constitute their primary markets. This facilitates the shifting of investment in production to facilities "overseas." By increasing and standardizing protections for investors' property in other countries, governments can reduce the risk that foreign investors will lose some or all of their investments due to unforeseen changes in government policies. This makes overseas investment more attractive, other things equal, with the largest effect in the countries where such "political risks" were previously greatest. How does the NAFTA increase international capital mobility, and how does this affect the market constraints faced by federal and provincial government policymakers? I consider each question in turn.

NAFTA AND CAPITAL MOBILITY

The NAFTA contributes to capital mobility in two ways. It eliminates all remaining tariffs among three countries over a period of 15 years, and most long before that. It also eliminates the need for import licences and a variety of other NTBs that restricted the movement of capital as well as consumer goods into Mexico. The NAFTA's contribution to these sources of capital mobility is modest because tariffs and NTBs between Canada and the United States had already been greatly reduced by successive rounds of the GATT and the FTA.[3] Similarly, Mexico's tariffs and NTBs against all countries have been even more rapidly reduced — though, from a much greater height, so that they remain more stringent — as part of the "liberalization" program that began in earnest under President Salinas in 1986. Mexico has since acceded to the GATT, so that the Salinas reductions are now embedded in a binding international agreement.[4]

The second and larger contribution that the NAFTA makes to increased capital mobility is through reducing the risk to private investors of investing in Mexico. The NAFTA does this by creating what amount to new continental private property rights that will protect foreign investors operating in all three countries. These new property rights are explicit in the Investment chapter, the chapter on monopolies and state enterprises, the Intellectual Property (IP) chapter, and the Financial Services chapter. However, the restrictions on government regulation found in the Standards-Related Measures chapter, and in the section of the Agriculture chapter dealing with Sanitary and Phytosanitary (SPS) standards, can also be understood as property rights. These latter chapters make it more expensive and difficult to regulate the behaviour of domestic and foreign corporations in ways that might reduce the value of their property.[5]

The most important of the new private property rights that the NAFTA creates are found in its Investment chapter.[6] Under the FTA, American investors were granted protection against four types of "performance requirements."[7] They were also protected against expropriation without "just compensation," as determined by an FTA panel.[8] Finally, American investors were protected against any "nullification and impairment" of benefits which they expected to derive from the agreement, even though such disappointment might not result from the violation of any specific provision of the FTA.[9] The NAFTA incorporates these rights and extends them in a number of ways. It prohibits three new types of "performance requirements," the most important of which are "technology transfer" and "product mandating" requirements. These rights are granted to all foreign investors, whether or not they originate in NAFTA countries.[10]

The NAFTA also creates a new investor-state dispute process, permitting NAFTA investors who believe that one of their rights has been violated to go to an international tribunal with binding arbitration powers, or to the domestic courts, whichever the aggrieved investor prefers. Under the FTA and the GATT, by contrast, private investors must persuade their national governments to undertake such a challenge. The NAFTA Investment chapter expands the number of corporations that will have access to these new property rights and legal procedures through its expanded definition of NAFTA "investors."[11]

The NAFTA Monopolies and State Enterprises chapter incorporates the FTA's restrictions on monopolies.[12] In addition, it requires that monopolies accord "non-discriminatory" treatment to NAFTA investors. The NAFTA also requires state enterprises to comply with the obligations set out in the Investment and Financial Institutions chapters when exercising any "regulatory, administrative, or other government authority."[13]

The NAFTA's Intellectual Property chapter has no predecessor in the Tokyo GATT or the FTA.[14] It applies to virtually every important form of intellectual property rights, in many cases granting more stringent forms of protection than were available under the domestic intellectual property laws of Canada and Mexico. The IP chapter also contains novel and important enforcement procedures.[15]

The main impact of the FTA's Financial Services chapter on capital mobility was the waiving (for American investors) of restrictions on foreign ownership of Canadian financial institutions chartered by the federal government.[16] The NAFTA's Financial Services chapter is much more comprehensive, incorporating the National Treatment principle, and the Investment chapter's provisions on the right to transfer profits, dividends, and the like freely across national borders.[17] It also incorporates the Investment chapter's investor-state dispute mechanism to protect these rights, subject to certain qualifications.[18] Finally, the financial institutions have the right to transfer financial data out of NAFTA countries for processing.[19]

The NAFTA also strengthens FTA restrictions on government regulations by increasing the burden that governments must meet in order to defend technical and SPS standards deemed trade restrictive. Like the Tokyo GATT and the FTA, the NAFTA recognizes a special class of "legitimate" regulatory objectives — the "safety or the protection of human, animal or plant life or health, the environment, or consumers" — which may be valid even if they restrict trade.[20] If a measure is found to be trade restrictive, a government seeking to defend it must first demonstrate that the intent of the measure was to realize one of these "legitimate objectives." In the FTA and the Tokyo GATT, if a trade-restrictive measure passed this first hurdle, the government had to show that this measure was also "necessary" to achieve that legitimate objective. If this second test was also met, then the measure survives the challenge. The NAFTA increases the difficulty of meeting this second test by requiring that governments prove that the measure chosen was the "least trade restrictive necessary" to achieve a legitimate objective.

Given the difficulty of successfully defending a regulation deemed "trade restrictive," the burden that a challenger must meet in order to show that a measure is indeed trade restrictive becomes very important. In many cases, the most promising way to meet this burden is to show that the measure violates the National Treatment principle. Under this principle, a measure is trade restrictive if it discriminates in favour of national producers or investors as against non-national exporters or investors. Over the years, GATT panels have developed a broad interpretation of what counts as "discrimination" — the "equal competitive opportunity" (ECO) interpretation.[21] On this reading, a government measure can apply the same rule to nationals and non-nationals and still be discriminatory if it has the *effect* of placing foreign exporters or investors at a competitive disadvantage.[22] Language reflecting this interpretation is explicitly included in the NAFTA's Financial Services chapter,[23] and it may be "read into" other chapters by future NAFTA panels, investor-state arbitration tribunals, or the courts.

In all of these ways, the NAFTA will make it faster and less expensive for an expanded list of eligible NAFTA investors to protect their new property rights against the depredations of NAFTA governments. The NAFTA will also increase the likelihood of successful challenges to a broad range of government regulations by the Mexican and American governments. This will result in more challenges to more government measures, other things equal, and hence, higher regulatory costs, even if governments successfully fend off all such challenges. Where governments lose, they will have to change their behaviour or pay compensation. Efforts to reduce the number and success of such challenges by ensuring that the "least trade restrictive necessary" test has been met, will cost money and reduce the range of policy instruments available to governments. All this is likely to have a chilling effect on efforts to raise national regulatory standards in existing fields or to introduce regulations in new areas, a prospect that private investors greet with approbation.

These changes will have the greatest impact on capital mobility where the risks of investment, in the absence of NAFTA property rights, were greatest. These risks were perceived to be much higher in Mexico, owing to the more interventionist character of its economic policies, memories of the oil company nationalizations, perceived nationalist hostilities to foreign investors, the lesser legal protections offered by their courts, and a range of other factors. Risks of investment in Canada were doubtless rated higher than in the United States, but they have already been reduced somewhat by the new investor property rights created in the FTA. Thus, the NAFTA's impact on the foreign private investor security is much greater in Mexico than the other two NAFTA countries. By making Mexico a substantially less risky place to invest than it was before, the NAFTA thus increases the pressure on Canadian and American governments seeking to retain or attract domestic and foreign private investment in industries (e.g., auto) that could be located in any of the three countries.

GOVERNMENT BARGAINING POWER WITH PRIVATE INVESTORS

By substantially increasing capital mobility, the NAFTA will significantly increase the bargaining power of private investors (in most cases, the transnational corporations (TNCs) that are best equipped to take advantage of these new opportunities) vis-à-vis governments. In a mixed economy, democratic governments must try to persuade private owners to invest a sufficient share of the economic resources that they control to make possible productivity growth, low unemployment, and the other economic desiderata. Private sector investors cannot guarantee good economic performance, but by refusing to invest, they can guarantee bad performance.

The only other private interest possessing anything approaching this kind of economic power is organized labour. But workers must organize and act collectively in order to exercise such power, which makes them highly visible and vulnerable to government restrictions on the right to strike. By contrast, private investors need not organize in order to withhold, withdraw, or transfer their investments. Independent action on the part of numerous investors who believe that the government is insufficiently pro-business is sufficient to put great pressure on governments to mend their ways.[24] Thus, even if private investors were constrained to make their choices about where (and whether) to invest within a single national economy, they would possess unparalleled power to influence government economic policy.[25]

The power of private investors is further increased if they are able to move their investments freely from one country to another. As long as private wealth holders are constrained to invest (or consume) within their country of origin, high consumption taxes can create strong incentives to re-invest profits in domestic businesses, even if government economic and social policies are not regarded as particularly congenial to business interests.[26] However, this tax instrument becomes less effective as capital mobility increases. Merely pointing to the existence of an increasingly attractive exit option substantially increases the leverage of private investors vis-à-vis governments seeking to maintain and increase investment. It becomes riskier to introduce new regulations or taxes that might have a negative impact on corporate bottom lines. Consequently, such taxes are not raised as much as would otherwise have been the case, and either taxes on other sectors of society are raised more or cuts in government spending are made.[27]

An increase in capital mobility can substantially affect the economic and political power of the labour movement. Where a strong labour movement exists, governments are constrained not to bend too far in the direction of private investor interests. This is reflected in the fact that countries in which labour movement power is high tend to have larger and more activist governments,[28] more egalitarian distributions of the benefits of economic growth,[29] and lower levels of inflation and unemployment.[30]

In Canada, increased capital mobility will tend to reduce both the membership and the political influence of unions, because membership levels tend to be very high in the manufacturing sector that is most directly and (I would argue) negatively affected by this change. Manufacturing plants may close as the TNC moves its operations to lower labour-cost zones, and union members who worked in those plants are lost. Or plants may be kept open, but in order to remain competitive with such low-cost production sites, new capital investments that reduce the need for labour are introduced. Because it is more difficult to organize most parts of the private-service sector than the manufacturing sector, members lost in the latter sector are not easily made up in the former.[31] Consequently, a decline in the manufacturing sector's share of total employment, other things equal, will be associated with a decline in union density.

In summary, the NAFTA would increase capital mobility and with it, the bargaining power of large private investors vis-à-vis Canada's federal and provincial governments. An agreement only between the U.S. and Mexico would also have this effect, with or without Canada. The NAFTA goes well beyond the high water mark established by the FTA in two ways: first, it substantially extends the scope of the new private property rights that are the principal source of increased capital mobility; and second, it protects these property rights in Mexico, which (given the current global competitive climate) arguably provides a much greater incentive to "social dumping"[32] than was the FTA's increased incentive to locate production in the United States.

All of the impacts of increased capital mobility on national government bargaining power with private investors hold *a fortiori* for provincial and local governments. An increased threat of exit, once acquired, is just as effective in negotiations with subnational governments as with national governments. Indeed, it is more effective because it is much easier for TNCs to play ten provincial, 50 U.S. state, and 30 Mexican state governments off against one another than it is to play the three national governments off against each other. Ninety state and provincial governments amount to a competitive market in which any one government is a TNC condition-taker; three national governments are an oligopoly, retaining the power to impose some conditions on TNC investment, although this is also diminished by international competition for investment among nation-states. This would be true even if none of the provisions of the NAFTA that enhance capital mobility applied to provincial government measures (though in fact, as we shall see below, most do).

SOCIAL DUMPING AND THE NAFTA SIDE-DEALS

The labour and environmental side-deals to the NAFTA, completed on 13 August 1993, are supposed to neutralize any encouragement that the NAFTA might give to "social dumping." Even if completely successful in this objective, capital mobility would still be substantially higher, and hence, government power significantly lower, under the NAFTA. But successful side-deals would at least reduce one of the most powerful incentives to use their mobility in economically inefficient and socially harmful ways. This would reduce, though not eliminate, some of the most important political costs of increased capital mobility. How effective are the side-deals likely to be in their stated purpose? The final legal text of the side-deals is not available at the time of writing. However, using the summary "highlights" of the final agreement released jointly by the three governments on 13 August 1993, and the legal texts from 9 August to 12 August 1993 (leaked to *Inside U.S. Trade*), it is possible to form a reasonably clear picture of how the side-agreements will work.[33] I first summarize and then evaluate these agreements.

DESCRIPTION

The main strategy for dealing with social dumping embodied in the side-deals is to improve the domestic enforcement of domestic labour standards and environmental laws by creating an international oversight mechanism to monitor this process. Where this mechanism finds a "persistent pattern of failure to effectively enforce" one of the domestic laws covered by the agreement, a national government can bring the matter before an arbitral panel provided that certain conditions are met. The panel is empowered to levy a fine against the country failing to enforce, should it find in favour of the complaining party. If the national government so sanctioned fails to pay the fine, the complaining party is entitled to levy trade sanctions against the non-complying party if it is the United States or Mexico. If the non-complying party is Canada, the complaining party has the right to go to the Canadian courts which will be mandated by federal statute to order the federal government to pay the fine. I will briefly expand on each of these features.

Oversight of domestic enforcement processes is the task of two commissions (Labour and Environment), each made up of a ministerial council, and a permanent secretariat mandated to provide technical, administrative and operational assistance to the council. Each ministerial council is comprised of Cabinet-level representatives from each country; each secretariat is comprised of officials with a degree of autonomy from the three national governments. The environmental secretariat is empowered to receive complaints from private parties, and to prepare a report on the facts relevant to the validity of the complaint. The labour secretariat does not have these powers, though it will prepare "analytical reports" on issues relevant to disputes at the request and under the terms of reference of its council. Neither secretariat has subpoena powers, and neither is entitled to make recommendations as to how the council should proceed.

The Labour Commission will be more complicated than its environmental counterpart in two ways. First, the Labour Commission will have a third component: national administrative offices (NAOs) will be located within each country, with top officials appointed by the national governments of that country. These NAOs will compile and transmit information to the secretariat and to receive complaints from other NAFTA governments.[34] NAOs would not be entitled to hear complaints from interested parties, and consultations among them could only be initiated by national governments. Second, the labour side-deal interjects an additional procedural step between the initiation of consultations by an NAO and the decision to initiate an arbitral panel. Should consultations fail to resolve the issue, a party can initiate the formation of an "Evaluation Committee of Experts" (ECE) provided that three criteria are met:[35] (i) the labour law in question is among those covered in the agreement, (ii) a systematic "pattern" of non-enforcement is alleged,[36] and (iii) such non-enforcement has "trade-related" consequences.[37] For purposes of the first criterion, labour laws are divided into three categories:

(a) child labour, minimum wage, and worker health and safety measures;
(b) forced labour, employment discrimination, equal pay for men and women, compensation in cases of work accidents or occupational diseases, and the protection of migrant workers; and
(c) all other matters covered by labour laws, including basic worker rights to organize, bargain collectively, and strike.

ECEs can only investigate alleged failures to enforce laws of types (a) and (b), which are defined as "technical labour standards." Type (c) laws and regulations are not covered by the agreement. The ECE process will be "non-adversarial." The ECE would issue a public report, which would have no binding force, but would be fed into ongoing consultations.

Under the labour side-deal, if consultations following the ECE's report still fail to resolve the issue, the complaining party can initiate the formation of an arbitration panel provided that two-thirds of the other parties to the agreement concur, and the law in question is of type (a).[38] Under the environmental side-deal, there is no ECE stage, and the complaining party may initiate an arbitral panel provided that the same two-thirds support is secured, and the complaint pertains to one of the types of environmental law to which the side-deal applies. The environmental side-deal applies to measures aimed at preventing pollution, controlling hazardous materials, and protecting flora and fauna and their habitats. Largely at Canada's insistence, the environmental side-deal will not apply to provisions governing the management of the "commercial harvest or exploitation, or subsistence or aboriginal harvesting, of natural resources."

If these conditions are met, the arbitration panel is empowered to impose a fine on the offending party. No minimum fine has been set. If and only if the offending party fails to pay any fine assessed within a specified period, the complaining party may impose trade sanctions in the form of quotas or tariffs commensurate with the scale of the harm caused by the failure to enforce. However, no such trade sanctions may be taken against Canada. Instead, the federal courts of Canada will be granted the power (by federal statute) to require the government of Canada to pay any fines levied against it by this body, with no possibility of appeal.[39]

The application of the side-deals in the Canadian case is characterized by a second important asymmetry. Without the cooperation of a minimum number of provinces, Canadian obligations will apply only to labour laws falling under exclusive federal jurisdiction (these cover about 10 percent of the workforce). The provincial labour laws that apply to the remaining 90 percent of the Canadian workforce will only be subject to the labour side-deal process if a sufficient number of provincial governments choose to participate to reach a minimum "threshold" level. The 9 August 1993 labour accord draft reveals continued disagreement as to the precise threshold level, but the range is between 30 and 40 percent of the total Canadian workforce, and 55 to 60 percent of the total employment in the sector to which the complaint pertains.[40] Conversely, the Canadian government will only be able to challenge lax enforcement in other NAFTA countries for the economic sectors over which it has exclusive jurisdiction, *and sectors under provincial jurisdiction where the required thresholds are met.* Provincial governments will indicate their participation by agreeing to list their (relevant) labour laws in Annex II of the labour agreement, and the Canadian government is obliged to encourage provincial governments to do this.[41]

The 10 August 1993 draft of the environmental side-deal reveals a parallel approach to provincial government adhesion. Canada may not seek panel proceedings against another party unless provincial governments representing at least 55 percent of Canada's GDP sign on to the agreement, and (if the matter is industry or sector-specific) at least 55 percent of the industry or sector in question is covered by the provinces adhering to the agreement. Conversely, no actions can be brought against Canada or any province that may adhere to the agreement until these thresholds are met.

EVALUATION

The exclusion of resource management schemes from the ambit of the environmental side-deal is problematic if its point is to prevent price competition based on unsustainable forms of environmental exploitation. Past inadequacies in the enforcement of such schemes — e.g., the failure of B.C. logging companies to meet their commitments to replanting — have contributed to a situation in which loggers now press to cut down the last stands of ancient timber in the hope of extending their employment for a few years. The exclusion of worker rights from coverage under the labour side-deal is even more damaging to the effectiveness of what is, in any case, the weaker of the two agreements. These rights are the single most important target of employers and governments wishing to engage in (or permit) social dumping. This is because unionization levels tend to be higher where worker rights are well protected, and wages and benefits tend to be higher where a larger share of the workforce is organized, other things equal.

Labour rights are also critical to the effective monitoring and enforcement of the (United States) kinds of labour standards that are covered by the labour side-deal. As the declining enforcement of the *Occupational Health and Safety Act* (OSHA) in the 1980s demonstrates, even countries as rich as the United States find it difficult to effectively monitor all the workplaces in the country effectively. Where workers are able to organize into independent unions, so that they are less fearful of reprisals if they assert their legal rights relating to workplace health and safety, they are ideally placed to discover and report infractions, and they have a strong incentive to do so. Conversely, it often appears to employers that the simplest way to reduce costs associated not only with worker wages and benefits but also with the effective enforcement of labour standards is to deny workers their rights.

Even if the side-deals covered worker rights and natural resource management laws, the strategy for combatting social dumping implicit in the side-deals is deeply flawed. As long as the relevant national standards can be unilaterally reduced as competitive pressures mount, mechanisms to improve the monitoring and enforcement of such laws are of very limited value. Moreover, Canada will not be able to use the side-deals to challenge enforcement in either of the other NAFTA countries unless a sufficient number of provincial governments agree to be bound by the side-deals. Nor will other countries be able to challenge lax enforcement in Canada unless these conditions are met.

To conclude, the side-deals are, for many reasons, unlikely to seriously retard, much less neutralize the social dumping pressures increased by the NAFTA's boost to continental capital mobility. Indeed, they may be worse than nothing, given the symbolic message sent by Article 32. Even if they did substantially reduce social dumping opportunities, this would only provide

The NAFTA, the Side-Deals, and Canadian Federalism 205

some respite from the intensified market constraints that the NAFTA will impose on both orders of government in Canada.

LEGAL IMPACTS ON PROVINCIAL POLICY INSTRUMENTS

The federal government is subject to the legal restrictions on its policy instruments outlined in the previous discussion of the NAFTA and its side-deals. However, the legal restrictions on provincial governments are not identical to the federal government's. Some restrictions apply only to the federal government. Moreover, there remain questions about whether some or all of these restrictions can be enforced effectively by the federal government. I first consider what the agreements claim provincial governments must do or refrain from doing. I then consider how the federal government might seek to enforce these claims, how hard it is likely to try, and whether it is likely to succeed.

SCOPE AND STRINGENCY OF RESTRICTIONS ON PROVINCIAL POLICIES

Prior to the Tokyo round, the GATT focused almost exclusively on the reduction of quotas and tariffs on imported goods. Such measures are matters of exclusive federal jurisdiction. With the Tokyo round, "non-tariff barriers" (NTBs) to trade became a major focus of all "trade" agreements. The best known forms of NTBs are probably subsidies and government purchasing (or "procurement") policies. But virtually any government policy that has the effect of placing foreign producers at a competitive disadvantage vis-à-vis domestic producers can be construed as an NTB. Signed in 1979 and phased in over the next eight years, the Tokyo round agreements included NTB "codes" on subsidies and countervailing duties, anti-dumping measures, government procurement, technical barriers to trade, import licensing procedures, and customs valuation.

By the inclusion of NTBs in the GATT, many provincial government and Crown corporation procurement and regulatory policies became potential objects of GATT regulation for the first time.[42] Accordingly, provincial governments insisted on (and got) an unprecedented level of participation in the Tokyo round.[43] As it turned out, however, the Tokyo codes had only a very limited direct impact on provincial policy instruments. Subnational governments were exempted from all provisions of the government procurement code. The subsidies code was too weak and preliminary to have much impact on provinces.[44]

Only the technical barriers code created obligations sufficiently specific and robust to provide the basis for GATT-based challenges to provincial government measures. Article 2.1 committed governments to ensure that technical standards and regulations "do not have the effect of creating unnecessary obstacles to international trade," and that products imported from other parties are accorded "treatment no less favourable than that accorded to like products of national origin" in relation to such standards and regulations.[45]

Canada-U.S. FTA

The restrictions on provincial policy instruments created by the FTA went well beyond those found in the Tokyo GATT. Indeed, the Ontario Ministry of the Attorney-General concluded that, while it did not "purport to change the formal division of powers prescribed in the Constitution Act, 1867,"

> the Agreement will permanently alter the capacity [of provincial governments] to make economic and social policy in Canada, sometimes shifting it to the federal government, sometimes abandoning it for all governments. This dramatic change in the ability of governments to respond to the legitimate expectations of their populations amounts to a constitutional change.[46]

Of the many areas examined by the Ontario Attorney-General, only the most important can be highlighted here. These include the new investor property rights and the restrictions on the operations and policies of provincial government monopolies, discussed above.

The National Treatment requirement of the FTA Investment chapter might, for example, prevent provincial governments from treating American insurance companies differently from their domestic competitors, even if there were sound industrial policy reasons for wishing to do so. The new monopolies provisions could make it much more expensive to introduce public auto insurance in provinces that do not already have it.[47] The FTA also prohibited provincial policies restricting the export of some unprocessed natural resources. Such policies have been used to promote job creation in the short run, and over the longer haul, the development of forward and backward industrial linkages from the exploitation of raw materials.[48]

The FTA included a commitment to develop an FTA subsidies code over a period of five to seven years.[49] This code would likely have had important implications for provincial policy, but the commitment to develop such a code has thus far been quietly dropped when it became clear that American negotiators were not willing to make substantial concessions on this matter.[50]

Provincial food and agricultural product standards ("sanitary and phytosanitary" or SPS standards), were already covered by the Tokyo GATT technical standards codes, but the FTA subjected such measures to a more stringent test than the GATT: standards must not create an "arbitrary, unjustifiable, or disguised restriction on bilateral trade."[51] Depending upon how these tests were interpreted, provincial governments might find it more difficult to maintain or increase environmental standards.

Despite its broad impact on provincial policy instruments, the FTA's dispute resolution mechanisms (Chapters 18 and 19), made no provision for provincial participation. Provincial governments had no role in the selection of Canadian panel members, and no right to participate in defending provincial measures against American challenges. Moreover, the federal government alone had the right to decide whether to contest a challenge, and if so, by what arguments, and whether to launch a challenge on behalf of a province or a private actor. Contrast this with the procedures employed in the German federation for negotiating and implementing EC provisions trenching on the jurisdiction of the Länder.[52]

The FTA's impact on current provincial government policies was mitigated in two important ways. First, many of its provisions were "grandfathered" (i.e., measures already in place prior to the implementation of the FTA on 1 January 1989 were exempt from coverage). The bulk of the FTA's burden was thus imposed on future provincial governments, which will find it impossible to develop many new classes of policy instruments, or to employ many traditional policy instruments in innovative ways, in response to new international challenges or new voter demands. The FTA's alcoholic beverages provisions were the only ones requiring an immediate change in provincial practices.[53] Second, Ottawa's approach to implementing legislation was calculated to present the smallest possible target to provincial government objections and a possible constitutional challenge. Three approaches were considered. The least immediately obtrusive was chosen after consultations with provincial governments indicated that the support of some was contingent on adopting this "minimalist" approach.[54] The federal legislation which implemented the FTA provided if necessary for federal regulations to implement the wine and spirits provisions, but put off their introduction to a later date. Beyond that, it simply reserved the right to introduce legislation to enforce other provisions of the agreement against any non-complying subnational government should this become necessary.

NAFTA and its Side-Deals

Most of the new types of restrictions on government measures found in the NAFTA apply to provincial government measures. Among these are the three new kinds of "performance requirements" found in the Investment chapter, the new restrictions on state enterprises in Chapter 15, and the substantial expansion of the rights of foreign financial service providers set out in Chapter 14. The NAFTA's new investor-state dispute process for enforcing these private property rights can be used to challenge provincial as well as federal measures. As with FTA and NAFTA panels, so with the new investor-state arbitration tribunals, provincial governments have no place in any of the dispute resolution processes set out in the agreement.

Consider the new performance requirement prohibitions. Product mandating and technology transfer are important industrial policy instruments for provincial as for federal governments, particularly in countries such as Canada that rely heavily on foreign investment. TNCs may not wish to see the wide diffusion of technologies that they develop, as this may increase the competition that they face. They may also resist pressures to include a full range of managerial and R&D employment in countries other than their home base.[55] The need for such requirements may be increasing, owing to changing TNC strategies that reduce the autonomy of their operations outside their home country.[56] The NAFTA's prohibition of these policy instruments was thus important for future provincial governments, even though most do not employ such measures at present.

The NAFTA also expands FTA restrictions on provincial governments in several ways. The new and wider definition of "investors" eligible for the rights created in the Investment and State Enterprise chapters increases the number of private actors that can directly challenge provincial government measures. In contrast to the FTA, the NAFTA applies to all provincial technical standards, and toughens the tests that provincial governments must meet in order to defend technical and SPS standards. It also expands the scope of provincially regulated financial institutions covered to include all such institutions.

As in the FTA, many of the NAFTA's provisions are "grandfathered," so that their principal burden falls on future provincial governments rather than current ones. Once again, federal implementing legislation minimizes requirements to change existing provincial laws, claiming instead the right to enforce the agreement through later legislation, should a party or investor mount a successful challenge to a provincial measure. These approaches minimize the immediate impact of the NAFTA on provincial governments, but they imply a federal claim to the jurisdiction to enforce such provisions at some future date.

Yet the government of Canada maintains that the only serious inroads into provincial jurisdiction in the NAFTA package are located in the provisions of the labour and environmental side-deals. Hence the complex procedures, outlined above, that permit individual provinces to opt-in, and make Canada's rights and obligations under these agreements conditional upon reaching a certain threshold of voluntary provincial participation. There is no doubt that jurisdiction over approximately 90 percent of Canada's paid workforce, and all of the laws and regulations applying to them *qua* workers, falls to the provinces.

The division of powers relevant to the matters covered in the environmental side-deal is more complex and less clear. Unanticipated by the framers of the constitution, environmental issues could fall under federal exclusive jurisdiction insofar as they have international and interprovincial dimensions, and under exclusive provincial jurisdiction insofar as they pertain to provincial ownership of and regulatory powers over natural resources. The actual working relationship that emerged out of this constitutional uncertainty in the 1970s may be characterized as a situation of *de facto* concurrent jurisdiction, in which the two orders of government interact as follows:

> Generally, the federal government agrees to establish national baseline effluent and emission standards for specific industrial groups and specific pollutants, and the provinces agree to establish and enforce requirements at least as stringent. Both parties agree to cooperative monitoring programs in areas of joint interest and to free exchange of data.[57]

So both side-deals bear on matters falling partially or primarily within provincial jurisdiction. Yet the side-deals in no way require provincial governments to alter their laws or regulations in these areas. Even if we set aside the possibility of provincial opt-out, all that the side-deals do is create a long and convoluted dispute resolution process. At the end of that process, the governments of Mexico and the United States are entitled to collect fines from the Government of Canada unless and until it is able to convince a non-complying provincial government to improve the enforcement of its own laws. In what sense can this be seen as a federal intrusion into provincial jurisdiction?

Federal pressure on a province to enforce its own laws could affect its budget priorities since the provincial government in question might prefer to allocate a larger share of its budget to something other than enforcing the particular labour or environmental standards in question. But there is surely a difference between federal actions that affect provincial spending priorities (e.g., capping the CAP), and outright federal intrusions into areas of provincial jurisdiction (e.g., federal claims to enforce investor property rights against provincial governments and their enterprises). The side-deals' provisions fall in the former category of indirect influence; it is the NAFTA itself, as the above example suggests, that includes a long list of provisions falling in the latter category of more direct intrusion.

Even the claim that the side-deals could, in principle, force provincial governments to alter their spending priorities may be over-blown, because the side-deals are actually highly solicitous of democratic governments' rights to set their own priorities. For example, Article 5.3 of the labour side-deal (9 August 1993 draft) states that:

> a Party has not failed to "effectively enforce its labour law" when an agency or official of that Party has not taken action authorized by law to prevent, halt or penalize violations, or ameliorate the consequences of such violations, of labour statutes and regulations, but such inaction: (a) reflects a reasonable exercise of the agency's or official's discretion with respect to investigatory, prosecutorial, regulatory, or compliance matters; or (b) results from *bona fide* decisions to allocate enforcement resources to violations determined to have higher priorities.[58]

The environmental side-deal has a similar provision, though it is located in an Annex containing definitions.[59]

Labour rights and standards are stronger and better enforced in most Canadian jurisdictions than in either the United States or Mexico. The same can confidently be said of environmental standards and their enforcement in Canada, relative to Mexico. The U.S.-Canada comparison on environmental standards is another matter; here there is evidence that American enforcement (of standards at least as stringent) is significantly better than Canadian, at least in some areas.[60] This implies that, with the possible exception of some environmental regulations, the Mexican and American governments are unlikely to challenge enforcement by Canadian provinces. They have no reason to fear Canadian social dumping, and little incentive to challenge enforcement practices in Canada that their domestic critics (and ours) will be quick to identify as tougher than their own. Since ordinary Canadians have no right to use the dispute resolution processes set out in the side-deals, challenges will not come from the Canadian labour or environmental movements either.[61]

The upshot is that in most of the areas covered by the side-deals, there is not likely to be anyone who is both willing and able to use them to pressure provincial governments to alter their enforcement or spending priorities, even if provinces lacked the right to opt-out. Yet the governments of Quebec and Alberta publicly express fears that the side-deals will trench on provincial jurisdiction in unacceptable ways.[62] This contrasts sharply with the FTA and the (main text of the) NAFTA, both of which purport to impose substantial legal restrictions on a wide range of provincial government policy instruments. Neither of these agreements has comparable provincial opt-in provisions, yet the same provincial governments have strongly backed both the FTA and the NAFTA, down-playing their potential impacts on provincial jurisdiction. I will return to this odd behaviour in the final section of the paper.

EXTENT OF FEDERAL OBLIGATION TO ENFORCE

All of the new provincial obligations that the FTA and the NAFTA purport to create may amount to little if the federal government has no serious obligation to enforce such provisions against provincial governments. How strong is this federal obligation in the NAFTA, and how does it compare with the obligations in the Tokyo GATT and the FTA?

The Tokyo round left untouched the GATT's original "federal state" clause, which states that: "Each contracting party shall take *such reasonable measures* as may be available to it to ensure observance of the provisions of this Agreement by the regional and local governments and authorities within its territory."[63] "Reasonable measures" was not defined in the original GATT, or in any of its subsequent iterations. With respect to the Tokyo GATT, the Government of Canada has taken the position that it cannot "reasonably" be expected to launch constitutional court cases aimed at establishing federal jurisdiction in areas long regarded by courts and politicians as falling under exclusive provincial jurisdiction.

The federal government's obligation to enforce the FTA against provincial governments was substantially strengthened under Article 103 of the agreement, which stated that: "The Parties [i.e., the two federal governments] to this agreement shall ensure that *all necessary measures* are taken in order to give effect to its provisions, except as otherwise provided in this Agreement, by state, provincial and local governments." The FTA does not specify what a party must do to meet this obligation. But it is widely agreed that this language is stronger than the GATT's "reasonableness" standard.[64] FTA dispute resolution panels will determine what counts as "all necessary measures" in the first instance. It appears that panels can be over-ruled on such interpretative matters by the Commission comprised of Cabinet-level officials operating on a consensus basis.[65]

Article 105 of the NAFTA incorporates the FTA's "all necessary measures" language, and the agreement appears to assign a parallel final appeal role to its Commission. It remains to be seen how this term will be interpreted. Consider the following scenario: a group of American insurance companies use the new investor-state dispute process to challenge the Ontario government's plan to create a public auto insurance system without compensating them for their lost business. They win their case at the arbitral tribunal. The federal government is obliged to convince Ontario to alter its policy. If it fails, it will have to pay the damages that result to the private insurance companies (or incur the loss of NAFTA benefits for failing to pay such damages).[66] Ottawa consults with Ontario, but the provincial government is adamant. Is the federal government obliged by Article 105 to do anything more, or can it just pay the damages and leave it at that?

It might be argued by the complainants that Ottawa has not met its Article 105 obligation to take "all necessary measures" until it employs the financial and constitutional levers at its disposal to try to stop the Ontario government from implementing this policy. After all, federal payment of damages for provincial non-compliance is not the same as provincial compliance, and Article 105 speaks of the federal government's obligation to ensure the latter. "All necessary measures," in plain English, means whatever measures are necessary to get the job done. If the parties wanted a weaker standard than that, it could be argued, they could have retained the weaker GATT standard.

If a NAFTA panel accepted such arguments, and ruled that the federal government must launch a constitutional challenge against Ontario's right to pursue such a policy in order to meet its Article 105 obligations, the NAFTA Commission would have to decide whether to back the panel's interpretation. The Commission, which must operate by consensus, could decide to override the NAFTA panel, perhaps on the not implausible grounds that such an exercise of *force majeure* could well provoke a constitutional crisis in Canada that would result in the abrogation of the NAFTA. On the other hand, with a lot of money at stake, there would be strong pressures on the American government to press its claims. It would have to consider not only the losses in the Ontario case, but also the implications for the security of American investments in Mexico — the single most important purpose of the entire treaty for the United States. In the absence of a Commission consensus to the contrary, the panel's interpretation would presumably stand.

We cannot know exactly how far the federal government might be compelled to go in order to meet its Article 105 obligations, or what would happen if the Government of Canada balked at a NAFTA panel's interpretation on this point. All that can be said with any conviction is that the high conflict scenario sketched above does not depend on manifestly implausible provincial government policy objectives, or wild interpretations of NAFTA investor rights or of the words of Article 105.

FEDERAL ENFORCEMENT STRATEGIES

By what means might the federal government seek to meet its Article 105 obligations, and how effective are these means likely to be? I first consider the constitutional division of powers as it bears on the federal government's capacity to enforce through legislation. I then turn to the non-legislative means by which the federal government might attempt to induce provincial government compliance, regardless of the constitutional division of powers.

The federal government could argue for its authority to make laws to implement and enforce the NAFTA under its treaty power, its trade and commerce power, or its "Peace, Order and Good Government" (POGG) power. The federal treaty power appears to be the least promising of these possibilities, owing to the near-sacred status that the JCPC's decision in the *Labour Conventions* case (1937) has acquired over the years.[67] The case involved federal legislation to implement three International Labour Organization (ILO) conventions that the Bennett government had ratified in 1935. Lord Atkin, for the Judicial Committee of the Privy Council, held that the federal government could only introduce the legislation necessary to implement treaties on matters falling within its jurisdiction. In areas falling under provincial jurisdiction, the federal government would have to persuade provincial governments to introduce the required implementing legislation, if legislation were required. In Canada, the federal government could not expand the scope of its jurisdiction simply by signing a treaty trenching on provincial jurisdiction.

The more likely strategy is to expand what has traditionally been understood to be the scope of federal jurisdiction so as to encompass the provincial practices that the federal government is required to alter. The most promising ways to realize this objective are to build on recent developments in the interpretation of the federal trade and commerce and POGG powers.

In the United States, the federal commerce power was dramatically expanded in a series of landmark cases upholding the constitutionality of much of President Roosevelt's New Deal legislation.[68] In Canada, however, the JCPC defined the Canadian trade and commerce power much more narrowly. In the 1960s, the Supreme Court of Canada began to broaden the interpretation somewhat.[69] But the most important trade and commerce power case for our purposes is a very recent one, *General Motors v. City National Leasing* (1989). In that case, the six Supreme Court of Canada judges participating in the decision unanimously upheld the federal *Combines Investigation Act* on the ground that it fell within the scope of the federal trade and commerce power. In so doing, the court affirmed the criteria developed by (then) Chief Justice Dickson in the *C.N. Transportation* case (1983): (i) the regulatory scheme must be national in scope, rather than local, and pertain to trade in general, rather that a particular business; (ii) provinces must be constitutionally incapable of implementing the type of regulation in question; and (iii) failure to include one or more provinces must jeopardize the successful operation of the regulatory scheme in other parts of the country.[70]

It is difficult to assess the federal government's capacity to meet these conditions. The first seems straightforward: the NAFTA is surely national in scope and pertains to trade in general. However, the NAFTA applies to much more than trade and commerce (i.e., to investment flows and investor and intellectual property rights). These latter provisions certainly affect trade and commerce, but then so do any number of other things (e.g., civil rights and language policies). It could therefore be argued that the first branch of Dickson's test screens out the federal government's power to enforce aspects of the NAFTA that fall outside some reasonably circumscribed definition of "trade and commerce."

The second test could also be difficult for the federal government to meet. Provincial governments are constitutionally capable of implementing the NAFTA provisions that bear on their practices; the problem is that they may not all want to implement such provisions. The third condition raises the question: What counts as "the regulatory scheme"? If it is the NAFTA as a whole, and one province fails to implement some or all of its provisions, this may not undermine the deal as a whole. If it does not, then it will continue to apply in the other provinces. If several provinces refuse to cooperate, however, the other NAFTA parties may threaten to pull out of the deal, which would have an impact on all provinces. On this reading, as much depends upon the behaviour of other provinces and other parties to the agreement as it does on the behaviour of a single non-complying province.

The leading case expanding the POGG power is *Crown Zellerbach* (1988). In that case, the Supreme Court of Canada upheld federal legislation prohibiting the dumping of any substance at sea, even though the definition of "sea" included provincial internal waters, and some kinds of dumping might have no direct effect on an expressly conferred federal jurisdiction such as the fisheries. The court upheld the federal law not on the ground that it was necessary to implement an international convention, but on the ground that it was necessary to realize an objective of "national concern." The court set out three conditions that federal legislation must meet in order to fall under the "national concern" dimension of the POGG power: (i) "it must have a singleness and distinctiveness of purpose that distinguishes it from provincial legislation; (ii) it must have a limited scale of impact so as not to cut a devastating path through provincial jurisdictions; and (iii) it must have been shown that the failure of a province or provinces to deal effectively with the problem would have significant extra-provincial impacts."[71]

It is not easy to assess the chances of a federal claim to enforce one of the agreements considered here under this new doctrine. Regarding the first condition, it could be argued that implementing the NAFTA is a single purpose, and one that falls outside provincial jurisdiction by virtue of its status as an international agreement. But "singleness of purpose" is a slippery concept. If the intent (or effect?) of the agreement is not only to permit the freer movement of goods and services across national borders, but also to alter the risks and other incentives facing investors in ways that will substantially alter international capital flows, does the NAFTA embody multiple "purposes"? As to the second condition, what counts as a "devastating" intrusion into provincial jurisdiction? Will courts look only to the impact that the NAFTA has on existing provincial policies, or will they consider what future provincial electorates might want their governments to do? The final condition should be relatively easy to meet. If a provincial government is found to have violated the provisions of one of these agreements and fails to alter its behaviour, then trade sanctions may be levied against Canada as a whole, rather than the offending province alone. Such sanctions would constitute a clear extra-provincial impact. Knowing this, other NAFTA parties keen to increase the federal government's enforcement capacity would have a strong incentive to threaten this sort of sanction.

In summary, all of the possible routes for justifying federal legislative enforcement are problematic. The federal trade and commerce and POGG powers are more promising than the federal treaty power, but it is by no means obvious that any of them are adequate to justify the scale of the shift in what we have heretofore understood to be the division of powers implied by the FTA and the NAFTA. Of course, the issue will only be decided *en masse* in this way, rather than on a case-by-case basis, if a government sends a more general reference to the courts. This is a high risk move for either side.

The language of the new conditions posited in these areas is far too vague to permit such weighty matters to be decided by a process of deduction from doctrinal first principles, even if there were a judicial consensus on a doctrine or model of federalism in Canada. In practice, the trade-offs implicit in the answers given by the courts, while buttressed by reason, will depend upon the ideological and political commitments of those who sit on the bench. These personal biases will be tempered and conditioned by the balance of political forces in the wider society, because unelected judges concerned to maintain the legitimacy of judicial review in a democratic society can never move very far away from any broad societal consensus that emerges.

The NAFTA does not require the federal government to override or strike down non-conforming provincial measures by legislative means. It is enough if the federal government can induce provincial governments to bring their measures into conformity with the requirements of the agreement through some form of positive or negative incentive. The two most plausible tools at this level are the threat to introduce enforcement legislation, and the use of the federal spending power.

If the federal government introduced enforcement legislation that clearly overrode significant provincial legislation, the affected provincial governments would be forced to either back down and lose face, or launch a constitutional challenge. If they launched such a challenge and lost, the ramifications for their jurisdiction might be larger and more negative than compliance with the particular provisions in the federal legislation as noted above. Depending on the importance of the measure at issue (e.g., public auto insurance versus an obscure effluent standard), and how risk averse the affected governments are, they might decide that bowing to the federal legislation is the lesser evil.

Another weapon in the federal enforcement arsenal, which can be used as a carrot or a stick, is its spending power. Given the level of federal transfers to provincial governments — particularly the share of total revenues that such transfers represent for the poorer provinces — the threat to make some part of those transfers conditional on meeting NAFTA obligations cannot be dismissed lightly. Some find this scenario implausible, but the federal government was willing to use this weapon to protect the principles of the *Canada Health Act.* It does not seem so far-fetched to think that a future federal government (perhaps even the current one) will put at least as much stock in the private property rights embodied in the NAFTA as in the principles of Canada's health-care system. Certainly, the current federal government has not been reluctant, in the name of budgetary responsibility, to violate the conventions governing unilateral changes to the five-yearly federal-provincial fiscal arrangements.[72] Is not the defence of "free trade," a good relationship with our major trading partner, and so on, at least as compelling as balancing the federal budget?

To conclude, the NAFTA main agreement (unlike the side-deals) purports to impose stronger legal restrictions on a broader range of actual and potential provincial policy instruments than any other trade agreement Canada has ever signed. The precise character of the federal government's obligation to enforce these restrictions against recalcitrant provincial governments is unclear, but it is likely to be more extensive than the GATT. The federal government's constitutional right to enforce these provisions legislatively is also unclear, but Ottawa has a number of potentially quite effective means to induce provincial compliance, short of outright legislation. In all of these respects, the NAFTA echoes and reinforces the FTA. Taken together, these considerations suggest that the NAFTA could become the legal basis for a significant narrowing of the provincial policy space, whether or not this is ever recognized as a formal shift in the division of powers.

CONCLUSION

Pulling together the discussion of the last three sections, the most general conclusion is that things are not always as they appear to be. It might appear that the greatest constraints on provincial government powers are to be found in the legal restrictions embodied in these agreements. But the largest and most powerful constraints on Canada's provincial governments are likely to result from the substantially increased capital mobility that depends most upon the legal restrictions imposed on the federal government of Mexico.

It might appear that the legal restrictions on the federal Government of Canada are greater than those that apply to the provincial governments, since all restrictions in these agreements apply to the federal government, while only some apply to provincial governments. Nevertheless, Ottawa has found a way to at least claim the right to regulate provincial governments to an extent far beyond anything ever attempted with the spending power, and provincial governments have thus far granted this claim sufficient credibility by refraining to test it in the courts. Moreover, the market constraints increased by the agreement will fall most heavily on provincial and local governments.

It might appear that the most substantial legal restrictions on provincial jurisdiction must be located in the side-deals, since these are the agreements that give provincial governments the right to opt-out, and indeed, to "deactivate" the entire agreement if most choose not to participate. Yet it seems most unlikely that the side-deals will require changes in existing provincial policies in the labour and environmental fields, or foreclose any future options that provincial governments might wish to pursue. Conversely, the NAFTA — which lacks all such opt-out and threshold mechanisms — is the source of a wide range of important legal restrictions on current and future provincial government policy instruments and options.

Finally, it might appear that the Meech Lake and Charlottetown Accords were about fundamental constitutional reform, while the FTA and NAFTA are about something quite different called trade policy. But the federal government has sought (among other things) to advance the same neo-conservative policy prescriptions in both processes. Efforts to bring expanded private property rights and increased court powers over provincial industrial policies through the front door of formal constitutional reform were blocked by provincial governments, social movements, and Canadian voters. It may be argued therefore that important steps towards the realization of these objectives were nonetheless made through the back door opened by the FTA and the NAFTA. These gains have been entrenched in the quasi-constitutional form of an international agreement that will be difficult if not impossible for subsequent national governments to amend in these areas, and more costly to abrogate with each passing year. In the constitutional shell game, the pea turns out to have been under the shell labelled "trade policy."

For a decade now, the attention of students of federalism has been rivetted on our marathon efforts to amend the constitution, in ever more baroque ways, in response to the burgeoning demands of the politics of collective identity. These reform efforts — those that succeeded and those that did not — have changed Canadians and, to some degree, the character of Canadian federalism. They have not, however, resulted in any major changes in the formal or the actual division of powers. The politics of identity may yet alter the character of Canadian federalism more profoundly, perhaps even leading to the exit of Quebec from the federation.

Meanwhile, however, the character of Canadian federalism is subject to change from another source: developments in the international and domestic political economy, and changes in the economic and social roles of the state. For the foreseeable future, the form that globalization takes will be the most important determinant of changes of this type. I would argue that two broad types of globalization are possible: one would extend the national and subnational deregulation trends of the 1980s; the other would build new supranational institutions to regulate international worker rights and labour and environmental standards. I called these the neo-conservative and the communitarian forms of globalization.

No matter which form of globalization prevails, federal intrusions into provincial jurisdictions can be expected to increase in scope, and both orders of government will be increasingly subordinate to new quasi-constitutional obligations located in international agreements backed by trade sanctions. The real issue is not whether such a reduction in "state sovereignty" — both federal and provincial — can be stopped, but what form this reduction takes, and what ends it serves. I have argued that neo-conservative globalization will substantially reduce the capacity of both national and provincial governments to pursue the kinds of public goods that their electorates value (e.g., low unemployment and rising real wages). Communitarian globalization, on the other hand, offers the prospect of increasing governments' capacity to realize such values, even though they restrict the policy instruments available to do so.

The international economic integration agreements such as the *Single European Market Act* and the FTA, the NAFTA, and the Maastricht Treaty will be among the most important determinants of which form of globalization emerges in the coming years. If implemented, the NAFTA will substantially encourage the neo-conservative form of globalization. In part, this flows from the new legal restrictions that the agreement imposes on a wide range of federal and provincial policy instruments. But even more important are the new market constraints on government power and policy options that flow from the increased capital mobility that this agreement promotes. The market constraints will exist even if Canada refuses to implement the NAFTA, provided that the United States and Mexico go ahead with it. The market constraints will also hit provincial governments harder than national governments. Only the defeat of the NAFTA in the United States or Mexico can prevent an acceleration of already existing tendencies towards the neo-conservative model of globalization in North America.

The labour and environmental side-deals to the NAFTA, insisted upon by the Clinton administration, and strongly resisted by the governments of both Canada and Mexico, represent a gesture — but little more than that — in the direction of communitarian globalization. They do not even begin to neutralize the NAFTA's acceleration and intensification of the trend towards neo-conservative globalization, much less to set the political economies of North America firmly on the path to communitarian globalization. When assessing the likely impact of these agreements on the character of Canadian federalism, then, we must view them as promoting subordinate federalism in the context of neo-conservative globalization. So understood, there are best-case and worst-case scenarios.

In the best case, where the economy performs well, subordinate federalism is likely to resemble the "classical" federalism of the 1920s more than anything else with which we are familiar. Both orders of government will do much less, with fewer policy instruments. They will therefore interact with one another less, whether in cooperation or conflict.

In the worst case, stronger versions of the neo-conservative economic policy prescriptions of the 1980s will only exacerbate current economic problems of high and rising unemployment, falling real wages for most Canadians, and increasing income polarization. In such an economic context, the federal government will have to try to enforce a wide range of NAFTA-type restrictions against provincial governments and electorates that are increasingly inclined to view them as counterproductive and unconstitutional. The result could be intense federal-provincial conflict and constitutional crisis.

NOTES

This chapter is based on a paper presented to the annual meeting of the Canadian Political Science Association at Carleton University, on 7 June 1993. Thanks to Alain Noel for organizing the session, and to Richard Simeon, Ronald Watts, and Yves Vaillancourt for their comments on that paper. My understanding of the NAFTA and its relation to provincial power has also been advanced through conversations with Frank Longo, Barry Appleton, Louise Barry, Sandra Morris, and Doug Brown over the course of the last year. Thanks are also due to Doug Brown and Patti Candido for their editorial work on this manuscript. Any remaining errors are my own. Research for this paper was made possible in part by a Post-Doctoral Research Fellowship from the Social Sciences and Humanities Research Council of Canada.

1. For the details of these developments, and an explanation of the periodization in the evolution of Canadian federalism that will be used throughout this chapter, see Richard Simeon and Ian Robinson, *State, Society and the Development of Canadian Federalism* (Toronto: University of Toronto Press, 1990).
2. See my forthcoming chapter "Globalization, Trade Policy and Canadian Federalism," in François Rocher and Miriam Smith (eds.), *New Trends in Canadian Federalism* (Peterborough: Broadview, forthcoming).
3. By the time the FTA was signed, the Tokyo GATT had been fully implemented. By 1987, about 70 percent of Canadian goods entered the United States duty free and vice versa. The average American tariff on the remaining 30 percent of Canadian goods was under 5 percent, though it was over 20 percent in the apparel sector. The average Canadian tariff against American goods was somewhat higher, but under 10 percent. See Michael Hart, *A North American Free Trade Agreement* (Halifax: Institute for Research on Public Policy, 1990), pp. 42-43.
4. For an overview of Mexican tariffs, border measures, and NTBs as of 1990, see Clyde Prestowitz, Jr. and Robert Cohen, with Peter Morici and Alan Tonelson, *The New North American Order: A Win-Win Strategy for U.S.-Mexico Trade* (New York: University Press of America, 1991), pp. 14-23, 113-16.
5. "Property rights" include but go beyond the exclusive ownership of a thing or an idea. A right to the value accruing from — or expected to accrue from — the use of some thing or idea is also a property right. Government regulations can reduce the value of property even though they do not expropriate it. Investor rights that restrict such government regulations — or provide for compensation for any lost value caused by such regulations — can thus be understood as a species of property rights.
6. The NAFTA's Investment chapter is the only one that American negotiators sought to protect with a clause guaranteeing that its provisions would continue to apply for a full decade after abrogation, should any party exercise its right to abrogate the agreement. This provision was cut in the final round of negotiations and does

not appear in the final text, but it indicates the unique importance attached to this chapter by American negotiators.
7. FTA Article 1603. Performance requirements are conditions that investors must meet if they are to do business in a province or nation. Most apply exclusively to foreign corporations, because the ownership structure of these corporations was thought to make them less amenable to other forms of government regulation, and more likely to behave in ways contrary to the public interest. The National Treatment principle would require governments to generalize performance requirements to all comparable investors, foreign and domestic. The four performance requirements listed are prohibited even if governments impose them equally on domestic investors.
8. FTA Article 1605. This may amount to importing American property rights jurisprudence into Canada. Under Canadian law, there is a convention of statutory interpretation to the effect that governments are bound to compensate private property holders who are expropriated unless the expropriating legislation clearly indicates that there is to be no compensation. See *Manitoba Fisheries* case [1979] 1 S.C.R. 101. Under American constitutional law, no matter what a government includes in a statute, the constitution has been interpreted to prohibit the expropriation of private property without "just compensation." See *Pennsylvania Coal v. Mahon* (1922) 260 U.S. 393.
9. See FTA Article 2011. The "nullification and impairment" clause states that a government measure need not conflict with the provisions of the FTA in order to violate this Article. Nor need the expected benefits be "directly" affected by the measure in question; it is enough if they are "indirectly" affected (whatever that means).
10. "Technology transfer" conditions require foreign investors to train Canadian workers and engineers in all stages of product development, manufacture, and sale. "Product mandating" requires the parent TNC to assign its operations in a particular country the mandate to develop, produce, and market one or more products in the continental or global market.
11. Foreign investors seeking the more limited protections of the FTA's Investment chapter had to own a majority of shares in, or otherwise control, the business claiming these protections. The NAFTA definition of "investment" merely requires *some* American or Mexican ownership or control. This appears to grant almost any publicly held business operating in Canada protection under this chapter, since most of them will have at least some American (or Mexican) ownership. Protection against the performance requirements listed in Article 1106 extends even further to include all foreign investors.
12. Article 2010 of the FTA imposed constraints on the creation of new monopolies and the operation of existing ones by governments. Governments had to try to "minimize or eliminate any nullification or impairment of benefits" to U.S. investors or exporters caused by such monopolies. Further, monopolies were required to act "solely in accordance with commercial considerations" and could not use their monopoly power to engage in "anticompetitive practices," such as "the discriminatory provision of the monopoly good or service, cross-subsidization or predatory conduct."

13. NAFTA Articles 1502, 1503 and 1505.
14. There were no *intellectual property* (IP) provisions in the Tokyo GATT or the FTA. Intellectual property rights were discussed during the FTA negotiations at American insistence, but no agreement was reached. See G. Bruce Doern and Brian W. Tomlin, *Faith and Fear: The Free Trade Story* (Toronto: Stoddart, 1991), pp. 67-74, 97-98, 153-57, and 281-82.
15. NAFTA Articles 1714-1718.
16. FTA Article 1703.
17. NAFTA Articles 1405 and 1401, respectively.
18. NAFTA Article 1415.
19. Article 1407.
20. NAFTA Article 904.
21. See "United States — Section 337, Report of the Panel (16.1.89)," *World Trade Materials*, 2, 1 (January 1990): 51-53.
22. For example, Northern Telecom has recently developed a non-ozone-depleting (i.e., CFC-free) way of cleaning printed circuits and microchips. Were Canada to require that all producers of such materials in that province and all exporters of such materials to that province employ a CFC-free process, this would place Northern Telecom's foreign rivals at a competitive disadvantage in Canada until they licensed its clean technology or developed their own. This would be enough to qualify such a regulation as discriminatory, hence trade restrictive, on the ECO interpretation. Thanks to Frank Longo for this example.
23. NAFTA Articles 1404.5, 1404.6, and 1404.7.
24. See Claus Offe and Helmut Weisenthal, "Two Logics of Collective Action," in Maurice Zeitlin (ed.), *Political Power and Social Theory*, vol. 1 (Greenwood, Conn.: JAI Press, 1980), pp. 67-115.
25. See C.E. Lindblom, "The Market as Prison," in Thomas Ferguson and Joel Rogers, (eds.), *The Political Economy: Readings in the Politics and Economics of American Public Policy* (Armonk, NY: M.E. Sharpe, 1984), pp. 3-11.
26. See Adam Przeworski and Michael Wallerstein, "Democratic Capitalism at the Crossroads, " in Ferguson and Rogers (eds.), ibid., pp. 335-48.
27. For estimates of the scale of the losses incurred by the Canadian government as a result of cuts in corporate income tax since the early 1970s, motivated in part by the intensifying international competition for investment, see David Wolfe, "The Politics of Deficits," in G. Bruce Doern (ed.), *The Politics of Economic Policy* (Toronto: University of Toronto Press, 1985), pp. 111-162.
28. See David R. Cameron, "The Growth of Government Spending: The Canadian Experience in Comparative Perspective," in Keith Banting (ed.), *State and Society: Canada in Comparative Perspective* (Toronto: University of Toronto Press, 1986), pp. 21-51; and John D. Stephens, *The Transition from Capitalism to Socialism* (Chicago: University of Illinois Press, 1986), pp. 89-176.
29. See Stephens, ibid., pp. 163-76; and Francis Green, Andrew Henley and Euclid Tsakalotos, "Income Inequality in Corporatist and Liberal Economies: A

Comparison of Trends within OECD Countries," Working Paper 92/13 (Leicester: Centre for Labour Market Studies, University of Leicester, November 1992).

30. See David R. Cameron, "Social Democracy, Corporatism, Labour Quiescence, and the Representation of Economic Interest in Advanced Capitalist Society," in John H. Goldthorpe (ed.), *Order and Conflict in Contemporary Capitalism: Studies in the Political Economy of Western European Nations* (Oxford: The Clarendon Press, 1984), pp. 143-178; and Miriam Golden, "The Dynamics of Trade Unionism and National Economic Performance," *American Political Science Review*, 87, 2 (June 1993): 439-54.

31. See Noah Meltz, "Unionism in the Private-Service Sector: A Canada-U.S. Comparison," in Jane Jenson and Rianne Mahon (eds.), *The Challenge of Restructuring: North American Labor Movements Respond* (Philadelphia: Temple University Press, 1993), pp. 207-225.

32. By "social dumping" I mean a competitive strategy that pushes the costs of labour and/or natural resource inputs below their real costs to society and/or the global ecosystem. Costs can be externalized in this fashion by repressing worker rights or maintaining labour standards far below the levels that productivity levels permit, and/or by exploiting the environment without any consideration for the standards necessary to maintain the sustainability of the resource. On social dumping in North America, see Jim Stanford, "Cheap Labour as an Unfair Subsidy in North American Free Trade," (Ottawa: Canadian Centre for Policy Alternatives, 1992). On social dumping in the EC, see Christopher Erickson and Sarosh Kuruvilla, "Labor Costs and the Social Dumping Debate in the European Community," photocopied ms. (October 1992).

33. The unbracketed portions are those on which there was already agreement among the negotiators by 9 August 1993. It is therefore less likely that there will be changes to these sections. The 9 August 1993 labour side-deal text was reproduced in full in *Inside U.S. Trade* (20 August 1993), pp. 7-13.

34. See Government of Canada, *Highlights of the Labour and Environmental Agreements* (August 1993).

35. It is not clear who is to determine whether these criteria have been met. It could be the government launching the ECE process, or it might be the first issue to be decided by an ECE once it is convened, or it might be decided in some other fashion.

36. Article 17.3 states that the Evaluation Committee of Experts provisions apply only to "matters occurring after the entry into force of this Agreement." A "pattern" of non-enforcement, according to the definitions in Part VII, must involve "a series of events and does not arise from a single instance or case." Does this mean that sustained failure to enforce prior to the agreement cannot be counted as part of the requisite "series of events"? The answer is probably yes. Article 29 of the environmental side-deal explicitly includes a "non-retroactivity" clause stating that "The provisions of this Agreement do not bind a party in relation to any act or fact which took place or any situation which ceased to exist before the date of entry into force of this Agreement."

37. See Article 17.2 of the 9 August 1993 draft text. Part XI defines "trade related" to mean "a situation involving workplaces, firms, companies or sectors that produce goods or services traded between the Parties or that compete with goods produced and services provided by another Party." This could mean that labour laws otherwise covered by the agreement pertaining to the public sector, and to substantial parts of the private-service sector that are not traded, would be exempt from the agreement. This was one of the Canadian government's original proposals.

38. I see nothing in the text of the 9 August 1993 draft, or in the subsequent dispute resolution provisions texts (see previous endnotes for references) that prevents the arbitral panel from examining complaints of failure to enforce type (b) labour laws. However, the "Summary of the North American Agreement on Labour Cooperation" released on 13 August 1993 indicates that the arbitral panel can investigate alleged violations of the agreement pertaining to "labour laws with respect to health and safety, child labour and minimum wage" (p.4). This is also Scott Otteman's interpretation. See "NAFTA Accord Reveals Watered-Down Deal," *Inside U.S. Trade* (20 August 1993), pp. 1, 6 at 6.

39. See "Kantor Highlights Enforcement Provisions of NAFTA Side Accords," *Inside U.S. Trade* (16 August 1993), pp. S1-S8, at S1. It is doubtful that a statute can deny the courts the right to hear appeals that raise constitutional questions. The agreement presumably refers to appeals based on other grounds.

40. See Annex II: Subnational Governments. The draft text provides for a ministerial council review and possible modification of threshold levels two years after the agreement enters into force. The point of this provision seems to be to make it possible to lower the thresholds if necessary. See "Provinces Could Limit Challenges to Canada Under NAFTA Side-Deals," *Inside U.S. Trade* (20 August 1993), pp. 1, 17 at 17.

41. At his 13 August 1993 press conference, Canadian Trade Minister Thomas Hockin argued that provincial governments have an incentive to participate so as to enable Canada to challenge enforcement failures in the U.S. and Mexico. Participating provinces would also be permitted to take part in a number of the "cooperative exercises" specified in the agreement, if they sign on. See ibid., p. 17. The cooperative exercises mentioned by the minister could be those listed in Part VI of the 9 August 1993 draft, the cooperative consultations process described in Part IV, or both.

42. For a detailed discussion of provincial NTBs, see John Quinn, "Federalism and Foreign Economic Relations," *Canada-United States Law Journal,* 10 (1985): 197-219.

43. For details of the federal-provincial process associated with the Tokyo round negotiations, see Douglas M. Brown, "The Evolving Role of the Provinces in Canada-U.S. Trade Relations," in Douglas M. Brown and Earl H. Fry (eds.), *States and Provinces in the International Economy* (Berkeley: Institute of Governmental Studies Press, University of California, Berkeley, 1993), pp. 107-111.

44. The subsidies code contained a "commitment" by the parties not to employ export subsidies (except for certain primary products). But it did not define an "export subsidy." Nor did it seek to distinguish between subsidies that should be

countervailable and those that should not, leaving this judgement to national legislation. The code's principal impact was on countervailing duties, rather than subsidies per se. National governments wishing to impose a countervailing duty were required to hold prior consultations with the alleged subsidizer, and to demonstrate that some of its producers had suffered material injury as a result of the alleged subsidy. They were also committed to ensure that the scale of any countervailing duties levied was commensurate with the scale of the subsidy that it is supposed to neutralize. Provinces provide subsidies, but they do not levy countervailing duties, so the code did not restrict their subsidy practices. If anything, it provided their subsidy practices with greater protection against massive (and disproportionate) retaliation than they had enjoyed prior to the Tokyo Subsidies Code.

45. See Article 2.1, Agreement on Technical Barriers to Trade, in *The Texts of the Tokyo Round Agreement* (Geneva: GATT, August 1986), pp. 2-3.

46. Ontario Ministry of the Attorney-General, *The Constitutional Impact of the Free Trade Agreement* (Toronto: Ministry of the Attorney-General, 1988), pp. 4-5.

47. Suppose that the provincial government of Ontario passes legislation creating a public monopoly in auto insurance. No private investor has been expropriated, but the value of private investments has been reduced. Should these investors be compensated for this loss of value? American courts have interpreted the constitutional prohibition on "takings" of property without just compensation to include reductions in the value of property. The Canadian convention that statutes will be interpreted to compensate expropriated property-owners — unless the statute explicitly states otherwise — does not conflate expropriation and value-diminishing regulation. Here, as with expropriation, the FTA moves Canadian law towards American property rights doctrines.

48. Controls on the export of logs and unprocessed fish on the east coast were exempted from this prohibition by Article 1203, but export controls on unprocessed minerals and west coast fish are prohibited. "Backward" industrial linkages related to minerals would include mining equipment; "forward" linkages would include refining plants, smelters, and the like.

49. The FTA subsidies code was to provide "rules governing government subsidies and private anti-competitive pricing practices such as dumping, which are not controlled through unilateral application of countervailing and antidumping duties." Government of Canada, *The Canada-U.S. Free Trade Agreement* (Ottawa: External Affairs Canada, 1988), p. 267, referring to Articles 1906 and 1907.

50. A decent interval was observed between the 1988 election and the quiet end of efforts to negotiate the subsidies code. With hindsight, it is remarkable that some trade experts took seriously the idea that this commitment would ever be realized. If the U.S. signed such a code with Canada (20 percent of its export market), and brought its subsidy practices into conformity with it, it would lose an important source of leverage to induce its other trading partners to make reciprocal concessions on their subsidy practices.

Recognizing this, Canadian trade officials now look to the Uruguay round of the GATT for a subsidies code sufficiently strong to discipline American legal definitions of unfair subsidies. However, the subsidies code outlined in the Dunkel draft promises to be highly intrusive with respect to provincial jurisdiction. It divides all subsidies into "general" and "specific" subsidies. All specific subsidies — i.e., those that are targeted on a particular firm, or sector, or region — are *prima facie* trade distorting. If the nation is the unit of analysis, then all subnational government subsidies are regionally specific, since they apply within a part of the nation's territory. All subnational government subsidies are therefore *prima facie* trade distorting and as such, countervailable. Existing inconsistent subsidy programs may be grandfathered for up to three years, but no more. See Matt Schaefer and Thomas O. Singer, "U.S. Multilateral Trade Agreements and the States: An Analysis of Potential GATT Uruguay Round Agreements" (Denver, CO: Western Governors' Association, May 1992), pp. 22-25. Exceptions are made for R&D and assistance to disadvantaged regions, but it is unclear whether provincial regional policies fall under the latter exception unless approved by the federal government. The Canadian government has made altering the subsidies code its top priority in the GATT negotiations, but so far there is no indication that it is succeeding in this effort. See *Inside U.S. Trade* (4 December 1992), p. 3.

51. FTA Article 708.2b. The GATT language, as we have seen, prohibited only "unnecessary" restrictions on trade.

52. See Rudolf Hrbek, "German Federalism and the Challenge of European Integration," in Charlie Jeffrey and Peter Savigear (eds.), *German Federalism Today* (Leicester and London: Leicester University Press, 1991), pp. 84-102. For suggestions on how Canadian practices and processes might be modified to address the same problems, see Richard Simeon, "Federalism and Free Trade," in Peter M. Leslie (ed.), *Canada: The State of the Federation, 1986* (Kingston: Institute of Intergovernmental Relations, Queen's University, 1986), pp. 189-214; and Douglas M. Brown, "The Evolving Role of the Provinces," pp. 123-134.

53. See Brown, ibid., p. 116.

54. For details, see Anonymous, "Issues of Constitutional Jurisdiction," in Peter M. Leslie and Ronald L. Watts, *Canada: The State of the Federation, 1987-88* (Kingston: Institute of Intergovernmental Relations, Queen's University, 1988), pp. 39-55, at pp. 45-46.

55. The federal government claims that it secured an exemption from both provisions in Annex I-C-5, but these exemptions apply only to conditions attached to the federal review of foreign acquisitions of Canadian companies under the *Investment Canada Act*. They do not exempt provincial regulations or conditions, they do not apply to foreign acquisitions of existing foreign investments, and they do not apply to any new foreign acquisitions of Canadian firms valued at less than $150 million.

56. Reed Scowen, "We Are Americans," *Montreal Gazette* (10 February 1993), p. B3, argues that "the role and even the existence of the Canadian head offices of U.S. firms is being questioned everywhere. What, exactly, is the purpose of a second head office in a single market?... The expansion, contraction, and the existence of Canadian factories and research facilities is being reconsidered." Isaiah Litvak, "U.S. Multinationals: Repositioning the Canadian Subsidiary," *Business in the Contemporary World*, 3, 1 (Autumn 1990): 111-19, also finds that many U.S. TNCs are considering moving managerial functions once performed in Canada to American head offices.

57. Testimony of the deputy minister of the environment for Ontario to the Ontario Select Committee on Ontario Hydro Affairs, reported in their published *Hearings* (29 July 1980), p. 27. For a detailed case study of federal-provincial interactions on labour and environmental standards issues, see Ian Robinson, "The Costs of Uncertainty: Regulating Health and Safety in the Canadian Uranium Industry," Working Paper No. 24 (Kingston: Centre for Resource Studies, Queen's University, April 1982).

58. See the text of the 9 August 1993 draft, *Inside U.S. Trade* (20 August 1993), pp. 7-8.

59. See the Annex to the environmental side-deal draft text (10 August), Section II on "Effective Enforcement," in *Inside U.S. Trade*, Special Report (20 August 1993), p. 9.

60. I am not aware of a systematic comparison of environmental standards and enforcement in Canada and the United States. However, Kathryn Harrison's recent paper on enforcement in the pulp and paper industries of the two countries finds that compliance in Canada is significantly lower than in the United States. See Harrison, "Is Cooperation the Answer? A Comparison of Canadian and U.S. Enforcement of Environmental Regulations," paper prepared for the annual meeting of the American Political Science Association, Washington, DC, 2-5 September 1993.

61. Regarding the labour side-deal, all that Canadian citizens groups can do is go to their NAO and request that it initiate consultations with another government alleged to be failing to enforce its laws; they cannot ask that their NAO enter into consultations (or anything stronger) with a provincial government. In the environmental side-deal process, Canadian citizens can request that the Environmental Secretariat investigate complaints of non-enforcement against their own country as well as the other signatories. However, the secretariat is not even allowed to compile a "factual record" on the allegations without the support of two of the three members (i.e., governments) of the Environmental Council. This would imply that both foreign governments would have to support the efforts of Canadian citizens to challenge their own government's enforcement record. Does this sound like good diplomacy? If not, what is the likelihood that it will ever happen?

62. See, e.g., Ian Austen, "Now Hard Part Begins: Provinces Hold Real Power and Have Good Reasons Not to Join," *Ottawa Citizen* (14 August 1993), and Barrie McKenna, "Ciaccia Blasts NAFTA Side Deal," *The Globe and Mail* (4 August 1993).

63. See GATT Article XXIV (12). Emphasis added.

64. See Anonymous, "Issues of Constitutional Jurisdiction," pp. 39-55, and Brown, "The Evolving Role of the Provinces," p. 115, for additional references.

65. FTA dispute resolution panels will have to decide the meaning of "all necessary measures" in the first instance. However, Article 1802.1 clearly assigns the Canada-U.S. Trade Commission, comprised of Cabinet-level representatives of the two national governments, the power "to resolve disputes that may arise over its [the FTA's] interpretation and application," and "to oversee its further elaboration." Article 1802.5 then states that the Commission's decisions shall be taken

by consensus. Are both national governments — challenger and defender — likely to agree to differ from the panel on such a key interpretative issue? On the face of it, this seems unlikely. If they do not, then the panel's interpretation presumably stands.

66. See Article 1135 (Final Award) which indicates that under the investor-state dispute process, the arbitral tribunal will award either monetary damages (plus interest) or restitution of property. It may also award costs in accordance with applicable arbitration rules. Article 2018 and 2019 contain the relevant provisions on what happens should the Canadian government fail to restore lost property values or pay the damages assessed by the tribunal.

67. *A.-G. Canada v. A.-G. Ontario* [1937] A.C. 326. See Peter W. Hogg, *Constitutional Law of Canada*, 2d ed. (Toronto: Carswell Co., 1985), pp. 251-54; and Anonymous,"Issues of Constitutional Jurisdiction," p. 42 n.7.

68. The leading cases from this period are *NLRB v. Jones and Laughlin Steel* 301 U.S. 1 (1937), *U.S. v. Darby* 312 U.S. 100 (1941), and *Wickard v. Filburn* 317 U.S. 111 (1942). The federal commerce power has been further expanded since the New Deal, as a basis for U.S. laws banning racial discrimination in public places. See Gerald Gunther, *Constitutional Law*, 11th ed. (Mineola, NY: The Foundation Press, 1985), pp. 157-76.

69. See Hogg, *Constitutional Law*, chaps. 17, 19, and 20; and John D. Whyte, "The Impact of Internationalization on the Constitutional Setting," in *Think Globally: Proceedings of the 42nd Annual Conference* (Toronto: Institute of Public Administration of Canada, 1991).

70. See *General Motors of Canada v. City National Leasing*, [1989] 1 S.C.R. 641 and *Attorney General of Canada v. Canadian National Transportation*, [1983] 2 S.C.R. 206, discussed in Whyte, "Impact of Internationalization," pp. 13-14.

71. See *The Queen v. Crown Zellerbach*, [1988] 1 S.C.R. 401, discussed in Whyte, "Impact of Internationalization," pp. 477-78; 480-81.

72. See James J. Rice and Michael J. Prince, "Lowering the Safety Net and Weakening the Bonds of Nationhood: Social Policy in the Mulroney Years," in Susan D. Phillips (ed.), *How Ottawa Spends, 1993-1994: A More Democratic Canada...?* (Ottawa: Carleton University Press, 1993), pp. 381-416, at 396-99.

IV

Chronology

10

Chronology of Events July 1992 – June 1993*

Anne Poels

An index of these events begins on page 255

1 July 1992 *Taxation*	Personal income taxes rise in British Columbia by one percent to 52.5 percent of federal tax payable, in Ontario by 1.5 percent to 54.5 percent and in Newfoundland by 2.5 percent to 64.5 percent of federal tax. The tax increases are expected to generate $900 million over the next two years. Analysts fear that provincial as well as municipal tax increases across Canada will have a direct impact on consumer spending and further delay economic recovery.
2 July 1992 *Fisheries –* *Northern Cod* *Moratorium*	Fisheries Minister John Crosbie announces a two-year shutdown of the northern cod fishery off Newfoundland's east coast to protect dwindling stocks and allow the resources time to recover. The moratorium leaves about 19,000 fishermen and plant workers out of work in the already depressed region. The northern cod fishery, worth $700 million, provides 31,000 jobs in Atlantic Canada. Ottawa plans to provide emergency aid.

---

* The author would like to thank Dwight Herperger for his much appreciated assistance with entries concerning constitutional reform.

7 July 1992
Constitutional Reform

Constitutional Affairs Minister Joe Clark and nine provincial premiers (excluding Quebec) reach an agreement deal after a last ditch, three-day effort to save the almost four month process of multilateral talks on constitutional reform; the deal, presented as a response to Quebec's demands for offers on renewed federalism, ultimately hinged on agreement on a modified Triple-E Senate (elected, equal, effective).

The agreement gives each province eight seats (Quebec currently has 24) and the territories two seats each in the reformed Senate. Aboriginal representation is to be determined later.

To compensate for the loss of seats by some provinces in the Senate, the Commons would be expanded to better reflect population distribution. Ontario would get ten more seats, British Columbia and Quebec three and Alberta one.

Other elements of the agreement:

- Quebec would be recognized as a distinct society;
- The aboriginal inherent right of self-government would be enshrined;
- All provinces would have a veto on amendments to federal institutions, but not on the issue of new provinces;
- Provinces would have exclusive jurisdiction over manpower training, culture, forestry, mining, housing, recreation, tourism and urban affairs;
- There would be a commitment to dismantle interprovincial barriers;
- There would be a statement of principles about social programs; and
- Quebec's right to three Supreme Court seats would be enshrined.

9 July 1992
Constitutional Reform – Quebec

Quebec Premier Robert Bourassa makes his first official response to the 7 July agreement, identifying positive elements in the constitutional package and leaving open the possibility of this province's return to the negotiating table; at the same time, Bourassa warns that the agreement, particularly the provisions relating to the Senate, would be "difficult to sell in Quebec" and are a "serious

Chronology of Events 1992-93   233

setback" for the province, and that changes would be needed; other areas of concern identified by the premier were provisions relating to the division of powers and aboriginal self-government.

10 July 1992 *Constitutional* *Reform*	At a news conference, Prime Minister Brian Mulroney hails the deal as containing "fundamental elements of an agreement" and says that Quebec could not expect much more from a constitutional settlement; indicating that the agreement would need some fine tuning, the prime minister cancels plans to recall Parliament 15 July to consider the constitutional deal.
14 July 1992 *Constitutional* *Reform - Ontario*	Ontario Premier Bob Rae announces that he will not return to the constitutional bargaining table unless Quebec Premier Robert Bourassa is present as an active participant.
15 July 1992 *Constitutional* *Reform*	Following a wave of criticism in Quebec towards the 7 July constitutional agreement, Prime Minister Mulroney appears to retreat from his remarks five days earlier by noting that his government would not support "any initiative whatsoever that would have the effect of isolating Quebec," particularly on the issue of Senate reform; in contrast, Constitutional Affairs Minister Joe Clark maintains that there will be no major structural changes to the proposal for an equal Senate, and or to other elements of the agreement.
17 July 1992 *Fisheries –* *Compensation*	Fisheries Minister John Crosbie announces that fishermen left jobless as a result of the moratorium on northern cod fishing will receive up to $406 a week depending on the average amount of their unemployment insurance benefits for the last three years. The payments are part of a plan that will offer retraining and early retirement to people wishing to leave the industry. The government hopes to reduce the number of people depending on the fishery for their livelihood by 5,000 over the next two years. Crosbie would not reveal the expected cost of the program, saying only it would be "well in excess" of $500 million.
22 July 1992 *Energy – Quebec*	The Cree of Quebec file a court order designed to stop Hydro-Québec from continuing construction on its Laforge 1 hydroelectric development. Hydro-Québec

maintains the project is not subject to environmental procedures specified in the 1975 James Bay agreement because it is part of the La Grande complex agreed to by the Cree. The Cree argue that Hydro-Québec made significant changes to the project since the 1975 agreement. Work on the $1.6 billion project began in 1988 and is expected to be completed late next year.

28 July 1992
Industrial Policy – Ontario

The Ontario NDP government presents its new industrial strategy. The strategy identifies six "competitive fundamentals" the government wants to advance through its spending and policy proposals. These include:

- increasing the technological and innovative capacities of Ontario companies;
- encouraging companies to place more of their "home-base" activities in Ontario;
- developing closer cooperation among companies in each sector while improving their international potential.

29 July 1992
Constitutional Reform – Quebec

Quebec Premier Robert Bourassa announces that he will drop his province's two-year boycott of constitutional talks and attend a lunch meeting of all first ministers at Harrington Lake to discuss the progress of the multilateral talks.

The Quebec premier cites several conditions for his return to the bargaining table, including: clarification regarding the creation of new provinces, changes to the provisions on a distinct society clause and an improved deal on immigration.

4 August 1992
Constitutional Reform – Federal-Provincial

Prime Minister Brian Mulroney and all the provincial premiers, including Quebec, meet at Harrington Lake to discuss how to proceed with the constitutional talks. Aboriginal leaders protest their exclusion from the talks.

12 August 1992
Free Trade – North America

Officials from Canada, United States and Mexico reach a tentative agreement on a "North American Free Trade Agreement." The deal, agreed to in Washington, provides for the phase-out of investment and trade barriers on thousands of items over the next ten years. The new agreement leaves intact the Canada-U.S. auto pact and at the same time opens up Mexico's highly protected auto market to duty free imports following a ten-year phase in period. In the textile and clothing industries Canada agrees to stricter rules which require more yarns and fabrics to be produced in North America.

Reaction to the agreement is mixed. Trade Minister Michael Wilson calls it a "good agreement for all three countries"; Bob White, president of the Canadian Labour Congress vows an all out fight against the agreement; and Ontario NDP Premier Bob Rae calls the agreement a "sell out" of Canada's economy.

17 August 1992
*Health Policy –
Saskatchewan*

Saskatchewan announces plans to introduce a "new era" in health-care delivery. Health Minister Louise Simard presents a "conceptual framework" that will shift the responsibility for the $1.6 billion health budget from the province to 20 or 30 newly created regional health boards. The province also plans to merge several government departments, such as health, environment and social services, to promote better health and disease prevention as well as to cut costs.

22 August 1992
Constitutional Reform

An agreement-in-principle is reached on a sweeping package of constitutional reforms after five days of intense, behind-closed-doors bargaining in Ottawa among all eleven first ministers and territorial and aboriginal leaders.

28 August 1992
*Constitutional Reform –
Charlottetown Agreement*

Prime Minister Mulroney meets with the ten provincial premiers, two territorial leaders and four aboriginal leaders in Charlottetown to put the finishing touches on the constitutional agreement reached a week earlier, and announces at a press conference that all the participants in the multilateral talks are leaning towards a national referendum.

Some of the provisions of the Charlottetown agreement are:

- An elected and equal Senate;
- 18 more Commons seats for Ontario and Quebec;
- Reduction of Senate seats to 62, six from each province and one from each territory;
- Senate veto for legislation involving natural resource taxation, and ratification authority over certain government appointments;

- A Senate double-majority (i.e., of both French and English-speaking Senators) requirement for legislation affecting French language and culture;
- The power to force a joint sitting of both houses by a majority vote against Commons bills;
- The recognition of an inherent right of aboriginal self-government, including provision for the courts to mandate progress towards implementation if negotiations are delayed;
- A set of principles outlining the social and economic union;
- Confirmation of provincial control over forestry, mining, tourism, recreation, housing, municipal and urban affairs, job training and culture. Federal control remains over national cultural institutions, and unemployment insurance;
- Provisions for constitutionally-protected agreements concerning immigration and regional development;
- Harmonization of federal and provincial rules on telecommunications.

The agreement must still be ratified by all governments; and legislation in British Columbia, Alberta and Quebec requires these provinces to hold their own referendums on the proposed constitutional amendments.

There appears to be wide support for the agreement across the country. With the exception of Parti Québécois most federal, business and union leaders pledge their support.

4 September 1992 *Aboriginal Peoples – Self-government*	In a step towards self-government, the Inuit of Northern Quebec assume control over the federal government's local employment and manpower training programs. It is the first time Ottawa has transferred such power to a regional government controlled by Aboriginal Peoples. The Innuit are currently negotiating with Quebec to transfer administration of provincial manpower programs as well.
8 September 1992 *Constitutional Reform – Quebec*	The Quebec National Assembly amends Bill 150 to allow for a referendum vote on the Charlottetown Accord, rather than on sovereignty as originally envisaged in the legislation.

Chronology of Events 1992-93

9 September 1992
Party Leadership – Alberta

Alberta Premier Don Getty stuns the country by announcing his resignation from government, with plans to step down this fall. Getty said he wanted to devote his time to selling the Charlottetown agreement in the referendum campaign without any question of his motives.

10 September 1992
Constitutional Reform – Referendum

The House of Commons, in a vote of 233-12, approves legislation for a national referendum on the question: "Do you agree that the Constitution of Canada should be renewed on the basis of the agreement reached on 28 August 1992?"

11 September 1992
Maritime provinces – Cooperation

In an effort to reduce the size and cost of government the three Maritime Provinces sign several cooperation agreements in Halifax. The three governments agree to harmonize their business taxes, jointly promote exports and tourism, harmonize their agriculture departments, deregulate the trucking and bus industries, and study the removal of barriers to job mobility.

The premiers of Nova Scotia, New Brunswick and Prince Edward Island make it clear that a full Maritime Union is not being considered.

13 September 1992
Constitutional Reform – Referendum

National Action Committee on the Status of Women President Judy Rebick announces that her organization will campaign for a "No" vote in the national referendum.

14 September 1992
Education – New Brunswick

The New Brunswick government announces plans to spend an extra $61.1 million to improve education in the province. The additional funds are aimed at giving students more testing in core subjects, smaller classes, improved curriculum content in subjects such as math, sciences and languages, as well as providing more support for remedial programs and libraries.

15 September 1992
Constitutional Reform – Referendum

The Senate gives final approval to the wording of the question for the national referendum, clearing the way for a campaign for the national vote; federal law will govern the vote in the nine provinces and two territories, while Quebec legislation will guide the vote there; federally, there will be an unlimited number of ("Yes" and "No") committees with relatively flexible spending limits, while in Quebec, there will be two umbrella committees with fixed spending limits.

16 September 1992 *Constitutional Reform – Referendum*	A taped telephone conversation between two senior Quebec constitutional advisors (outgoing Deputy Minister of Intergovernmental Affairs Diane Wilhelmy, and Andre Tremblay, a senior advisor to the premier), is leaked to the press. The conversation contends that the Charlottetown agreement is "humiliating" to Quebec and that Premier Bourassa "caved in" during negotiations. A court injunction obtained by Wilhelmy two days earlier did little to prevent the leaks and did not apply to publication of the transcripts of the conversation outside the province.
16 September 1992 *Social Assistance*	A bill to end the family allowance, known as the "baby bonus," passes in the Commons by a vote of 99-62. It will be replaced by a system designed to give more assistance to the working poor. Many fear that the bill marks the beginning of the end for universal social programs in Canada.
17 September 1992 *Health Policy – Funding*	Canada's health ministers meet in St. John's and call for a national information network to be set up. The network's mandate would be to analyze how well health dollars are spent, how costs can be cut, and services improved.
21 September 1992 *Constitutional Reform – Referendum*	The national referendum campaign officially begins.
21 September 1992 *Aboriginal Peoples – Land Claims – British Columbia*	The British Columbia Treaty Commission is established. The committee will work to facilitate negotiations, with various aboriginal groups, involving land claims in British Columbia.
22 September 1992 *Aboriginal Peoples – Land Claims – Saskatchewan*	Prime Minister Brian Mulroney and Premier Roy Romanow sign a $450 million land deal with Saskatchewan Indian Bands. The money provided by both Ottawa and Saskatchewan will enable bands to purchase between 170,000 and 640,000 hectares of new lands for reserve status.

Chronology of Events 1992-93 239

26 September 1992 *Constitutional Reform – Referendum*	Angus Reid/Southam News releases a poll indicating significant loss of support for the "Yes" side across the country — particularly in British Columbia, Alberta and Quebec.
29 September 1992 *Constitutional Reform – Referendum*	In a dramatic gesture Prime Minister Brian Mulroney rips up a list of Quebec's gains while speaking in Sherbrooke, Quebec.
1 October 1992 *Constitutional Reform – Referendum*	Former Prime Minister Pierre Trudeau gives a speech at Maison du Egg Roll in Montreal in which he urges Canadians to vote "No" in the 26 October referendum. The speech is seen as a significant boost to the "No" forces in the referendum campaign.
1 October 1992 *Aboriginal Peoples – Justice*	The government of Nova Scotia and native leaders sign an agreement which will allow some of the minor criminal cases to be tried by a native panel on the Indian Brook reserve. The agreement is seen as a step toward a native justice system, recommended by a provincial inquiry into the case of Donald Marshall Jr., a Micmac wrongly convicted of murder.
7 October 1992 *Free Trade – North America*	Trade ministers from Canada, the United States and Mexico initial the legal text of the North American Free Trade Agreement in San Antonio, Texas. Prime Minister Mulroney attends the ceremony and says that "the North American free-trade agreement provides us all with a pathway to prosperity."
7 October 1992 *Aboriginal Peoples – Royal Commission*	The Royal Commission on Aboriginal Peoples releases a report entitled *Framing the Issues* in which it calls for a complete restructuring of relations between natives and non-natives in Canada. The report stresses that aboriginal self-government is a crucial first step towards reconciliation.
10 October 1992 *Constitutional Reform – Charlottetown Agreement*	The legal text of the Charlottetown Accord is released in Quebec, quieting allegations that vital information was being withheld from voters and fears that the original Charlottetown agreement was being watered down; the text was released early in Quebec to accommodate a televised debate between Premier Bourassa and PQ leader Jacques Parizeau.

13 October 1992
Constitutional Reform – Charlottetown Agreement

The 51-page "best efforts" legal text of the Charlottetown Accord is released across Canada. At the same time two political accords, which were included as part of the Charlottetown Accord, are made public by Ottawa; the first dealing with aboriginal representation on the Supreme Court, and the second relating to the provision of land and resources to Métis communities. The accords are not legally binding.

18 October 1992
Constitutional Reform – Aboriginal Peoples

Assembly of First Nations chiefs meet in Vancouver, inviting Constitutional Affairs Minister Joe Clark and premiers Harcourt, Romanow and Rae to speak; they fail to provide their support for the "Yes" campaign, in contradiction of the position taken by the AFN Grand Chief Ovide Mercredi.

26 October 1992
Constitutional Reform – Referendum

The Canada-wide referendum vote is held, with an overall vote of 44.6 percent for the Charlottetown Accord and 54.4 percent against. A majority "No" vote is delivered in six of the ten provinces. Percentage results by province and territory are:

	Yes	No
Newfoundland	62.9	36.5
Prince Edward Island	73.6	25.9
Nova Scotia	48.5	51.1
New Brunswick	61.3	38.0
Quebec	42.4	55.4
Ontario	49.8	49.6
Manitoba	37.8	61.6
Saskatchewan	44.5	55.2
Alberta	39.7	60.1
British Columbia	31.7	68.0
Yukon	43.4	56.1
Northwest Territories	60.6	38.7

29 October 1992
Economic Policy

A federal advisory committee, appointed by Prime Minister Mulroney to make recommendations concerning the economy, co-chaired by David Camus and Marie-Josée Drouin, presents its report. The study, entitled *Inventing our Future — An Action Plan for Canada's Prosperity*, says Canada should trim federal and provincial deficits through spending cuts, not tax increases.

Chronology of Events 1992-93

30 October 1992 *Party Leadership –* *Prince Edward* *Island*	Joe Ghiz resigns as premier of Prince Edward Island after holding office for six years.
30 October 1992 *Aboriginal Peoples* *– Land Claims*	Inuit, federal and territorial leaders sign a political accord in Iqaluit for the division of the Northwest Territories and the creation of a new territory of Nunavut by the end of the century. Ottawa agrees to cover costs of setting up the new territorial government, including training programs to help the Inuit develop the skills and workforce necessary to run the government. The land agreement would give the Inuit title to 350,000 square kilometres, as well as $1.15 billion over 14 years.
5 November 1992 *Fiscal Policy –* *British Columbia*	In an effort to reduce a mounting deficit of almost $2.7 billion, British Columbia announces $83 million in spending cuts. Finance Minister Glen Clark blames his province's financial woes on reduced personal and corporate income tax revenues from Ottawa — about $500 million below projection this year.
7 November 1992 *Health Policy –* *Ontario*	The Ontario Medical Association and the Province of Ontario agree on a cost-cutting agreement. A number of medical services, such as examinations for life insurance, school entrance, motor-vehicle or pilots' licence, and sick notes will now be billed directly to the patient.
12 November 1992 *Aboriginal Peoples* *– Land Claims*	Referendum results, in which the Inuit of the eastern Arctic endorse by 69 percent the proposed land claim settlement and the creation of a new territory of Nunavut, are released in Iqaluit.
12 November 1992 *Telecommunications* *– Manitoba*	Manitoba becomes the ninth province to allow long--distance telephone competition. Saskatchewan remains the only province where competition for long-distance telephone service is not allowed.
19 November 1992 *Transportation –* *Royal Commission*	The federal Royal Commission on transportation, appointed by Prime Minister Mulroney in October 1989 following public protests over Ottawa's intention to cut Via Rail service by 50 percent, presents its report. The Commission recommends that Canadian governments should phase out their $5 billion-a-year transportation

subsidies within ten years and make passengers responsible for the full cost of road, rail, water and air travel.

20 November 1992
*Environment –
Quebec*

The Federal Court of Appeal, in a 3-0 decision, rules that federal environmental review regulations cannot be applied retroactively to government decisions made before the regulations came into effect in 1984. The court's decision was made in reference to the $1.5 billion Eastmain hydroelectric development in northern Quebec. The James Bay Cree, who are seeking the environmental review for Eastmain, say they will appeal.

25 November 1992
*Fisheries –
Compensation*

Federal Fisheries Minister John Crosbie announces that Ottawa will spend about $5 million on make-work projects designed to help unemployed fishery workers in Quebec and Atlantic Canada qualify for unemployment insurance.

Crosbie also announces that another $100 million will be made available to older workers, aged 55 to 64, who decide to leave the fishery by the end of the year.

26 November 1992
*Fiscal Policy –
Ontario*

Ontario Treasurer Floyd Laughren announces an expenditure restraint package designed to help bring the province's deficit under control. Ontario's schools, hospitals and municipalities will receive the promised 2 percent increase in their transfer payments for the fiscal year 1993-94 but not the following year. University and college tuition will rise by 7 percent and the implementation of job equity in the public sector will be delayed until 1998. These new measures are expected to save $600 million in the fiscal year beginning in April 1993 and another $1.2 billion the following year.

26 November 1992
Environment

Federal and provincial environment ministers meet in Aylmer, Quebec. At the conclusion of a two-day conference they announce a new plan to control national air quality starting next year. The ministers were responding in part to a report released by Pollution Probe claiming that toxic air pollutants are contaminating soils, crops and waterways across Canada.

2 December 1992
Fiscal Policy

Finance Minister Don Mazankowski presents a special economic statement in the Commons. The government is proposing to cut $8 billion in spending. Taxes are not expected to rise. One widely criticized measure is the

Chronology of Events 1992-93　　　　243

plan to save $2.5 billion from the unemployment insurance budget by denying benefits to people who quit jobs without just cause or are fired for misconduct. Other cost saving measures proposed by the government:

- a two-year freeze on salaries for federal public servants and judges; and
- a 3 percent cut in government departmental operating budgets for 1993-94.

3 December 1992
Trade –
Interprovincial

Provincial trade ministers meet in Toronto and agree to start a negotiating process aimed at dismantling interprovincial trade barriers by 1995. The ministers plan to meet again in March.

4 December 1992
Budgets –
Newfoundland

Newfoundland's Finance Minister Winston Baker presents a mini-budget. Personal income tax will rise 4.5 percent to 69 percent of basic federal tax. Tobacco and gasoline will cost more as will obtaining a driver's licence and registering of vehicles. Newfoundland is hoping that the new measures will help to cut the 1992-93 provincial deficit in half to $78.6 million.

14 December 1992
Resources

Federal Health Minister Benoît Bouchard and Quebec Energy Minister Lise Bacon announce in Montreal that the Canada-Quebec Agreement on Mineral Development will be extended to 1998. The agreement is expected to pump $100 million into the depressed sector. Ottawa and Quebec will split the cost.

16 December 1992
Education –
New Brunswick

The Senate approves a constitutional resolution guaranteeing English and French communities in New Brunswick the right to their own cultural and educational institutions. (The bilateral Canada-New Brunswick amendment had been part of the Charlottetown Accord set of amendments.)

16 December 1992
Transportation –
Prince Edward
Island

Ottawa, New Brunswick and Prince Edward Island sign a federal-provincial agreement in Charlottetown for the construction of an $800 million bridge linking Prince Edward Island to the mainland.

17 December 1992
Fiscal Policy

Canada's finance ministers meet in Ottawa and agree to cut spending for two or three years to control the ever rising deficits. Federal Finance Minister Don Mazankowski fails to persuade his provincial counterparts to put tax increases on hold. In view of Ottawa's limits on growth in transfer payments to the provinces, for health care, education and welfare, provincial finance ministers feel they have few other options.

17 December 1992 *Free Trade –* *North America*	Prime Minister Brian Mulroney signs the North American Free Trade Agreement. In order for the agreement to become law legislation must still be passed in all three countries.
17 December 1992 *Energy – Manitoba*	Manitoba announces it will not go ahead with its $5.8 billion Cinawapa dam project. In 1989 Ontario Hydro agreed to buy 1,000 megawatts of electricity, for 22 years beginning in 2000, from Manitoba. Recently, however, demand has decreased and Ontario Hydro, facing financial problems and a surplus of electricity, backed out of the deal.
18 December 1992 *Fisheries – Quotas*	In an effort to preserve what is left of the groundfishery on the East Coast the federal government further slashes quotas, in some cases by as much as 70 percent, and limits fishing licences. Fisheries Minister John Crosbie says that people forced out of the industry will receive employment training aid but no special compensation.
21 December 1992 *Sovereignty –* *Quebec*	Speaking at a Quebec City news conference, Parti Québécois Leader Jacques Parizeau predicts that Quebec could become a sovereign country within two and a half years.
23 December 1992 *Fiscal Policy –* *Alberta*	Alberta Treasurer Jim Dinning announces that this year's provincial deficit will be $300 million higher than expected. Dinning blamed the increase on welfare and education costs and a drop in income tax revenues. Alberta is expected to have a $2.6 billion deficit this year.
23 December 1992 *Telecommunications*	The Federal Court of Appeal rules that major Canadian telephone companies must pay millions of dollars to enable their competitors to hook up to their systems.
8 January 1993 *Energy –* *Aboriginal Peoples* *– Quebec*	The Cree of Northern Quebec sign a deal in Montreal with Hydro-Québec. The agreement is designed to compensate the Cree for the social, economic and environmental disruption on their communities of the La Grande

hydroelectric project. The Cree will receive a minimum of $125 million over 50 years.

13 January 1993 *Aboriginal Peoples – Land Claims*	The Sahtu Dene of the Great Bear Lake region of the Northwest Territories reach a land-claims agreement with the federal government. The agreement, signed in Yellowknife, will give the Sahtu Dene and Métis 41,437 square kilometres of land, a tax-free payment of $75 million over 15 years and a share of the government's resource royalties from the southern Mackenzie Valley.
15 January 1993 *Energy – Hibernia*	Ottawa steps in to increase its share of the $5.2 billion Hibernia oilfield project in order to keep the project going. Energy Minister Bill McKnight confirms that the federal government will spend $360 million on an 8.5 percent share in the oilfield, located off the coast of Newfoundland.
19 January 1993 *Energy – British Columbia*	Premier Mike Harcourt announces that the government of British Columbia will hold public hearings to determine ways to reduce the environmental impact of the $1 billion Kimano hydroelectric project. Harcourt also emphasizes, however, that the British Columbia government will not stop the completion of the project.
19 January 1993 *Health Policy – Quebec*	Quebec's Finance Minister Gérard-D. Levesque and Treasury Board President Daniel Johnson release a discussion paper in which they suggest imposing user fees for health services, raising university tuition and school taxes, privatizing Crown holdings, contracting-out services and holding down civil servants' wages and benefits. The measures outlined in the report are designed to attack the provincial deficit which has risen to more than $4.2 billion this year.
20 January 1993 *Labour Training*	Federal-provincial ministers meet in Toronto for talks on labour and training issues. Federal Employment Minister Bernard Valcourt refuses to relinquish control over manpower and job training to the provinces, a move Ottawa agreed to in the Charlottetown Accord, in spite of pressure from Quebec.
22 January 1993 *Social Assistance – Ontario*	The government of Ontario agrees to take over the costs of general welfare now paid for by municipalities. Municipalities in turn agree to maintain more roads and pay

the $135 million cost of providing property assessment services. The province will also reduce its grants to municipalities by $165 million to reflect their savings on welfare.

The change, to take effect next January, will bring the province's share of welfare costs to approximately 70 percent, with the other 30 percent being paid by Ottawa.

25 January 1993 *Aboriginal Peoples*	The Ontario Court of Appeal rules that Indians in Canada do not have a historical right to bring commercial goods across the U.S. border.
25 January 1993 *Party Leadership –* *Prince Edward* *Island*	Catherine Callbeck is sworn in as premier of Prince Edward Island, succeeding the retiring Joe Ghiz.
2 February 1993 *Health Policy –* *British Columbia*	British Columbia's Health Minister Elizabeth Cull announces major reforms to the province's health-care system. The responsibility for planning and management of the province's $6 billion yearly budget will now fall to local authorities. Newly created community health councils and regional boards will have the responsibility of deciding which services best meet the needs of the population and which services should be cut. The Health Ministry will continue to set standards and establish core services that all community councils must provide.
3 February 1993 *Fiscal Policy –* *British Columbia –* *Deficits*	A study commissioned by British Columbia's NDP government shows that Ottawa is "offloading" its financial problems on the provinces contributing to soaring provincial deficits. Federal Finance Minister Don Mazankowski responds by saying that British Columbia is looking for a scapegoat to justify its own out-of-control deficit expected to reach $2.3 billion this year.
9 February 1993 *Aboriginal Peoples* *– Newfoundland*	Federal Minister of Indian Affairs, Tom Siddon announces that the federal government will pay for the relocation of the Innu village of Davis Inlet in northern Labrador. In 1967 the Newfoundland government moved the community to its remote location. Davis Inlet has been progressively devastated by poverty and suicide.

24 February 1993 *Party Leadership –* *Federal*	Prime Minister Brian Mulroney announces his plans to resign in June after a successor is chosen to lead the Progressive Conservative Party.
25 February 1993 *Fiscal Policy –* *Equalization* *Payments –* *Transfer Payments*	Six provinces, Newfoundland, Prince Edward Island, Nova Scotia, Quebec, Manitoba and Saskatchewan, are told by Ottawa that they will have to repay more than $600 million in equalization payments. The changes in transfer payments result from new estimates of the population by Statistics Canada. However, Ottawa now owes the provinces more under the EPF program. The census recalculation also affects the equalization program as a bigger proportion of the undercount is in provinces that define the equalization standard. The amount the poorer provinces will have to pay back more than exceeds the increase they will get under the EPF. On the other hand, Ontario, British Columbia, Alberta and New Brunswick will benefit from the revision and are expected to receive an extra $200 million next year and $400 million in back payments.
1 March 1993 *Fiscal Policy –* *Ontario,* *Saskatchewan,* *British Columbia*	Canada's three NDP premiers, Rae, Romanow and Harcourt, agree at a meeting in Toronto to form a common front when dealing with Ottawa on fiscal matters. The three premiers complain that the federal government blames them for running high deficits while it continues to reduce the amount it pays towards cost-sharing programs. The premiers also condemn the proposed North American Free Trade Agreement saying it will further contribute to Canada's unemployment.
4 March 1993 *Education –* *Manitoba*	In a unanimous decision the Supreme Court of Canada rules that Manitoba must establish an independent French-language school board and hand over exclusive control of French-language education to the francophone community.
9 March 1993 *Fiscal Policy –* *Federal*	Moody's Investors Services releases a report in which it paints a grim picture of Canada's financial health. The report also backs provincial claims that Ottawa has been off-loading its debt problems on the provinces by reducing transfer payments for social programs. Since 1990, Moody's has downgraded Ontario, Alberta and

Saskatchewan, making it more expensive for them to borrow money.

12 March 1993
Constitutional Reform – Official Languages – New Brunswick

Following the passage of constitutional resolutions in the New Brunswick Legislature and the House of Commons and Senate, the Governor-General of Canada proclaims the amendment of the *Constitution Act, 1982* to add a new section 16.1 entrenching the equality of the English and French linguistic communities in the province of New Brunswick, including the right to distinct educational and cultural institutions. The amendment is the first of the provisions that had been part of the Charlottetown Accord to become constitutional law.

17 March 1993
Fiscal Policy – Stabilization Payments

Ontario, Saskatchewan and Prince Edward Island will receive special fiscal stabilization payments from the federal government. Stabilization payments are made to provinces facing a year-over-year decline in revenues because of economic downturn. Final amounts have not yet been determined.

18 March 1993
Budgets – Saskatchewan

The Saskatchewan government presents its 1993-94 budget in which it proposes to cut its deficit in half to $296 million. Taxes will rise, hospitals, municipalities, schools and universities will have their grants reduced and farmers will receive 19 percent less in support payments. The universal prescription drug plan and a children's dental plan will apply only to the needy. The government will spend an additional $15 million on social services and another $51 million on research and development on ways to stimulate the economy and create jobs.

18 March 1993
Budgets – Newfoundland

The Newfoundland government presents its budget. There will be no new tax increases, instead money will be saved by cuts in public spending. Public sector workers will have their compensation packages cut by $70 million and another $29 million will come from cuts to programs and services.

The government plans to bring its 1993-94 provincial deficit to $51 billion.

Chronology of Events 1992-93

19 March 1993 *Economic Policy –* *Federal-Provincial* *– Alberta*	Federal Finance Minister Don Mazankowski, Alberta Premier Ralph Klein and Cabinet ministers from both levels of government meet in Calgary. Ottawa and Alberta hope to coordinate economic policies and eliminate overlap in areas of shared concern. Among other things they agree to improve highways throughout Alberta and to combine environmental assessment reviews for major projects.
20 March 1993 *Budgets – British* *Columbia*	Glen Clark, British Columbia's finance minister, brings down the provincial budget. Taxes will rise and spending will increase by 5.7 percent. The deficit is projected to be $1.5 billion for 1993-94 which will bring the province's accumulated debt to $26.4 billion.
25 March 1993 *Budgets – Yukon*	The Yukon government presents its budget. Taxes will rise but the territory hopes to balance its $483 million budget and eliminate the $57 million deficit left over from the previous NDP administration.
29 March 1993 *Elections – Prince* *Edward Island*	Catherine Callbeck, leader of Prince Edward Island's Liberals, becomes Canada's first elected female premier. The Liberals win 31 of the 32 seats in the Island legislature. Pat Mella, the Conservative leader, captures the sole remaining seat to become the official opposition.
31 March 1993 *Budgets – New* *Brunswick*	New Brunswick presents its budget. The budget contains tax increases, spending cuts and job losses. The budget deficit for 1993-94 is forecast to reach $350 million, raising the province's net debt to $4.1 billion.
2 April 1993 *Aboriginal Peoples* *– Royal Commission*	The Royal Commission on Aboriginal Peoples releases its second report. Commission member Alan Blakeney resigns in frustration over how the Commission is proceeding. Blakeney is reported as being dissatisfied with the slowness in finding practical solutions to the problems of Aboriginal Peoples. Ovide Mercredi, national chief of the Assembly of First Nations, also voices his dissatisfaction saying the Commission has yet to offer "concrete and substantive solutions."
6 April 1993 *Budgets – Manitoba*	Manitoba releases its budget designed to reduce the deficit through spending cuts and tax hikes. Finance Minister Clayton Manness forecasts total spending of

	$5.4 billion in fiscal year 1993-94, down 1.2 percent from last year, and a deficit of $367 million compared with $562 million in 1992-93.
6 April 1993 *Transportation –* *New Brunswick*	New Brunswick Premier Frank McKenna and the federal government come to an agreement on a deal to upgrade the Trans-Canada Highway running through the province. The agreement commits each government to spend $150 million over the next four years. Ottawa and Nova Scotia also recently signed an agreement to upgrade the highways in that province, worth $140 million.
22 April 1993 *Parti Québécois –* *Manifesto*	The Parti Québécois publishes a new manifesto entitled "Quebec in a New World." The manifesto proposes that a sovereign Quebec and Canada break all political ties but establish three bi-national institutions to manage their economic association. A Council of Ministers, made up of elected members from the two states, a Secretariat, an administrative branch of the Council of Ministers and a Tribunal that would act as a dispute-settlement mechanism on trade matters. The manifesto will serve as a discussion document as the Parti Québécois prepares a new platform in the coming months in anticipation of the 1994 provincial election.
23 April 1993 *Fisheries –* *Compensation*	Fisheries Minister John Crosbie announces a further $190 million aid package to the East Coast groundfishery. Fishermen whose catch consists of 50 percent groundfish and workers in plants who process 25 percent groundfish will qualify for assistance.
26 April 1993 *Budgets – Federal*	Finance Minister Don Mazankowski delivers what is termed a "pre-election" budget. There will be no rise in taxes and no significant cuts in government spending. The deficit is expected to be $32.6 billion. The accumulated federal debt is expected to be in excess of $450 billion this year.
3 May 1993 *Elections –* *Newfoundland*	Newfoundland's Premier Clyde Wells is re-elected for a second term. The Liberals capture 34 seats in the 52 seat legislature, the Conservatives 17 and the NDP one.
6 May 1993 *Budgets – Alberta*	Alberta's Treasurer Jim Dinning presents what is expected to be a pre-election budget. There will be no tax

increases, and deficit reduction will come through spending cuts. The deficit is expected to be $2.5 billion for 1993-94 down from $3.2 billion last year.

6 May 1993 *Fiscal Policy –* *New Brunswick*	The New Brunswick legislature passes a balanced budget bill that makes it illegal for the government to show a cumulative deficit on its current account (day-to-day) expenditures. There are no penalties in case the government fails to abide by the new law. Alberta also passed a similar deficit elimination bill this month.
13 May 1993 *Fisheries – Reform*	Fisheries Minister John Crosbie introduces legislation in the Commons that would see the creation of two independent agencies, the Atlantic Fisheries Board and the Pacific Fisheries Board, representing the east and west coasts. The agencies would have the authority to decide who could catch fish and how much they could take. The proposal is met with opposition from Newfoundland's premier, Clyde Wells, who feels that the plan compromises his province's fishing interests. Wells wants Newfoundland to have more control over the fishery.
13 May 1993 *Environment –* *Prince Edward* *Island*	Federal Public Works Minister Elmer McKay announces that his department has completed a court-ordered environmental impact assessment of the proposed bridge between Prince Edward Island and New Brunswick and found it to be insignificant. He added that the governments of Prince Edward Island, New Brunswick and Nova Scotia "concur with the process followed to date." Ottawa now has 30 days to decide whether to hold public hearings on the potential environmental effects of the $840 million project.
17 May 1993 *Education –* *Manitoba*	Manitoba introduces a bill aimed at the establishment of a new francophone school board. The legislation is in response to a recent Supreme Court ruling that gave Manitoba's francophone parents control over the education of their children.
19 May 1993 *Budgets – Ontario*	Ontario's NDP government introduces a budget that includes $1.6 billion in tax increases, the biggest increase in the province's history. Ontario's Finance Minister Floyd Laughren says that the tax increases coupled with $4 billion spending cuts are necessary to keep the projected deficit for 1993-94 to $9.2 billion. Laughren

estimates that Ontario's total expenditures will be $53.1 billion overall, about the same as last year.

20 May 1993 *Budgets – Quebec*	Quebec's Finance Minister Gérard-D. Levesque tables a budget that eliminates deductions, closes loopholes and leaves Quebecers $1.3 billion poorer. Levesque's aim is to hold the province's 1993-94 deficit at $4.1 billion, down from $4.9 billion in the last fiscal year.
25 May 1993 *Elections –* *Nova Scotia*	The Liberals, led by John Savage, win a resounding majority in Nova Scotia's provincial election winning 40 out of 52 ridings. The Conservatives manage to hold on to nine seats while the NDP fail to add to their existing three seats.
27 May 1993 *Free Trade –* *North America*	The Commons passes legislation that would bring Canada into the proposed North American Free Trade Agreement by a vote of 140-124. The bill now goes to the Senate for approval. The agreement, if ratified in Canada, United States and Mexico, is scheduled to take effect 1 January 1994.
28 May 1993 *Aboriginal Peoples* *– Land Claims*	The federal government introduces legislation to create Canada's third territory. The Inuit of the Eastern Arctic and Prime Minister Mulroney signed the final agreement to create the territory of Nunavut on 25 May in Iqaluit, N.W.T. Ottawa agreed to create the territory by 1999. The Inuit will own one-fifth of the new territory and have the right to fish and trap in the rest. They will also get $1.14 billion over 14 years and representation on boards and commissions concerning Nunavut.
29 May 1993 *Aboriginal Peoples* *– Land Claims*	The federal government and First Nations in the Yukon sign a land claims agreement in Whitehorse. The settlement, known as the Umbrella Final Agreement, gives the 14 First Nations involved $280 million and 41,400 square kilometres of land to divide among themselves. The agreement provides for the establishment of a joint management board system between the Indians and the territorial government in such areas as wildlife and land use. It also envisions eventual Indian self-government with jurisdiction over taxation, education, justice and environmental protection.

31 May 1993
Fiscal Policy –
Debt and Deficit
Reduction

Federal and provincial finance ministers meet in Ottawa to discuss the debt and deficit reduction. Bank of Canada governor John Crow also attends the two day meetings.

The nine ministers agree to work over the summer on issues such as duplication of services and the reduction in costs of social programs.

9 June 1993
Fiscal Policy –
Federal Debt

Moody's Investors Service, a prominent New York bond-rating agency, releases a report in which it downplays Canada's debt crisis. Moody's vice-president William Streeter, speaking in Toronto, says "we do not subscribe to the notion that there is an impending credit crisis." Streeter expects, however, that the provinces will have to pay more for the money they borrow.

10 June 1993
Aboriginal Peoples
– Land Claims

Legislation providing for the creation of Canada's third territory, Nunavut, passes in the Senate.

13 June 1993
Party Leadership –
Federal

Kim Campbell becomes the new Conservative leader at the party's leadership convention in Ottawa. Campbell wins on the second ballot with 1,817 votes over 1,630 for Environment Minister Jean Charest. Campbell will become Canada's first female prime minister when she officially takes over from Brian Mulroney 25 June.

15 June 1993
Transportation –
Prince Edward
Island

Legislation allowing the federal government to proceed with plans to build a bridge between Prince Edward Island and New Brunswick passes in the Commons by a vote of 146-17. Before it becomes law the bill must also be approved in the Senate.

15 June 1993
Elections – Alberta

Alberta's Conservatives under Premier Ralph Klein are re-elected with a majority government. The Tories win 51 seats, the Liberals become the official opposition with 32 seats, and the NDP fail to elect a single member, losing all 15 seats they held in the previous legislature.

17 June 1993
Budget – Prince
Edward Island

Prince Edward Island Treasurer Wayne Cheverie brings down a deficit-fighting budget. There will be job cuts affecting civil servants as well as government workers in the health-care and education fields. There will be no new hospitals or schools built and road construction will be limited. The new budget cuts spending by $25.4 million to $792.6 million for fiscal year 1993-94.

Cheverie expects a deficit of $25.4 million this year down from last year's $83.4 million.

| 18 June 1993 *Fisheries – Reform – Compensation* | Fisheries Minister John Crosbie holds out little hope for a significant recovery of cod stocks before the late 1990s. Crosbie would not commit to future aid for those left unemployed as the result of a two-year fishing moratorium, imposed last July, when a federal compensation program runs out next year. Crosbie says that Ottawa is willing to set aside proposals for fisheries reform, which the federal government introduced in May, if Newfoundland stops its push for joint management of the resource. |

| 21 June 1993 *Aboriginal Peoples – Land Claims – British Columbia* | The federal government and the government of British Columbia sign a memorandum of understanding aimed at settling aboriginal land claims in the province. Ottawa agrees to provide most of the money and British Columbia most of the land. It is hoped that the agreement will facilitate negotiations between the Aboriginal Peoples and the province. |

| 22 June 1993 *Fiscal Policy – Quebec* | Moody's Investors Service cuts Quebec's credit rating from AA minus to A plus citing continuing budgetary pressures that hinder deficit fighting. Quebec now rates lower than British Columbia, Ontario, Alberta and New Brunswick. |

| 25 June 1993 *Aboriginal Peoples – Land Claims – British Columbia* | The British Columbia Court of Appeal rules that the Gitksan and Wet'suwet'en Indians have a valid claim to aboriginal rights for the use of territory in the northwestern part of the province. In a unanimous decision the court agrees that aboriginal rights to the land have not been relinquished during colonial times before British Columbia joined Confederation in 1871. However, the court declines to extend ownership as such of the lands involved to the Gitksan and Wet'suwet'en. |

Chronology: Index

Aboriginal Peoples 1 October 1992, 25 January 1993, 9 February 1993

Aboriginal Peoples – Land Claims 21 September 1992, 22 September 1992, 30 October 1992, 12 November 1992, 13 January 1993, 28 May 1993, 29 May 1993, 10 June 1993, 21 June 1993, 25 June 1993

Aboriginal Peoples – Royal Commission 7 October 1992, 2 April 1993

Aboriginal Peoples – Self-Government 4 September 1993

Budgets 4 December 1992, 18 March 1993 (two entries), 20 March 1993, 25 March 1993, 31 March 1993, 6 April 1993, 26 April 1993, 6 May 1993, 19 May 1993, 20 May 1993, 17 June 1993

Constitutional Reform 7 July 1992, 9 July 1992, 10 July 1992, 14 July 1992, 15 July 1992, 29 July 1992, 4 August 1992, 22 August 1992, 28 August 1992, 8 September 1992, 10 October 1992, 13 October 1992, 18 October 1992, 12 March 1993

Constitutional Reform – Referendum 10 September 1992, 13 September 1992, 15 September 1992, 16 September 1992, 21 September 1992, 26 September 1992, 29 September 1992, 1 October 1992, 26 October 1992

Economic Policy 29 October 1992, 19 March 1993

Education 14 September 1992, 16 December 1992, 4 March 1993, 17 June 1993

Elections 29 March 1993, 3 May 1993, 25 May 1993, 15 June 1993

Energy 22 July 1992, 17 December 1992, 8 January 1993, 15 January 1993, 19 January 1993

Environment 20 November 1992, 26 November 1992, 13 May 1993

Fiscal Policy 5 November 1992, 26 November 1992, 2 December 1992, 17 December 1992, 23 December 1992, 3 February 1993, 25 February 1993, 1 March 1993, 9 March 1993, 17 March 1993, 6 May 1993, 31 May 1993, 9 June 1993, 22 June 1993

Fisheries 2 July 1992, 17 July 1992, 25 November 1992, 18 December 1992, 23 April 1993, 13 May 1993, 18 June 1993

Free Trade – North America 12 August 1992, 7 October 1992, 17 December 1992, 27 May 1993

Health Policy 17 August 1992, 17 September 1992, 7 November 1992, 19 January 1993, 2 February 1993

Industrial Policy 28 July 1992

Labour 20 January 1993

Maritime Provinces 11 September 1992

Parti Québécois 22 April 1993

Party Leadership 9 September 1992, 30 October 1992, 25 January 1993, 24 February 1993, 13 June 1993

Resources 14 December 1992

Social Assistance 16 September 1992, 22 January 1993
Sovereignty 21 December 1992
Taxation 1 July 1992
Telecommunications 12 November 1992, 23 December 1992
Trade 3 December 1992
Transportation 19 November 1992, 16 December 1992, 6 April 1993, 15 June 1993

List of Titles in Print

The Following Publications are Available From:
Renouf Publishing Co. Ltd.
1294 Algoma Rd.
Ottawa, Ontario K1B 3W8
Tel.: (613) 741-4333 / Fax: (613) 741-5439

Canada: The State of the Federation

Douglas Brown and Robert Young, eds., *Canada: The State of the Federation, 1992.* ($20)
Douglas M. Brown, ed., *Canada: The State of the Federation, 1991.* ($18)
Ronald L. Watts and Douglas M. Brown, eds., *Canada: The State of the Federation, 1990.* ($17)
Ronald L. Watts and Douglas M. Brown, eds., *Canada: The State of the Federation, 1989.* ($16)
Peter M. Leslie and Ronald L. Watts, eds., *Canada: The State of the Federation, 1987-88.* ($15)
Peter M. Leslie, ed., *Canada: The State of the Federation 1986.* ($15)
Peter M. Leslie, ed., *Canada: The State of the Federation 1985.* ($14)
Canada: L'état de la fédération 1985. ($14)

Conference Proceedings

2. Douglas Brown, Pierre Cazalis and Gilles Jasmin, eds., *Higher Education in Federal Systems*, 1992. ($20). French version: *L'enseignement supérieur dans les systèmes fédératifs* ($30)
1. Daniel Bonin, ed., *Towards Reconciliation? The Language Issue in Canada in the 1990s/Vers la réconciliation? La question linguistique au Canada dans les années 1990*, 1992. ($20)

Research Papers/Notes de Recherche (Formerly Discussion Papers)

31. Steven A. Kennett, *The Design of Federalism and Water Resource Management in Canada*, 1992. ($8)
30. Patrick Fafard and Darrel R. Reid, *Constituent Assemblies: A Comparative Survey*, 1991. ($7)
29. Out of print.
28. Ronald L. Watts, Darrel R. Reid and Dwight Herperger, *Parallel Accords: The American Precedent,* 1990. ($6)
27. Out of print.

26. Ronald L. Watts, *Executive Federalism: A Comparative Analysis*, 1989. ($6)
25. Denis Robert, *L'ajustement structurel et le fédéralisme canadien: le cas de l'industrie du textile et du vêtement*, 1989. ($7.50)
24. Peter M. Leslie, *Ethnonationalism in a Federal State: The Case of Canada*, 1988. ($4)
23. Peter M. Leslie, *National Citizenship and Provincial Communities: A Review of Canadian Fiscal Federalism*, 1988. ($4)

Reflections/Réflexions

11. C.E.S. Franks, *The Myths and Symbols of the Constitutional Debate in Canada*, 1993. ($9)
10. Out of print.
9. Donald J. Savoie, *The Politics of Language*, 1991. ($4)
8. Thomas J. Courchene, *The Community of the Canadas*, 1991. ($5)
7. Gordon Robertson, *Does Canada Matter?* 1991. ($3)
6. Thomas J. Courchene, *Forever Amber: The Legacy of the 1980s for the Ongoing Constitutional Impasse*, 1990. ($5)
5. Patrick J. Monahan, *After Meech: An Insider's View*, 1990. ($6)
4. Albert Breton, *Centralization, Decentralization and Intergovernmental Competition*, 1990. ($3)
3. Peter M. Leslie, *Federal Leadership in Economic and Social Policy*, 1988. ($3)
2. Clive Thomson, ed., *Navigating Meech Lake: The 1987 Constitutional Accord*, 1988. ($4)
1. Allan E. Blakeney, *Canada: Its Framework, Its Foibles, Its Future*, 1988. ($3)

Bibliographies

Aboriginal Self-Government in Canada: A Bibliography 1987-90. ($10)
Aboriginal Self-Government in Canada: A Bibliography 1986. ($12)
Bibliography of Canadian and Comparative Federalism, 1986. ($20)
Bibliography of Canadian and Comparative Federalism, 1980-1985. ($39)

Aboriginal Peoples and Constitutional Reform

New Releases

Douglas Brown, ed., *Aboriginal Governments and Power Sharing in Canada*, 1992. ($7)
Thomas J. Courchene and Lisa M. Powell, *A First Nations Province*, 1992. ($7)

Background Papers

16. Bradford W. Morse, *Providing Land and Resources for Aboriginal Peoples*, 1987. ($10)
15. Evelyn J. Peters, *Aboriginal Self-Government Arrangements in Canada*, 1987. ($7)
14. Delia Opekokew, *The Political and Legal Inequities Among Aboriginal Peoples in Canada*, 1987. ($7)
13. Out of print.
12. C.E.S. Franks, *Public Administration Questions Relating to Aboriginal Self-Government*, 1987. ($10)

11. Richard H. Bartlett, *Subjugation, Self-Management and Self-Government of Aboriginal Lands and Resources in Canada*, 1986. ($10)
10. Jerry Paquette, *Aboriginal Self-Government and Education in Canada*, 1986. ($10)
9. Out of print.
8. John Weinstein, *Aboriginal Self-Determination Off a Land Base*, 1986. ($7)
7. David C. Hawkes, *Negotiating Aboriginal Self-Government: Developments Surrounding the 1985 First Ministers' Conference*, 1985. ($5)
6. Bryan P. Schwartz, *First Principles: Constitutional Reform with Respect to the Aboriginal Peoples of Canada 1982-1984*, 1985. ($20)
5. Douglas E. Sanders, *Aboriginal Self-Government in the United States*, 1985. ($12)
4. Bradford Morse, *Aboriginal Self-Government in Australia and Canada*, 1985. ($12)
2. David A. Boisvert, *Forms of Aboriginal Self-Government*, 1985. ($12)
1. Noel Lyon, *Aboriginal Self-Government: Rights of Citizenship and Access to Governmental Services*, 1984. ($12)

Discussion Papers

David C. Hawkes, *The Search for Accommodation*, 1987. ($7)

Position Papers

Inuit Committee on National Issues, *Completing Canada: Inuit Approaches to Self-Government*, 1987. ($7)

Martin Dunn, *Access to Survival, A Perspective on Aboriginal Self-Government for the Constituency of the Native Council of Canada*, 1986. ($7)

Workshop Report

David C. Hawkes and Evelyn J. Peters, *Implementing Aboriginal Self-Government: Problems and Prospects*, 1986. ($7)

Bibliographies

Evelyn J. Peters, *Aboriginal Self-Government in Canada: A Bibliography 1987-90*. ($10)

Evelyn J. Peters, *Aboriginal Self-Government in Canada: A Bibliography 1986*. ($12)

Final Report

David C. Hawkes, *Aboriginal Peoples and Constitutional Reform: What Have We Learned?* 1989. ($7)

The Following Publications are Available From:
The Institute of Intergovernmental Relations
Queen's University
Kingston, Ontario K7L 3N6
Tel.: (613) 545-2080 / Fax: (613) 545-6868

Institute of Intergovernmental Relations, *Annual Report to the Advisory Council, 1991-92*/Institut des relations intergouvernementales, *Rapport annuel au Conseil consultatif, 1991-1992*. (Charge for postage only)

William M. Chandler and Christian W. Zöllner, eds., *Challenges to Federalism: Policy-Making in Canada and the Federal Republic of Germany*, 1989. ($25)

Peter M. Leslie, *Rebuilding the Relationship: Quebec and its Confederation Partners/Une collaboration renouvelée: le Québec et ses partenaires dans la confédération*, 1987. ($8)

A. Paul Pross and Susan McCorquodale, *Economic Resurgence and the Constitutional Agenda: The Case of the East Coast Fisheries*, 1987. ($10)

Bruce G. Pollard, *Managing the Interface: Intergovernmental Affairs Agencies in Canada*, 1986. ($12)

Catherine A. Murray, *Managing Diversity: Federal-Provincial Collaboration and the Committee on Extension of Services to Northern and Remote Communities*, 1984. ($15)

Peter Russell et al., *The Court and the Constitution: Comments on the Supreme Court Reference on Constitutional Amendment*, 1982. (Paper $5, Cloth $10)

Allan Tupper, *Public Money in the Private Sector: Industrial Assistance Policy and Canadian Federalism*, 1982. ($12)

William P. Irvine, *Does Canada Need a New Electoral System?* 1979. ($8)

The Year in Review

Bruce G. Pollard, *The Year in Review 1983: Intergovernmental Relations in Canada*. ($16)

Revue de l'année 1983: les relations intergouvernementales au Canada. ($16)

S.M. Dunn, *The Year in Review 1982: Intergovernmental Relations in Canada*. ($12)

Revue de l'année 1982: les relations intergouvernementales au Canada. ($12)

S.M. Dunn, *The Year in Review 1981: Intergovernmental Relations in Canada*. ($10)

R.J. Zukowsky, *Intergovernmental Relations in Canada: The Year in Review 1980, Volume I: Policy and Politics*. ($8) (*Volume II not available*)

Discussion Papers

22. Robert L. Stanfield, *National Political Parties and Regional Diversity*, 1985. (Charge for postage only)
21. Donald Smiley, *An Elected Senate for Canada? Clues from the Australian Experience*, 1985. ($8)
19. Thomas O. Hueglin, *Federalism and Fragmentation: A Comparative View of Political Accommodation in Canada*, 1984. ($8)
18. Allan Tupper, *Bill S-31 and the Federalism of State Capitalism*, 1983. ($7)
17. Reginald Whitaker, *Federalism and Democratic Theory*, 1983. ($7)
16. Roger Gibbins, *Senate Reform: Moving Towards the Slippery Slope*, 1983. ($7)
14. John Whyte, *The Constitution and Natural Resource Revenues*, 1982. ($7)

**Bibliothèques
Université d'Ottawa
Echéance**

**Libraries
University of Ottawa
Date Due**